Education and Cultural Studies

Education and Cultural Studies

Toward a Performative Practice

Edited by Henry A. Giroux
with Patrick Shannon

ROUTLEDGE

New York and London

Published in 1997 by
Routledge
29 West 35th Street
New York, NY 10001

Published in Great Britain by
Routledge
11 New Feller Lane
London EC4P4EE

Library of Congress Cataloging-in-Publication Data
Education and cultural studies : toward a performative practice/edited by Henry A. Giroux
with Patrick Shannon.
    p. cm.
    Includes bibliographical references and index.
    ISBN 0-415-91913-4. — ISBN 0-415-91914-2 (pbk.)
    1. Critical pedagogy 2. Culture—Study and teaching.
I. Giroux, Henry A. II. Shannon, Patrick, 1951–   .
LC196.E38 1997
370.11′5—dc21
          97-11239
          CIP

In remembrance of Paulo Freire:
for his political courage and moral compassion

Contents

Pedagogy, Education, and Cultural Studies

Acknowledgments

Most of the chapters in this book were previously published in *the review of Education/Pedagogy/Cultural Studies*, a journal of Gordon and Breach Publishers.

David Theo Goldberg (1994). Whither West? The Making of a Public Intellectual. *the review of Education/Pedagogy/Cultural Studies 16*, 1, 1–14.

Douglas D. Nobel (1994). Let Them Eat Skills. *the review of Education/Pedagogy/Cultural Studies 16*, 1, 15–30.

Robert Miklitsch (1994). Punk Pedagogy or Performing Contradiction: The Risks and Rewards of Anti-Transference. *the review of Education/Pedagogy/ Cultural Studies 16*, 1, 57–68.

Stanley Aronowitz (1994). A Different Perspective on Educational Inequality. *the review of Education/Pedagogy/Cultural Studies 16*, 2, 135–52.

David Trend (1994). The Fine Art of Teaching. *the review of Education/Pedagogy/Cultural Studies 16*, 2, 197–206.

Harvey J. Kaye (1995). Beyond the Last Intellectuals. *the review of Education/Pedagogy/Cultural Studies 17*, 1, 7–14.

Sharon Todd (1995). Psychoanalytic Questions, Pedagogical Possibilities and Authority. *the review of Education/Pedagogy/Cultural Studies 17*, 1, 15–26.

Cameron McCarthy (1995). The Problem with Origins: Race and the Contrapuntal Nature of the Educational Experience. *the review of Education/Pedagogy/Cultural Studies 17*, 1, 87–106.

Henry A. Giroux (1995). Is There a Place for Cultural Studies in Colleges of Education? *the review of Education/Pedagogy/Cultural Studies 17*, 2, 127–42.

Claudia Mitchell and Jacqueline Reid-Walsh (1995). And I Want to Thank You, Barbie: Barbie as a Site of Cultural Interrogation. *the review of Education/Pedagogy/Cultural Studies 17*, 2, 143–56.

Douglas Kellner (1995). Man Trouble. *the review of Education/Pedagogy/ Cultural Studies 17*, 2, 175–84.

Carol Becker (1995). The Artist As Public Intellectual. *the review of Education/Pedagogy/Cultural Studies 17*, 4, 385–96.

Jeffrey Williams (1995). Edward Said's Romance of the Amateur Intellectual. *the review of Education/Pedagogy/Cultural Studies 17*, 4, 397–410.
Deborah P. Britzman (1996). Towards a Polymorphous Perverse Curriculum. *the review of Education/Pedagogy/Cultural Studies 18*, 1, 1–14.
Mike Hill (1996). Trading Races: Majorities, Modernity, Critique. *the review of Education/Pedagogy/Cultural Studies 18*, 3, 279–90.

Cultural Studies and Pedagogy
As Performative Practice

Toward an Introduction

Henry A. Giroux with Patrick Shannon

Education was one of the first disciplines in the United States to incorporate the ongoing work of British cultural studies. For instance, Paul Willis's book, *Learning to Labor*, played a significant role in the educational debates of the late 1970s and early 1980s concerning theories of reproduction and resistance within critical educational thought. In the eighties and nineties, a small number of cultural-studies scholars in the United States attempted to address the importance of pedagogy as a continuing and significant dimension of cultural studies, but such attempts were uneven and often ignored.[1] Surprisingly, few critical educators attempted in the 1980s either to keep up with the developing work in cultural studies or to incorporate some of its best insights into the field of critical pedagogy. Fortunately, more and more critical educators are incorporating cultural studies into their work in the 1990s. This book reflects some of that work.

Though critical educators and cultural-studies scholars have traditionally occupied separate spaces and addressed vastly different audiences, the pedagogical and political natures of their work overlap and continue to leak into each other. At the risk of overgeneralizing: both cultural-studies theorists and critical educators engage in forms of cultural work that locate politics in the in-between space of representations, audience, and text; both engage cultural politics as an experience of sociality, and learning as the outcome of diverse struggles rather than a passive reception of information; both critical traditions have emphasized what theorists such as Lawrence Grossberg and Paul Gilroy call the act of doing, being in transit,[2] and the importance of understanding theory as the grounded basis for "intervening into contexts and power . . . in order to enable people to act more strategically in ways that many change their context for the better."[3] Moreover, theorists working in both fields have argued for the primacy of the political by calling for and struggling to produce critical public spaces, regardless of how fleeting they may be, in which "popular cultural resistance is explored as a form of political resistance."[4] But although both groups share certain pedagogical and ideological practices, they rarely speak to each other, in part because of the disciplinary boundaries and institutional borders that atomize, insulate, and prevent diverse cultural workers from collaborating across such boundaries.

This book brings together a number of critical educators and cultural-studies scholars whose work addresses in diverse ways the centrality of a project designed to address how the shared interests of politics, culture, and education can be articulated through what we call a pedagogy of performative practice. The concept of *the project* is taken from Jean-Paul Sartre's *Search for a Method*. For Sartre, the project has a double meaning. It refers to critically engaging that which exists and a praxis that opens into that which "has not yet been. A flight and a leap ahead, at once a refusal and a realization."[5] Framing each of the articles in this book is the recognition of a project that formulates the interrelationship between cultural studies and critical pedagogy within a language of critique and possibility, a theoretically rigorous discourse that affirms the critical but refuses the cynical, and that affirms hope as central to any sense of human agency and critical practice but eschews a romantic utopianism. The concept of the performative in this text provides an articulating principle that signals the importance of translating theory into practice while reclaiming cultural texts as an important site in which theory is used to "think" politics in the face of a pedagogy of representation that has implications for how to strategize and engage broader public issues. Pedagogy in this context becomes performative through the ways in which various authors engage diverse cultural texts as a context for theorizing about social issues and wider political considerations.

In what follows, we want to analyze how the intersection of the language of the pedagogical and performative might provide cultural-studies theorists and educators alike an opportunity to address the effectiveness of pedagogical practices that are not only interdisciplinary, transgressive, and oppositional but also connected to a wider public project to increase the scope of racial, economic, and social justice while expanding and deepening the imperatives of a radical democracy. But first, we want to explore the different registers that inform what we call the pedagogical as performative practice or performative pedagogy.

A performative practice in its more orthodox register focuses largely on events as cultural texts that link the politics of meaning to deconstructive strategies of engagement. Such a pedagogy in Judith Butler's terms focuses on representations and "discourses that bring into being that which they name."[6] Within this form of pedagogical practice, there is a great deal of emphasis on texts and how they are "presented, 'licensed,' or made 'excessive.' "[7] A growing tendency is appearing within cultural studies as it becomes more popular, especially in its North American versions, to reduce the discipline to a methodological reading of texts. The exclusive emphasis on texts, however, runs the risk of reproducing processes of reification and isolation, as when the performative is framed outside of issues of power and politics. In this instance, texts occupy a formalistic space that might disavow a universalistic aesthetic yet views issues such as one's commitments to the other, the ethical duty to decide between what is better and what is worse, and, by extension, human rights as either meaningless, irrelevant, or leftovers from a bygone age. In its most reductive moment, Lewis Gordon argues, performativity as a pedagogical practice often falls prey to a "focus on politics as rhetoric . . . [in which] the political dimension of the political is rendered invisible by virtue of being regarded as purely performative—or, as in more Foucauldian/Nietzchean articulations of this drama, purely manifestations of will to power. What one performs is rendered immaterial. Whatever 'is' is simply a performance."[8] Progressive cultural-studies theorists recognize that the complex terms of cultural engagement are produced performatively, but, unlike Gordon, many believe that the issue is still open regarding how the performative can have some purchase in social action or help produce new forms of identity and politics while simultaneously developing a political and ethical vocabulary for making connections and struggling to create multiple public cultures.

We want to frame the relevance of a politically progressive notion of the performative and its relevance as an articulatory principle that highlights the mutually determining role of theory and practice, on the one hand, and the related project of making the political more pedagogical on the other. This is especially important as pedagogy becomes more central to shaping the political projects that inform the work of educators and cultural workers in a variety of sites, especially within a present marked by the rise of right-wing politics, a resurgent racism, and punitive attacks on the poor, urban youth, and people of color. The invocation of a wider political context suggests that the intersection of cultural studies and critical pedagogy be analyzed more critically in light of a cultural politics in which power is addressed primarily through the display of texts, bodies, and representations. The importance of a pedagogy of the performative as an articulatory principle for connecting critical educators and cultural-studies scholars might begin with Raymond Williams's insight that the "deepest impulse (informing cultural politics) is the desire to make learning part of the process of social change itself."[9] For Williams, a cultural pedagogy signals a form of permanent education that acknowledges "the educational force of our whole social and cultural experience . . . [as an apparatus of institutions and relationships that] actively and profoundly teaches."[10] Education as a cultural pedagogical practice takes place across multiple sites and signals how, within diverse contexts, education makes us both subjects of and subject to relations of power.

As a performative practice, the pedagogical opens up a narrative space that affirms the contextual and the specific while simultaneously recognizing the ways in which such spaces are shot through with issues of power. Central to this referencing of the ethical and political is a pedagogical practice that refuses closure, insists on combining theoretical rigor and social relevance, and embraces commitment as a point of temporary attachment that allows educators and cultural critics to take a position without standing still. The pedagogical as performative also draws upon an important legacy of cultural-studies work in which related debates on pedagogy and cultural studies can be understood and addressed within the broader context of social responsibility, civic courage, and the reconstruction of democratic public life. Cary Nelson's insight that cultural studies exhibits a deep concern with "how objects, discourses, and practices construct possibilities for and constraints on citizenship"[11] is central to the project behind the diverse essays that make up this reader, one that brings together various educators, students, and theorists both within and outside of the field of cultural studies.

The performative dimension of cultural studies and critical pedagogy is also made manifest through an emphasis on "doing" pedagogical and political work that has a moral focus and addresses "the central, urgent, and disturbing questions of a society and a culture in the most rigorous intellectual way . . . available." At stake here is a notion of the performative that provides diverse theoretical tools for educators and cultural workers to move within and across disciplinary, political, and cultural borders that allow them to address the challenges presented within multiple public spheres, including the academy.[12]

Rooted in ongoing cultural exchanges, translations, and border engagements, the pedagogical as a performative practice rejects any rendering of the pedagogical that conveniently edits out the difficulties and

struggles posed by institutional constraints, historical processes, competing social identities, and the expansive reach of transnational capitalism.
Similarly, the pedagogical as performative practice acknowledges the full
range of multiple, shifting, and overlapping sites of learning that, in part,
produce, mediate, legitimate, and challenge those forces that are waging
an assault on democratic public life in the United States and other parts of
the world. In this instance, the political becomes more pedagogical as
diverse cultural workers recognize the need to work together to create/
perform/construct those spaces in which desire, memory, knowledge, and
the body reconfigure discourses of critique and possibility that enable
multiple ways of speaking and acting as part of an ongoing engagement
with the crucial issues of identity, agency, and democracy. By focusing on
the pedagogical and political dimensions of culture, educators and
cultural-studies advocates can interrogate texts as a form of ethnography,
expanding the range of ideological critique and pedagogical encounters to
images, symbols, myths, and narratives as well as diverse systems of belief.

As a form of cultural production, pedagogy takes on the goal of challenging canonicity and interrogating the forms of exclusion and inclusion in the
production, distribution, and circulation of knowledge. Critical pedagogy,
in this instance, joins cultural studies in raising questions about how culture
is related to power—why and how it operates in both institutional and textual terms—within and through a politics of representation. But a performative pedagogy does more than textualize everyday life and contest
dominant forms of symbolic production; it also calls for resistant readings
and the development of oppositional practices. Pedagogical work, in this
sense, informs and extends cultural studies' longstanding concern with
mobilizing knowledge and desires that may lead to significant changes in
minimizing the degree of oppression in people's lives. What is at stake in
making the pedagogical more fundamental to the diverse work done in cultural studies is a political imaginary that extends the possibilities for creating
counter-public spheres. For it is within such counter-public spheres that the
principles of equality, liberty, and justice become the normative rather than
absolute standards for a cultural politics that translates knowledge back into
practice, places theory in the political space of the performative, and invigo-
rates the pedagogical as a practice through which collective struggles can be
waged to revive and maintain the fabric of democratic institutions.

Envisioning the pedagogical as a performative practice also points to the
necessity of an integrative language for reconstituting educators and
cultural-studies scholars as public intellectuals. Seizing upon the role that critical theorists and educators might play as part of a wider oppositional strategy
of engagement, cultural critics such as Stuart Hall, Lawrence Grossberg,

Carol Becker, Stanley Aronowitz, Kobener Mercer, Tony Bennett, and Meghan Morris have attempted to create critical discourses and forms of social criticism through which people can understand and produce culture within democratic and shared structures and spaces of power. Rejecting the well-policed distinctions that pit form against content, professionalism against politics, and subjective experience against objective representations, many critical educators and cultural-studies theorists have endeavored in different ways to break down the rigid boundaries and binary oppositions between teaching and politics, ethics and power, high and low culture, margins and center, and so on. Rather than take up the notion of public intellectual as academic fashion plate ready for instant consumption by the *New York Times*, a number of critical theorists have reconstituted themselves within the ambivalences and contradictions of their own distinct personal histories while simultaneously recognizing and presenting themselves through their role as social critics and public intellectuals. By connecting the biographical, pedagogical, and performative, cultural workers such as Suzanne Lacy and Guillermo Gomez-Pena rearticulate the relationship between the personal and the political without collapsing one into the other.[13] As public intellectuals, such cultural workers not only refuse to support the academic institutionalization of social criticism, thus contributing to "its effective demise as a socially active force"; they also take seriously their role of critic as teacher and the potentially oppositional space of all pedagogical sites, including but not restricted to the academy.[14]

Of course, few of these cultural workers define themselves self-consciously as public intellectuals. And yet, what is so remarkable about their work is the way in which they render the political visible through pedagogical practices that attempt to make a difference in the world rather than simply reflect it. In this book, the pedagogical as performative takes on a dimension that gives readers the opportunity to grapple with new questions and, as Peggy Phelan puts it, with ways of "mis/understanding" that address and critically engage the most urgent social problems of our time.[15] For instance, the pedagogical as performative does not merely provide a set of representation/texts that imparts knowledge to others; it also becomes a form of cultural production in which one's own identity is constantly being rewritten. In this instance, cultural politics and the authority to which it makes a claim are always rendered suspect and provisional—not to elude the burden of judgment, meaning, or commitment but to enable cultural workers to challenge those forms of disciplinary knowledge and social relations that promote material and symbolic violence. The authority that cultural theorists and educators legitimate in any pedagogical site, in this instance, becomes both an object of autocritique and a critical referent for expressing a more "fundamental dispute with authority itself."[16]

The relationships between critical pedagogy, cultural studies, and the performative are largely taken up in this text through what Jacques Derrida calls "performative interpretation." That is, "an interpretation that transforms the very thing it interprets."[17] As a pedagogical practice, performative interpretation suggests that how we understand and come to know ourselves and others cannot be separated from how we represent and imagine ourselves. This is an attempt not so much to reassert the pedagogical/political significance of cultural criticism as a performative practice as to reaffirm such discourses as an integral component of memory-work and of the need for people to speak affirmatively and critically out of their own histories, traditions, and personal experiences. Refusing to reduce politics to the discursive or representational, performative interpretation suggests reclaiming the political as a pedagogical intervention that links cultural texts to the institutional contexts in which they are read, and the material grounding of power to the historical conditions that give meaning to the places we inhabit and the futures we desire. Within this notion of pedagogical practice, the performative becomes a site of memory, a location and critical enactment of the stories we tell in assuming our roles as public intellectuals willing to make visible and challenge the grotesque inequalities and intolerable oppressions of the present moment.

All of the authors in this volume share the task of making the performative pedagogical by viewing cultural texts as exemplary of a broader set of theoretical and political considerations. Here, texts become not merely serious objects of struggle over how meaning is constituted, but also practical sites that register how power operates so as to make some representations, images, and symbols under certain political conditions more valuable as representations of reality than others. Texts in this instance become pedagogical sites through which educators and others might analyze the mechanisms that inform how a politics of representation operates within dominant regimes of meaning to produce and legitimate knowledge about gender, youth, race, sexuality, work, public intellectuals, pedagogy, and cultural studies. At stake here is a politics and pedagogy of representation that interrogates how texts/textuality work to make specific claims on public memory, how they shape how we construct our relations to others, and what it might mean to use such knowledge as part of a larger struggle to engage and transform the economic, political, and cultural life of a society.

We want to emphasize that critical pedagogy as a theory and practice does not legitimate a romanticized notion of the cultural worker who can only function on the margins of society, nor does it refer to a notion of teaching/performance/cultural production in which either formalism or the fetish of method erases the historical, semiotic, and social dimensions of pedagogy as the active constructions of responsible, risk-taking citizens. On the contrary, we are suggesting, in our attempt to collect work that interrelates cultural studies and an expansive notion of the pedagogical, that educators and other cultural workers who take a political stand and recognize the performative as that space where theory and practice seize upon power as a pedagogical practice do so without having by default to engage in pedagogical or cultural terrorism. Pedagogy and other cultural practices whose aim is to inform and empower are rarely as doctrinaire or impositional as critics claim. Pedagogy as a performative practice—with or without a concerted notion of cultural authority or politics—is never neutral, just as it is never free from the influence of larger social and political forces. Seizing upon this insight, all of the authors in this book self-consciously foreground a number of crucial considerations that frame their own work. Central to such considerations are analyses regarding how cultural texts are produced, engaged, distributed, and sustained to secure particular forms of authority. In addition, many of the authors in this volume critically scrutinize the terms of exclusion and inclusion that define the performative interpretations that rewrite cultural texts; and many of them provide critical renderings of the interests that structure particular social relations legitimated through diverse pedagogical and performative practices.

In conclusion, we want to argue that pedagogy as a critical and performative practice becomes a defining principle among all those cultural workers— journalists, performance artists, lawyers, academics, representatives of the media, social workers, teachers, and others—who work in popular culture, composition, literary studies, architecture, and related fields. In part, this suggests the necessity for cultural workers to develop dynamic, vibrant, politically engaged, and socially relevant projects in which the traditional binarisms of margin/center, unity/difference, local/national, and public/ private can be reconstituted through more complex representations of identification, belonging, and community. As Paul Gilroy has recently argued, cultural workers need a discourse of ruptures, shifts, flows, and unsettlement, one that functions less as a politics of transgression than as part of a concerted effort to construct a broader vision of political commitment and democratic struggle.[18] This implies a fundamental redefinition of the meaning of educators/cultural-studies workers as public intellectuals. As public intellectuals, we must begin to define ourselves not as marginal, avant-garde figures, professionals, or academics acting alone, but as critical citizens whose collective knowledge and actions presuppose specific visions of public life, community, and moral accountability.

Crucial to this democratic project is a conception of the political that is open yet committed, respects specificity without erasing global considerations, and provides new spaces for collaborative work engaged in productive social change. Such a project can begin to enable educators and other cultural-studies scholars to rethink how pedagogy as a performative practice can be expressed by an "integrative critical language through which values, ethics, and social responsibility"[19] are fundamental to creating shared critical public spaces that engage, translate, and transform the country's most vexing social problems. The time has come for educators and other cultural workers to join together to defend and construct those cultural sites and public spheres that are essential for a viable democracy. We hope this book will make a significant contribution to such a project.

Notes

1. We are thinking specifically of the work of Roger Simon, Linda Brodkey, bell hooks, Lawrence Grossberg, Stanley Aronowitz, Henry A. Giroux, Peter McLaren, and David Trend.

2. See bell hooks, "Performance Practice as a Site of Opposition," in Catherine Ugwu, *Let's Get It On* (Seattle: Bay Press, 1996), 210–21; Paul Gilroy, " '. . . To Be Real': The Dissident Forms of Black Expressive Culture," in Ugwu, *Let's Get It On*, 12–33.

3. Lawrence Grossberg, "Toward a Genealogy of the State of Cultural Studies," in *Disciplinarity and Dissent in Cultural Studies*, ed. Cary Nelson and Dilip Parameshwar Gaonkar (New York: Routledge, 1996), 143.

4. David Bailey and Stuart Hall, "The Vertigo of Displacement," *Ten 8* 2:3 (1992): 19.

5. Jean-Paul Sartre, *Search for a Method*, trans. Hazel E. Barnes (New York: Vintage, 1968), 92.

6. Peter Osborne and Lynne Segal, "Gender as Performance: An Interview with Judith Butler," *Radical Philosophy*, no. 67 (Summer 1994): 33.

7. Simon Frith, *Performance Rites* (Cambridge: Harvard University Press, 1996), 204.

8. Cited in Joy James, *Transcending the Talented Tenth: Black Leaders and American Intellectuals* (New York: Routledge, 1997), 175.

9. Raymond Williams, "Adult Education and Social Change," in *What I Came to Say* (London: Hutchinson-Radus, 1989), 158.

10. Raymond Williams, *Communications* (New York: Barnes and Noble, 1967), 15.

11. Cary Nelson, "Cultural Studies and the Politics of Disciplinarity," in Nelson and Gaonkar, *Disciplinarity and Dissent*, 7.

12. bell hooks, "Performance Practice As a Site of Opposition."

13. See Suzanne Lacy, "Introduction: Cultural Pilgrimages and Metaphoric Journeys," in *Mapping the Terrain: New Genre Public Art*, ed. Suzanne Lacy (Seattle: Bay State Press, 1995), 19–47; Guillermo Gomez-Pena, *The New World Border* (San Francisco: City Lights Bookstore, 1996).

14. Terry Eagleton, *The Function of Criticism* (New York: Verso, 1984), 65.

15. Peggy Phelan, *Unmarked: The Politics of Performance* (New York: Routledge, 1993), especially "Afterword: Notes on Hope."

16. R. Radhakrishnan, "Canonicity and Theory: Toward a Poststructuralist Pedagogy," in *Theory/Pedagogy/Politics*, ed. Donald Morton and Mas'ud Zavarzadeh (Urbana: University of Illinois Press, 1991), 112–35.

17. Jacques Derrida, *Specters of Marx* (New York: Routledge, 1994), 51.

18. Paul Gilroy, *The Black Atlantic* (Cambridge: Harvard University Press, 1994).

19. Both of these quotes are taken from Lacy, "Introduction: Cultural Pilgrimages," 20, 43.

Education and the Crisis of the Public Intellectual

1

The Artist As Public Intellectual[1]

Carol Becker

Surely this is one of the most startling historical junctures any of us in America can recall. It is a time when many feel that much of the collective work of the sixties, seventies, and eighties—to rid society of conformism and prejudice, to introduce progressive legislation into labor, to change the way in which people are educated and the content of their education—is being eroded daily. It is a backlash, a "counter counter-cultural backlash," as the *New York Times* has called it, using words like "radical" and "revolutionary" to denote their opposite and reminding us that not even progressive language is safe from appropriation. Those of us in the arts and education suspect we might be seeing the end of the National Endowment for the Arts as well as the National Endowment for the Humanities. We know we are experiencing serious threats to these organizations—attacks that have little to do with budgetary necessities and everything to do with politics. We have for quite some time seen the decimation of the public school system in America; and we may well be witnessing the end of the concept of the public sector. Given this upheaval, where are the forums for serious debate? Certainly they are not to be found on talk shows, where all social issues are personalized, psychologized, and trivialized. Serious political debates are conceptually at the heart of a democratic society, yet we rarely experience them any longer. We are also seeing a return of the most reactionary use of the term "values" thrown at us with a vengeance. An issue of *Newsweek* magazine was devoted to "Shame: How Do We Bring Back a Sense of Right and Wrong?" On the cover was a sepia-toned photo of what appeared to be a nineteenth-century child with a gigantic dunce cap on his or her head. What are we supposed to think? Is shame the way to gain control of inner-city youths, gang violence, drug lords?—to return America to its puritanical origins, the proud Hester Prynn with the bold letter A plastered to her chest? America must find a way to grapple with what it has become, the extremes to which it has fallen. But because these reactionary conditions and values are not confined to America alone, now is a crucial time to look closely at the relationship between the personal and political, to articulate where we are positioning ourselves, and to find a group with whom to work and to think through the complexity of this moment so as to be most effective—in other words, to take one's life as a public citizen quite seriously. It is also necessary to evaluate our individual life goals against the pedagogical intentions of the institutions within which we study and work.

Because I cross worlds and live on the borders of several disciplines, I often find myself juxtaposing categories and thus bringing together what are often understood as disparate realities. In this essay, I will bridge some of these realities. I will first discuss the educational situation within which I work, then offer some relationship between the concept of the public intellectual and the artist—focused on the pedagogical work of each—then finally state specifically why I believe in the importance of the place of art and artists in society, especially at this most pressing time.

I am dean of faculty at the School of the Art Institute of Chicago. The school was founded 128 years ago, and the museum followed some years later. Together they form an institute, a very nineteenth-century construct—a school and museum brought into partnership as one educational entity. The school has grown considerably from those early days, when mostly men with smocks over suits and ties painted and sculpted mostly women who were often naked. Now it has almost 2,000 students and 350 faculty members, and at least half of each group are women. The school has 23 departments, from the most traditional to the most cutting edge: painting and drawing, of course, printmaking, ceramics, sculpture, fiber, art education/art therapy, liberal arts, art history, theory and criticism, filmmaking, video, performance, sound, art and technology, electronics, kinetics, holography, arts administration, historic preservation, interior architecture, and, beginning this coming fall, creative writing.

Some students still work in clay or make paper by hand, and others work only in cyberspace or make computer-generated holograms. Some hide in their studios, so shy they can barely stand next to their paintings and discuss them in a critique situation, and some love to create public spectacles involving hundreds of Chicagoans. Two years ago, Matthew Wilson, a former international student from the United Kingdom who now teaches part-time at the school, staged a piece to commemorate Earth Day. He asked two hundred people—many of them students—to dress up in business attire, and to meet in front of the Picasso sculpture in Daley Plaza on an assigned day, and at noon to fall to the ground as if dead and remain there for fifteen minutes. With hundreds of people routinely eating lunch in the plaza that day, the effect was startling.

Some students would define their goal in life as having a loft in Tribeca, a gallery in SoHo, an international arts career, and reproductions of their work on the cover of *Art in America*. In other words, they hope to become art stars/art-world celebrities. Others imagine a more serious and perhaps less lucrative life as an artist, struggling to make work that externalizes a vision of the world that grows from the inside out, a sense of communicating by whatever means necessary, or a representation of how they see the world or how they prioritize their personal concerns and position themselves in relation to their work. Some students whose intent is overtly political (as they would say) see themselves almost as interventionists, wanting to make strong statements about the world to the world through the medium of art. Our students come from a range of class, racial, and ethnic backgrounds and from some thirty-three countries. They are undergraduates and graduates, many returning to school after having lived lives in other professions. They come back determined to be artists, knowing there is no clear career path to follow but determined nonetheless. We also teach about 200 younger students on weekends in our multi-age programs, where students range from ages five to eighty. This Saturday program has gone on for decades; some of our faculty actually began their careers as artists by attending its classes.

But in a world that does not offer artists many possibilities and does not understand the complexity of the making of art, what do we who are art-school educators think we are doing as we turn out hundreds of artists each year into an unsympathetic economy? I should say first that we at the school educate our students to become *artists*. We do not train them only as painters or sculptors, or as those who create virtual realities. What we mean by training artists (and probably almost every faculty member would have a different way of stating this) is imparting a commitment to the notion that being an artist means developing a creative approach to the complexity of the world, and solving the problems that one poses to oneself through a visual medium, whatever that medium may be. To encourage this, students at the school are given the maximum space in which to develop. We do not place stuctural boundaries around their development; for example, they are not evaluated on the basis of a final product. They are measured by their commitment to the process, a much less tangible result, which is why there are no grades—

only credit or no credit. They are not wedded to one or two disciplines but may explore as many as are needed to find the form within which they work best. That is to say, at the undergraduate level there are no majors, and at the graduate level, although students are admitted in particular disciplines—painting, art and technology, performance—they can roam among disciplines. Those who come in as painters and then decide that they want to say something in performance art or video or film are free to move among these mediums until the right form or the right combination of forms enables them to actualize their vision. They may invent a new medium altogether. Several years ago, two of our students invented computer-generated holography; as a result, one can now create a three-dimensional holographic image from a two-dimensional, computer-generated image, thus greatly broadening the range and complexity, of possible holographic subjects. It is this spirit of invention at its best that makes the analogy between art making and scientific experimentation appropriate.

What we hope to achieve through this seemingly free-wheeling approach is the development of individual artists as well as the development of new forms in art—the realization that art changes and transforms, and that, ideally, artists themselves determine the future direction of art and art schools. When artists want to cross or transgress boundaries, they need a place to work that will allow and encourage such new forms to evolve. We are also committed to the idea that breaking down the barriers between forms—divisions that have often proved in the history of twentieth-century art making to be artificial—helps to create an environment that allows for this fluidity.

At the same time that we are interested in the mastery of form and the obliteration and transformation of form, we are also interested in turning out artists who have a solid foundation in liberal arts and art history, who can discuss, defend, and explicate their work, and who can attempt to position themselves within history. Traditionally, art students have learned history through art history, never envisioning a world larger than that framed through art historical references. We are trying to help students to imagine themselves as citizens within the world—not only the art world. This is the most difficult, least understood, and perhaps most radical venture we are engaged in.

There is no doubt that the predominant image for the artist in American society is the romantic, one of the artist on the fringes—wild, mad, visionary, alone, ahead of his or her time, misunderstood, somewhat like the prophet raging in the desert. And there is also the image of the artist as bohemian, somewhat irresponsible, less than adult, immersed in the pleasure principle, who at times makes something truly extraordinary and at times fools the general public with work that passes for art but is really fraudulent, or is so esoteric that only a handful of people "get it" or want to "get it." And we do have an image of artists as working out of their intuitive selves, envisioning the future. But we do not have in our collective consciousness, or probably unconsciousness as well, images of artists as socially concerned citizens of the world, people who could help determine, through insight and wisdom, the correct political course for us to embark on as a nation. We would not "ask" artists what they think about the degeneration of our cities, our school systems, our young people. On one hand we revere artists, give them a lofty place, and, when we like what they do, pay exhorbitant prices for the objects they create—a recognition and profit that often comes too late. On the other hand we mistrust them, see them as self-serving and lacking in the practical skills that would enable them to be statesmen, to represent our best interests as public personalities, or to run the world. Artists have also played into these contradictions, defining themselves as a subgroup relishing their otherness. And, as a traditionally puritanical culture, Americans fear the power of graven images and want to inhibit the right of secular individuals to create images that might become icons or focal points of adoration or controversy. Perhaps this is why Americans do not condemn the moving images of pornography, degenerateness, violence, and voyeurism of various kinds that appear on TV but become indignant as a society when such images are frozen in time, transformed and manipulated by artists, then presented back to us.

I mention this because it is this ambivalence, predominant in the culture, that our students suffer from in themselves, often in their work, and in their general ontological insecurity—the primal fear and uncertainty with which they go out into the world to meet an unarticulated and probably precarious fate. And I have tried for years in my own writing to articulate the vital place of artists in society because I believe in the educational process that produces artists, a process that encourages the crossing of all creative and intellectual boundaries and affirms the importance of the type of work that results from such training. Were artists to be taken seriously within American society, were they sought out for their opinions and concerns, they would enter their chosen profession with a much greater sense of self-esteem. Were society ready to accept them into its fold as participating citizens whose function might well be to remain on the margins asking the difficult questions, refusing to become assimilated, socialized in the traditional ways, refusing to accept the simplistic moral values that reflect the present political climate, there would be a great deal of psychic relief and a great deal less clamoring for the top of the art-world pyramid. Artists would

be freer to focus on what they do best—concentrated visual experimentation on the relationship of form and content, a type of work that, when
successful, advances the entire civilization's ability to see.

In their role as spokespersons for multiple points of view and advocates
for a critique of society, artists may well be understood as public
intellectuals—those who believe in and take seriously the importance of the
public sphere and who create, for an increasingly shrinking collective arena
able to house real debate, work they expect the world to respond to. It is the
absence of that response and the miscommunication of artists' intent when
there is response that are most devastating for artists. In their role as critics
of society and as mirrors of society, I have come to see artists as negotiating
the public realm—often ignored, unheard, and misunderstood, but
nonetheless tenacious in their insistence on presenting society with a reflection of itself without regard for whether society seeks such representation or
chooses to look at it when it is offered.

My way of understanding this role of the artist is furthered by the work of
Edward Said, especially in a series of essays called the Reith Lectures, which
were presented in 1993 and then broadcast on the BBC. Out of these lectures
came a very important small collection called *Representations of the
Intellectual.*[2] The way in which Said posits the place of the intellectual and distinguishes the various aspects of the role of the intellectual allows me to use his
arguments as touchstones to explicate what artists do, how they think about
what they do, and how their actions play out in, or could affect, American
society. Writers have criticized Said's understanding of the role of the
intellectual, citing the narrow theoretical basis for his analysis or the degree to
which he presents himself as the prototype for the engaged intellectual.[3]
However, I find the structures he creates useful, especially to illuminate the
potential role of the artist in American society.

Said refers to Gramsci's notion of the organic intellectual. In the *Prison
Notebooks*, Gramsci says, "All men are intellectuals, one could therefore say:
but not all men have in society the function of intellectuals."[4] And within
this category of those who function as intellectuals there are two groups.
The first are the priests and teachers, those for whom knowledge remains
stable, steady, transmittable, and at times even stagnant. These might be
called professional intellectuals, distinct from what he calls "organic intellectuals," those who are "always on the move, on the make,"[5] constantly
interacting with society and struggling to change minds and expand
markets. These fluid intellectuals may also be what he refers to as amateur
intellectuals, forever inventing themselves and renegotiating their place on
the border zones between disciplines, never stuck in any one discipline.
These amateurs, wedded to no fixed body of knowledge, are open to all

thought and to the renegotiation of ideas as that becomes necessary, whether through the merging of disciplines to solve complex problems as in the creation of cultural studies, or in the evolution of knowledge, as a discipline questions its own history, motivations, and methodologies and becomes self-reflexive—as in the philosophy of science. Important to these distinctions is the idea that the intellectual "is an individual with a specific public role in society that cannot be reduced simply to that of a faceless professional, a competent member of a class just going about her/his business." The organic intellectual is the one "whose *raison d'être* is to represent all those people and issues that are routinely forgotten or swept under the rug. The intellectual does so on the basis of universal principles: that all human beings are entitled to expect decent standards of behavior concerning freedom and justice from worldly powers or nations, and that deliberate or inadvertent violations of these standards need to be testified and fought against courageously."[6] In a sense there is "no such thing as a private intellectual, certainly not a private organic intellectual, since the moment you set down words and then publish them you have entered the public world." "Nor," says Said, "is there only a public intellectual, someone who exists just as a figurehead or spokesperson or symbol of a cause, movement, or position."[7] He states: "My argument is that intellectuals are individuals with a vocation for the art of representing, whether that is talking, writing, teaching, appearing on television."[8] I add to this the most obvious form of representing—the re-presentation of reality through images used in art making. Said goes on to say, "That vocation [of the intellectual] is important to the extent that it is publicly recognizable and involves both commitment and risk, boldness and vulnerabilty; when I read Jean-Paul Sartre, or Bertrand Russell, it is their specific, individual voice and presence that makes an impression on me over and above their arguments because they are speaking out for their beliefs. They cannot be mistaken for an anonymous functionary or careful bureaucrat."[9] What makes them unique is that their voice of the particular writer/thinker is heard—booming from their particular orientation, carrying their unique inflection. We might say to ourselves,"It could be no one other than Jean-Paul Sartre, Toni Morrison, Walter Benjamin, Nadine Gordimer." But we could just as well say, "Picasso, Max Ernst, Louise Bourgeois, Bettye Saar, Bill T. Jones, Anselm Kiefer, Andres Serrano, Carrie May Weems, Bruce Nauman," and so forth. The voices of these artists and writers are unmistakable.

I would like to stop here for a moment to talk about some implications of these ideas as they relate to art, artists, and art making. Said's two categories of intellectuals—those who simply represent the information that they were trained to pass along and those who are innovative, daring, and public in their re-presentation of their own personal interaction with the world—hold for artists as well. Most of the artists whose NEA funding has been revoked in the past six years might be said to be organic artists in Said's terms. In each instance the work that was targeted for public denunciation was art that took on serious issues, passed through the individual, the private sphere, and was placed into the public sphere. It was work that crossed borders, took a powerful stance and risked upsetting the moral status quo by exposing conventional hypocrisies. What truly terrified mainstream America was that the work seemed to debunk so-called traditional values. The myriad discussions about this art never communicated the very strong political messages that the work put forth about gender, class, and sexual equality, or the fact that these artists cared about society enough to put their bodies on the line to represent its injustices to a general audience. The integrity of the artists and their commitments to social causes were never discussed.

Said quotes Isaiah Berlin, who in discussing Russian writers of the nineteenth century talks about how conscious they were that they were "on a public stage, testifying."[10] It is fair to say that several artists whom politicians have tried to humiliate because of the nature of their work were most assuredly "testifying." Ron Athey, one performance artist who lost his NEA grant, performs works focused on his HIV-positive condition. He actually does piercing and tattooing on stage and makes imprints of the blood let from these exercises onto paper towels. The blood prints are not made from the blood of HIV-positive people, but when Athey hangs them high above the audience on clotheslines, they are a looming reminder of our own fear of the proximity of AIDS. The content of the work is precisely a testimony about what it means to be young, creative, talented, successful, and to know that you probably will not live out a normal life. The literalness of the sacrifice involved is reminiscent of Kafka's *Penal Colony*, in which an elaborate machine engraves into the flesh of the sinner words denoting the crime that society has deemed the individual guilty of. Through protracted pain supposedly comes the realization of the crime and the possibility of redemption. Through physical torture comes the spiritual recognition of sin. Redemption through the body is the task Ron Athey has set for himself. But the literalness of these performances—the stark painfulness of them—frightens those who hear about the work and makes Athey an easy target for politicians eager to discredit the symbolic value and cathartic function he attempts to give to these pieces. There is no public discussion of or interest in his actual intention.

These artists have seen their task as that of making their own personal conditions public and of taking that which is in the public domain and translating it into the personal. And yet these functions, so well articulated by Said for intellectuals, are not valued enough in this society to have these arguments secure the public funding that would support such work. Despite this complexity, all that the media have finally been interested in are the sensationalism and supposed "pornography" of the art, rather than its testimony to what Said describes as "resistant intellectual consciousness,"[11] a term he uses to describe Stephen Dedalus, Joyce's prototypical autobiographical protagonist in *Portrait of the Artist As a Young Man*. Such artists resist assimilation. They defy simplistic descriptions or literal analysis. They attempt to reach large audiences, but they refuse to render themselves benign to do so. They see themselves as engaging in these activities to "advance human freedom and knowledge."[12] And they will not compromise. But all of this is beyond Republican Newt Gingrich, who has likened the NEA and its funded projects to a "sandbox" for the rich cultural elite.

Right-wing intellectuals, especially those who write for *The New Criterion*, denounce such artists as working against the public good. But they in fact dislike these artists because, instead of falsely elevating society, they appear to drag it down; instead of offering solutions, they expose society's, inherent contradictions; and instead of pursuing absolute truth, they offer complexity, ambivalence, and at times aggressive confrontation with the status quo. This offends right-wing art critics who continue to believe that artists should idealize beauty. But these organic artists refuse to re-present the past romanticality or to create art that they feel can no longer be made in good conscience in America in the 1990s. Instead they choose to confront that which haunts their own reality.

If the work cannot bring the American psyche together under one homogeneous whole, if it can no longer re-present harmonius images, this is because the world within which these artists live does not allow for such image making. They are true to their historical moment and to that which they feel has been silenced and must be stated within the public realm. Because they defy the prevailing norms and are unable to create order and continuity in their work, they are rightly understood as subversive to the silent complicity around them. They also refuse the depoliticized talk-show mentality, which gives the illusion of a public realm but in fact focuses on the personal and psychological, often negating or denying the historical/sociological moment from which these personal problems evolve. To use Oscar Wilde's phrase, they see themselves in "symbolic relationship with their time."[13]

Said adds another important distinction that I would like to extend to include artists when he says that to the intellectual's responsibility "of representing the collective suffering, and testifying to its travails . . . there must be added something else." This is to "universalize the crisis, to give greater human scope to what a particular race or nation suffered, to associate that experience with the sufferings of others."[14] I would add that all great writing, art, poetry has this capacity. Even the poetry of Neruda or the paintings of Picasso that he alludes to are not exempt from this requirement. No matter how particular its historical references, the work itself through form and the emotional weight it achieves as it moves through the individual is able to recreate and touch a deep level of human suffering. The best art goes so far into the personal that it broadens its own particularity and touches the world. Through the strength of its execution it becomes emotionally, intellectually, and aesthetically available to a more heterogeneous audience. So no matter how particular the images of Picasso's *Guernica* may be, he has plunged into the nature of civil strife so deeply and found images so rooted in the historical/collective consciousness and unconsciousness that the subject becomes bigger than the Spanish Civil War, and the painting is transformed into an icon for all the monumental horror and devastation of war.

Artists also identify with the exile, the one who is spiritually, if not literally, removed from his or her own land—and is neither assimilated nor assimilable. Adorno, Said reminds us, always placed a great premium on "subjectivity," always mistrusting the "totally administered society."[15] It is finally the refusal of the artist to fit in, to conform to this regimentation, that makes the image of the artist so powerful within the culture. The artist is the living negation of the society; at the same time, he or she is the best representer of that society. Once artists admit that society makes no place for them, they feel a sense of freedom and abandon. It is a lonely position but also an enviable one, and can readily be attributed to the intellectual as well. Artists and intellectuals alike rarely expect to have direct impact on society. Rather, they long to be understood, to be read, in Said's words, as "they intended the text to be read"[16] or to have their work seen as they intended it to be seen. They are grateful when they connect to one other person through their work, if that connection does not simplify or distort their intention.

Very few people in American society grasp the complexity of the role of the artist or the potential pedagogical function of art. Few artists themselves are able to articulate the range of possible roles they might play, and even fewer have been trained to see their function as parallel to that of the intellectual—and yet it is and should be. Artists stand at the edge of society. Few ever dare to hope they might create an image or representation that actually affects or changes society. This is because the task of artists, which is to pull what is personal into the public sphere and to give shape to what is public as it occurs in the private sphere, is rarely valued. Few artists would describe themselves as attempting to enter political life through their work; however,

Said quotes Genet as once saying, "The moment you publish essays in a society you have entered political life; so if you want not to be political do not write essays or speak out."[17] This is also true of artists. Once work is hung on a wall, placed on a floor, projected into a space in public view, performed, its statement becomes part of the public sphere, the public discourse, and is subject to all the strengths and limitations of the society it has entered. Artists reject the notion that they are not in control once work enters the public sector. Even those artists who have made very provocative work often do not understand why people respond as they do. Once the work is in the public domain, the public feels it has the right to respond as it wishes. And however much artists try to imagine what the response will be, they often cannot. The deeper the work goes, the more likely it is to upset someone who will feel violated by the work's intent. And if the work is making a strong statement in America, it had best not be funded with public dollars or else its function as a vehicle for public debate about real societal concerns will surely be eclipsed. American society has tried to position art in a small, insignificant, restricted, commercial, and mystified space, yet it keeps being pulled into a more complex relationship to society arena. This is infuriating to some.

At a time when America is pitted against itself and the push to conformity shocks our waking hours, intellectuals and artists would do well to align. The battle is about to be too gory and go on too long for any one group to enter into it alone, especially when the desired goals of each group are so well suited to the other.

I return now for a moment to my roles as writer, educator, and arts administrator. I should say that although I see the role of the artist as a public one, only certain artists would choose to embrace this identity, and would identify their task and their life's purpose as serving the public sector through the rigor and unconventionality of their work. As radical as artists and art students often seem, unfortunately many will fall into Said's category of "professionals." They will find a form within which to work—one that is safe, one that receives a certain level of recognition. They will be content within traditional art-world parameters—and that is where they will stay. They will become, in their own ways, as conservative as intellectuals who remain claustrophobically within their circumscribed fields, never expanding, venturing forth, crossing over, making alliances with any other worlds, speculating on the relationship of their work to the larger whole, or attempting to place their work in a more public arena. And, as Said asks, what would it mean, anyway, to be a private intellectual? And I would add, what would it mean to be a private artist? One would have to write books, make paintings, and simply lock them in a closet to achieve such an end. I suggest only that I see the job of those of us who teach and take seriously our pedagogical roles—those of us who will be writers, artists, and educators training the next generation of public intellectuals—to up the ante in our own educational environments, to provide every opportunity imaginable for our students to be challenged in both form and content, to encourage them to become as radical in form as they are in content, to help them learn to ask themselves the most difficult questions, to push themselves as far as they can go, and to be educated in such a way that they cannot hesitate to take their stand within the public arena.

Notes

1. An earlier version of this essay was presented as part of Henry Giroux's Waterbury Lecture Series at Pennsylvania State University on February 16, 1995.

2. Edward W. Said, *Representations of the Intellectual* (New York: Pantheon, 1994).

3. Michael Walzer, "The Solipsist as Hero," a devastating review of *Representations of the Intellectual,* in *The New Republic,* 7 November 1994, 38–40.

4. Antonio Gramsci's *Prison Notebooks,* as cited by Said in *Representations of the Intellectual,* 3.

5. Said, *Representations of the Intellectual,* 4.

6. Ibid., 12.

7. Ibid.

8. Ibid., 13.

9. Ibid.

10. Ibid.

11. Ibid., 15.

12. Ibid., 17.

13. Ibid., 43.

14. Ibid., 44.

15. Ibid., 55.

16. Ibid., 57.

17. Ibid., 110.

2

Beyond the Last Intellectuals

Harvey J. Kaye

I may be naive, but I assume that most of us took up intellectual labors in the belief that we could thereby contribute to the advancement and enhancement of American culture and political life. Didn't we pursue graduate study in hopes that it would better enable us to engage as citizen-scholars in the public debates and struggles of the day? And didn't we believe that, in alliance with working people and the oppressed, we could participate in the making of history, expanding and deepening liberty, equality and democracy? But, of course, the intervening years have not transpired as we had hoped.

Instigated by a shared apprehension about the struggles of blacks, students, women, and labor, the defining feature of post-sixties' American political history was the ascendance of a New Right coalition of free marketeers, old-time and neoconservatives, cold warriors, and moral majoritarians under the banner of Reagan Republicanism. Expressing the anxieties of the "governing class"—the fear that a broad alliance for social democracy and racial and gender justice and equality was in the making and promising of even more radical-democratic developments—neoconservative political scientist Samuel Huntington stated in the Trilateral Commission's 1975 report, *The Crisis of Democracy*, that "some of the problems of governance in the United States today stem from an 'excess of democracy.'"

The most immediate threat, according to both the Trilateralists and the emergent leadership of the New Right, was the growing influence of the "adversary culture ... of the media, foundations and universities."

Thus, the corporate elites set about establishing new foundations to under-write a predominantly extra-academic "counter-intelligentsia" to command media attention, reshape the public agenda, and marginalize the activities of "the value-oriented intellectuals who often devote themselves to the deroga-tion of leadership, the challenging of authority, and the unmasking and delegitimation of established institutions." The goal was not simply to enfeeble the political and intellectual Left; it was to create a new conserva-tive national consensus in favor of capital and the powers that be.

Admittedly, the forces of the New Right have failed to fully accomplish their goals, and they may never do so: Their coalition is in disarray, and, for the meantime, at least, a neoliberal Clinton administration holds office. Nevertheless, there is little reason to be joyful. Their campaigns have wrought confusion, disarray, and hardship. By all accounts their policies provided for the rich to grow richer and working people poorer, and our material, social, and moral infrastructures suffered steady decay. Moreover, even if they failed to create a new postliberal consensus, in one important respect the New Right succeeded. The (feared) radical-democratic coalition never transpired; in fact, the struggles of the sixties are fragmented and enervated, and political expectations and aspirations are dramatically reduced. Meanwhile, the political center has shifted to the right, and the Clinton administration has yet to show the commitment to working people and the poor that it has shown to the ambitions of multinational capital (for example, NAFTA).

At the same time, the anger and hostilities displayed in the Los Angeles riots/uprising in the spring of 1992 and the alienation and dissatisfaction expressed in the course of the '92 election campaigns surely attest to a deep crisis in American social and political life. As Philip Mattera put it: "These days there is not much collective dreaming in America."

What is sorely missing is a democratic politics to engage popular frustra-tions and the awareness of the increasing distance between American ideals and American realities. Sadly, as many of us are all too well aware, the past twenty years also have witnessed the undeniable "retreat" of the intellectual Left. And all fingers seem to point to the academy, the universities and the professoriat, and especially to faculties in the humanities and social sciences, including education.

Commonly referred to as the "culture wars," the New Right's media-grabbing campaigns against higher education and the academic Left have taken the form of assaults on teachers in the humanities and social studies, cleverly formulated as "the crisis of history," "the collapse of the canon," "the decline of cultural literacy," "the closing of the American mind," and, most recently, "PC" or "political correctness."

Though not to the extent that its critics have asserted, a generation of New Left scholars has indeed secured itself in colleges and universities with tenure and professorships. Furthermore, having done so according to the traditional rules of the game—arguably, with more verve and imagination than were usually called for—we of that generation have achieved positions of some import in our departments and professional associations and, in the process, have critically transformed our disciplines by opening them to new approaches and subjects.

Unfortunately, in the process we also, whether by necessity or desire, too often repressed the dream that originally motivated us: that is, to contribute to the popular and democratic struggles of the day. Instead, we have regularly directed our intellectual efforts and agencies to merely scholarly forums and academic politics. As the establishment not long ago of Teachers for a Democratic Culture reveals, even when the academic Left aspires to overcome its isolation, it often ends up recreating it anew.

The founding of Teachers for a Democratic Culture (TDC) in the autumn of 1991 would appear to have been a most welcome and timely development. Although its organizers were overwhelmingly from literature departments, the placement of the TDC "manifesto" in newsletters and campus mailboxes across the disciplines promised the making of a broad coalition, and its very title (recalling Students for a Democratic Society/SDS) hinted at a new "cultural politics" on the part of the academic Left.

The authors of the TDC manifesto commenced by celebrating the growing "diversity" and "democratization" of university classroom and curriculum alike. Acknowledging the outrageous and false accusations being leveled by the New Right and neoconservatives, they went on to proclaim that, contrary to the assertions of a "vociferous band of critics," recent "curricular reforms . . . have greatly enriched education rather than corrupted it" and that the controversies related to "admissions and hiring practices, the social functions of teaching and scholarship, and the status of such concepts as objectivity and ideology are signs of educational health, not decline."

The manifesto's authors then proceeded to accuse the New Right critics of "blatant hypocrisy" in accusing the academic Left of "politicizing" and "subverting" academic life even as they themselves have advanced and sought to impose an avowedly conservative political agenda on the humanities and social study. In fact, they specifically identified a few of these New Right critics as hypocrites. They referred first to the corporate-funded, on-campus activists of the National Association of Scholars (NAS) and, then, to Dinesh D'Souza, the author of *Illiberal Education* (1991), as an example of the extra-academic "ideologues" recruited and retained by the likes of the neoconservative American Enterprise Institute and John M. Olin Foundation for the purpose of popularizing the accusations against the academic Left; and, finally, illustrating the complicity of the Reagan-Bush administrations, the manifesto's authors highlighted the ambitions of Lynne V. Cheney who, as chair of the National Endowment for the Humanities, vigorously promoted the New Right agenda for teaching and research and sought, contra its congressional mandate, to pack the National Council on the Humanities with "politically correct" conservatives.

The founders of Teachers for a Democratic Culture closed by declaring that the purpose of their organization was to defend "democratic culture and education," and they called for others to join them in their efforts to "refute malicious distortions" and to "educate the interested public about matters that still too often remain shrouded in mystery—new literary theories and movements such as deconstruction, feminism, multi-culturalism, and the new historicism, and their actual effects in classroom practice."

In addressing the political character of our antagonists' attacks and in calling for actions directed beyond the academic realm, the manifesto of Teachers for a Democratic Culture represented a critical advance beyond the beautifully crafted but academicist defense of the humanities offered in the American Council of Learned Societies' 1988 report, *Speaking for the Humanities*. However, the TDC document was most disappointing.

Although the authors of the TDC manifesto smartly denied that the academic realm stands outside of, and separate from, public culture, they did so not by insisting on the connections between them but, rather, by conflating academic culture with public culture as a whole. In effect, they reduced democratic culture and education to merely academic, indeed, higher academic, pursuits and practices: "In our view, a democratic culture . . . is a culture in which terms like 'canon,' 'literature,' 'artistic value,' 'common culture,' and even 'truth' are seen as disputed and not given. This means not that standards for judging art and scholarship must be discarded, but that standards should evolve out of democratic processes in which they can be thoughtfully challenged." Their equation of academic with public culture was also evident in their proposed program of action, which, again, was limited to combating distortions and misrepresentations and educating the interested public about the significance of recent higher academic and theoretical movements.

To be sure, Teachers for a Democratic Culture was to be supported for its commitment to defending the ongoing diversification and democratization of higher education. But, in the end, its conceptions of democratic culture and education were too limited and too narrow, effectively abandoning the extra-academic public spheres to the New Right politicians and intellectuals. Where in the TDC manifesto was there an appreciation of the fact that the attacks on the humanities and social studies have been bound up with an even grander politics and project of the New Right, threatening not only intellectual and academic life but also public culture and debate, indeed, democratic movements and possibilities more broadly? And where in its program of action was there a recollection of the vision that first drew us to the humanities and social studies, in which our labors were to contribute not simply to the transformation of our disciplines but, as part of the democratic struggles of the day, to the formation and reformation of political and cultural thought and action?

The manifesto of Teachers for a Democratic Culture was an elitist document, not simply because its organizers were faculty from upper-crust private and public institutions of higher education, but also because its "call to arms" seemed to boil down to protecting academic priorities and privileges. The TDC manifesto registered a narrowing of vision, a lowering of aspirations, and a continuing failure to grasp the challenges before us.

To be clear about it: We do need organizing, but not simply to secure our own academic accomplishments. We need it to work more effectively and more broadly for democratic culture, politics, and social change. To recall the words of the great Jewish sage Hillel: "If I am not for myself, who will be? But if I am only for myself, what am I? If not now, when?"

Of course, criticism of the academic Left has emanated not only from the Right. While neo- and paleoconservatives alike have been bewailing the occupation of the academy by "tenured radicals," many of us on the Left have been wondering what academy they are talking about and have been agonizing about our increasingly peripheral status in politics and public life. Indeed, we sometimes think that the only evidence we have of our extra-academic significance are the shots fired against us by the hired guns of the Right.

Whatever our criticisms of it, the work that actually "named" our experience and anxiety—the realization that for all of our radical rhetoric we are not just marginal to public debate but incapable of addressing the very people whose oppression we claim to understand—was Russell Jacoby's *The Last Intellectuals: American Culture in the Age of Academe.*[1] Previously known for writings in European intellectual history, Jacoby had been teaching part-time (mostly at UCLA) while trying to secure himself as a freelance scholar and writer. Arguably, this experience afforded him a particular view of both higher education and his colleagues on the Left (a view described by some as "critical perspective" and by others as "crankiness").

In *The Last Intellectuals*, Jacoby argued that the decline, or crisis, of American culture was due to the absence of a "class" of public intellectuals contributing to and enriching public life and discourse. In particular, he contended that in contrast to previous generations of young intellectuals, the sixties' cohorts—who had promised to radically reconstruct American polity and society—had turned their backs on politics and public culture in favor of merely academic pursuits.

The book was not warmly received by its subjects; and, in fact, there were good reasons to be critical. Jacoby (nostalgically) exaggerated the "public" presence and influence of earlier generations of American intellectuals. Also, he did not fully appreciate what the academic Left had accomplished. Furthermore—and I think this is crucial—Jacoby did not adequately account for the ways in which the corporate-dominated media have actively excluded critical Left voices, making our absence from "public life" seem to be solely of our own doing. Nevertheless, *The Last Intellectuals* was timely and important, for therein Jacoby pointedly described how an imaginative and politically committed generation of young intellects had participated in its own alienation from public culture and debate. Again, it named the problematic of a generation.

In *Dogmatic Wisdom*, Jacoby offers a historically informed and critical discussion of the culture wars in academe.[2] His basic argument is registered in the volume's subtitle, *How the Culture Wars Divert Education and Distract America*. As he explains: "Conservatives protest that education has lost its mind. Radicals respond that it is better than ever. The debate stays within the boundaries of curricula, books, and speech. Both sides suffer nearsightedness" (xii). Stated bluntly, the battles being waged are deflecting attention from the grander material and moral crises of American education and society.

Jacoby soberly looks at several of the issues around which the culture wars are conducted, but he concerns himself especially with the battles over liberal arts curricula and canons, and "political correctness," and speech codes. On the former, he observes that the biggest and most publicized debates about courses and syllabi have been staged at the truly elite institutions (the Dukes and Stanfords) and are essentially irrelevant to most campuses because the overwhelming majority of college students are at schools where faculty/ student ratios dictate large lecture-hall classes, textbook reading, and multiple-choice tests—that is, forget discussion, forget literature and the classics past and present, and forget essay writing. Moreover, as Jacoby also points out, at most colleges and universities the so-called core curriculum or general education in the liberal arts has for some time been reduced to choosing from a "menu"; that is, pick what you like from set categories.

Conservative critics rightly condemn cafeteria-style education for its lack of intellectual coherence and integrity, but they ignore the real culprit. What is undermining liberal education, Jacoby writes, is not radicalism, but an "illiberal society . . . [a]n unbridled desire for practical knowledge and good money" (8). In other words, the market rules! He adds that, sadly, in contrast to contemporary conservatives, earlier conservatives who spoke in defense of the academy at least appreciated the threat to education of "grubby commercialism."

On the subject of "PC" and academic freedom, Jacoby rightly insists that the matter has been blown entirely out of proportion by the Right and the media. Conservative claims that leftists are pursuing "McCarthyism" against "politically incorrect" profs are absurd. In the 1940s and '50s, hundreds of academic leftists lost their jobs for political reasons; conservatives do not suffer so. Looking at the incidents reported by the Right, Jacoby observes: "The loss of livelihood eviscerates freedom; and only the obtuse could miss the news that during the late forties and early fifties teachers were losing their jobs. . . . The recent cases belong in another category. . . . Those targeted do not become unemployed. . . . Cold shoulders, mortifying looks, and nasty comments do not constitute an infringement of academic freedom, much less fascism" (34, 36, 38).

Noting that the besiegers of academe are richly sponsored by New Right foundations, Jacoby does not fail to make clear that the opposing sides in the academic culture wars are unevenly matched. Radicals may be tenured, but we are neither as well financed nor as well connected to the media as are the public intellectuals of the Right. Nevertheless, as Jacoby goes on to illustrate, merely because the Right finds the culture wars lucrative does not mean the academic Left is innocent of all charges.

Here Jacoby returns to the theme of *The Last Intellectuals*, the retreat of the intellectual Left from public life into academe. He repeats his criticisms of the academic Left's convoluted and poor prose, especially characteristic of the writings of lit-crit postmodernists and poststructuralists. This, he says, was not true of the writings of those figures so admired by the Left (Marx, Freud, and—it nauseates me to so include him—Nietzsche). However, it's not just the language question that infuriates Jacoby, both the jargon and the "linguistic turn" of the postmodernists; it's also the "rank careerism," the "celebration of academic hierarchy, professions and success" (referring, for example, to the likes of Stanley Fish, Duke University English professor [182]).

To be honest, I get a certain pleasure out of Jacoby's criticisms of the elite of the (so-called) academic Left. I envy the teaching loads of humanities and social science faculty at the "big-time" schools, their graduate seminars and assistants, high salaries (reportedly well into the six figures), and monopoly of research awards. (Without assistants, I teach seven classes a year, including, each semester, an introductory course with up to 200 students, and my salary is a far cry from six figures.)

More important, I am regularly angered by the radical poses and self-serving rhetoric of my more affluent colleagues. If nothing else, consider

that for all their talk about democracy and culture, they fail to address—
indeed, they actively avoid—matters of public education and schooling, the
domain of public culture most energetically contested by the New Right. If
they were truly interested in being public intellectuals, they would start by
tearing down the walls that separate them from education faculty and public schoolteachers.

Meanwhile, curricula and buildings alike disintegrate, public school
funding is capped or cut, enrollments rise, and social antagonisms multiply.
Enough is enough. It's time we overcame the last intellectuals' syndrome.
Jacoby's new book doesn't tell us what to do, but it should further remind
us that we aren't doing what we set out to.

Notes

1. Russell Jacoby. *The Last Intellectuals: American Intellectuals in the Age of Academe* (New York: Basic Books, 1987).

2. Russell Jacoby. *Dogmatic Wisdom: How The Culture Wars Direct Education and Distract America* (New York: Anchor Books, 1995).

3

Whither West?

The Making of a Public Intellectual

David Theo Goldberg

As a philosophical and political doctrine, liberalism is committed to individual liberties and the protection of privacy. The critical focus on liberalism and the interest in analyzing social identities have led since the 1980s to theoretical explorations of the public sphere (Habermas 1989) and public culture (Black Public Sphere Collective 1995), and of the influence of each on identity formation. In turn, these interests and the material conditions they at once reflected and represented prompted a renewed concern about public intellectuals and their commitments.

Public intellectuals speak in, to, and about public spheres and public cultures, articulating a grammar of political morality (Brenkman 1995, 7) that challenges conformity and bias. Public intellectuals want to generate new ideas, to examine these ideas and their premises critically, and to weigh arguments on crucial issues regarding public well-being and democratic flourishing. They test the limits of the given, the prosaic, and the sacred; and they seek in an open forum to debate and deliberate about the least contested and most basic of social values with a view to promoting social involvement, social intercourse, and transaction, coalitions across sometimes antagonistic social groups, mutual recognition and respect, civil agreement and acceptance, multiplicity and heterogeneity—that is, civic incorporation (Goldberg 1993, 220–23) and public visibility.

Public intellectuals accordingly pose difficult questions to a wide audience while avoiding orthodoxy of value and vocabulary. They enlarge a social, political, economic, or cultural issue so as to engage the public, to render the issue sufficiently general so as to *publicize* it—to make it a public and not parochial concern. Public intellectuals excavate local issues for their underlying general principles to effect local outcomes, challenging the powerful in the name of freedom and (in freedom's absence) of emancipatory commitment (see Said 1993; Becker 1995; Williams 1995; Giroux 1997).

For the past decade or more, Cornel West has been keeping us intellectually honest. He has an admirable ability to weave together a wide range of theoretical scholarship while showing how seemingly disparate (if not conflicting) views have compatible premises or purposes. He has been at the forefront of the related drives to make analysis of race and racism intellectually vital, especially in the humanities, and to emphasize the importance of interdisciplinary insight. He has deepened our knowledge of the range and limits of philosophical pragmatism by articulating its genealogy, of engaged theology by exploring its possibilities, and of critical multiculturalism by refusing to accept its silences. West's appeal has turned upon an inexhaustible capacity to renew, if only momentarily, a flagging faith and a hopeful confidence in the emancipatory project by mixing insightful intellectual critique with incisive social criticism.

The publication of *Race Matters* marked not so much a new direction for Cornel West (1993a) as a new mix: intellectual critic becomes public intellectual; critical intellectual shows up as the social critic. Yet, in this new mix, in taking center stage in the public and not just the academic theater, Cornel West—like any public figure—is no longer so clearly in command of his meaning.[1] For public representation designed to intervene at the level of civic debate and public policy commands a certain language and style of analysis, and these are hardly value free. They pull at their users, dragging them *center* stage. If one chooses to stand on this political stage—and if one's book is to sell in the marketplace of popular policy analysis—one risks at least *sounding* centrist. Presidential hopefuls suffer this strategy only too well. As economic and cultural capital project the next fifteen-minute icon from which to generate soundbites and surplus value, critical language becomes muted, internalized, sometimes self-directed. The power of language gives way, if only silently and subtly, to the language of power, if not to the gaps within language.[2] Where the subject is race, silences speak louder than words.

So this is West's dilemma, that of the critical intellectual turned public critic, as he sets out to offer a "balanced" analysis of the contemporary condition of America in racialized terms, of racialized America: to speak the language of truth to power as power speaks to truth!

Race matters, West suggests emphatically and repeatedly, and matters deeply to racialized America, but it is not all that matters, and certainly not all that defines the conditions of everyone who lives the racial condition, the matters of race in America. Racism is *a* determinant of the divide between black and white America, but it is one determinant among several. Any account that either elevates racism to the status of sole determinant of the conditions of blacks, and so also of whites, or denies its determinacy altogether dramatically overstates the truth.

This much has been pointed out by any number of analysts, academic and public alike, though the mix may vary from one to another, and the advice often goes unheeded, both in theoretical and practical political analysis. Nevertheless, *Race Matters* makes formative moves in new directions, blending theoretical critique with more straightforward political commentary to fashion a cutting critical account of, and a contrasting vision for, race in contemporary America.

West's framework is expressed in terms of a single critical principle: black Americans face "a nihilistic threat," a threat to their very existence that cannot be reduced simply to economic terms of material deprivation but is more deeply experienced as an existential depression, a sense of self-worthlessness, and social despair (12),[3] and which prompt meaningless, hopeless, and loveless lives (14–15). This is an important point, for though figures show that about one-third of blacks in the United States now are considered members of the middle class, this membership is economically more tenuous than it is for nonblacks occupying the same socioeconomic positions. In any case, the history and contemporary legacy of discrimination, struggle, and shifting ceilings leaves almost no black person, middle class or marginalized poor, existentially untouched. Public representation of blackness, the fabricated racial image, is one of lawlessness and violence, of threat and pollution. A feeling of deep social and personal despair is a (psycho-)logical consequence of this imagined, though imaginary, dehumanizing projection.

So, for West, the principal opponent of "black survival in America is not oppression or exploitation but the nihilistic threat" (15). It follows that the two prevailing but reductive paradigms for explaining the social situation of American blacks are both inadequate. Liberal structuralism reduces the condition of blacks to strictly economic terms and responds with more government programs and money; conservative moralism blames the victims, reducing poor blacks' current conditions to the impoverishment of values and moral degeneration. West criticizes the former for failing to comprehend that both structural programs and personal values are necessary to confront "the nihilistic threat," that people must be encouraged not to give in to their structured circumstances. The latter position, he contends, reduces the culture of moral poverty to the level of personal responsibility, to the poverty of culture, and so fails to acknowledge the institutional implications of culture. For culture, argues West, is rooted in and distributed through such social institutions as families, schools, religion, and the media. Thus, the crisis of morality, which West acknowledges confronts black Americans, is not so much a personal failing (though he thinks individual blacks also have to admit some responsibility) as it is an institutional one, pervading social culture.

If the history of black America has been one of struggle against not annihilation but "nihilism" (15), then the obvious question West must confront is why this threat is more pressing now than in the past, and moreso for blacks than for others. He offers two reasons, though he focuses primarily upon the second. The first is that black culture and life have been pervaded by market forces and market moralities, by profit making and the pleasure principle, creating habits of consumption that undermine traditional morality and habits of the heart. Combined with the legacy of white supremacist beliefs, this pervasion of market forces prompts a nihilistic self-loathing among blacks, a deep existential angst, for blacks have to deny their identity, their very being, to operate in the world defined by the market. This in turn extinguishes the flame of hope, and dramatically shrinks the range of possible meanings black people can draw on, leading to a deep-seated and pessimistic rage (17–18).

Given that nonblacks also face intensified commodification and the morality of the market, it is surprising that West says almost nothing about the way market mechanisms exacerbate white supremacy. If blacks suffer this commodified condition more intensely than others, the continuing legacy of white supremacy constitutes something like a multiplier effect on blacks' degrading and exclusionary experience (Goldberg 1993, 91). These effects necessitate an analysis of how historical shifts in the modes of accumulation transform white supremacy, and how such transformations have served both to license and rationalize different exploitative practices in relation to whites and blacks. West was drawn for popular purposes to frame his analysis in existential terms, thus drawing the focus away from political economy and entailing that structural issues remain largely hidden from view.

The second reason West offers for why blacks face a more intense nihilistic threat is the "present crisis in black leadership" (15), both political and intellectual, and the underlying social irresponsibility of middle-class blacks. Indeed, this argument goes much of the way in tying together the otherwise disparate essays in the book.[4] West places the emergence of the contemporary black middle class in the 1960s.[5] This emergence, he thinks, expresses an obsessive drive for status and an addiction to the stimulation of new commodities and experiences. The result is dramatic deterioration in personal, familial, and communal relations among African Americans, accompanied by a renounced moral commitment and reduced critical engagement in social causes (36–37). This atomistic individualism and self-serving egoism in turn pervade black leadership, middle-class movers who are left politically powerless and intellectually impotent. Lacking the virtues of personal integrity, political savvy, moral vision, prudent judgment, courageous defiance, and organizational patience, black leaders are adrift from the communities they purport to represent. Their expensive clothes set them apart, symbolically and materially, from any organic links they might have with their constituents, just as the shabby dress of black intellectuals imprisons them in their academic ivory towers (38–40).[6]

West's critique nevertheless identifies an important insight. In the American social formation, formal political leadership tends to be from the wealthy and powerful down. Even if a leader emerges from a grass-roots organizational setting, running a campaign takes capital; and campaigning, electioneering, and governing take time. Prospective political leadership, like prospective leadership generally, therefore becomes consumed with and by those who have, or have access to, capital. Once in power, even a grass-roots representative is pressured—by the interests of capital, by colleagues and their discourses, by forms of debate and representation, and by his or her own relation to and control of resources—to represent capital's (now his or her own) interests. So, by process (one might say almost by definition), a grass-roots representation, once it aspires to formal political representation from the inside, will very likely be sociostructurally transformed into the representation of capital's interests. West moralistically and simplistically dismisses the dress and culture of contemporary black leadership, which seem to function here as a metaphor for this phenomenon.

Despite this insight, West's two arguments nevertheless fail to sustain his claim that blacks suffer "the nihilistic threat" more than others. Absent the qualifier "black," both arguments apply to America at large. In one direction, West has overgeneralized the scope of "the nihilistic threat," perhaps for rhetorical reasons, though it essentializes in its totalizing reference to "blacks" and "the black community." "The nihilistic threat" is perhaps less pervasive for relatively successful blacks than West implies. In the other direction, the weight of "the nihilistic threat" experienced by most blacks is sustained more heavily than West seems ready to indicate here by the legacy of institutional and representational racisms. It is at this intersection of race and class that the multiplier effects of economic exploitation and racist exclusion weigh most heavily.

West concludes this line of analysis by noting that black intellectuals have suffered more than others the professionalization of knowledge, the bureaucratization of the academy, and the proliferation of arcane jargon.[7] Again, he offers two arguments to support the charge. In the first instance, the American academy has become insulated from its social situation because of professionalization, thus both reducing the likelihood of radical political critiques and disarming the ones offered (41). But all this shows is that critiques by black scholars have suffered as those by whites have. (This also has the uncomfortable consequence of being self-referential: *Race Matters* may be implicated inadvertently.) To sustain the claim to intensified suffering, West assumes here what he has argued elsewhere (1993b), namely, that black scholars are more vulnerable in the academy than nonblacks.

This vunerability seems to be the import of his second argument, for here West bemoans the poverty of black intellectual life. Citing no supporting evidence, he harshly dismisses black intellectuals who are independent of the academy—journalists, artists, writers, feminist groups—as "mediocre." Thereby, he offers no support to independent black intellectual culture. I suppose he is contrasting contemporary black intellectuals to the likes of those identified with black modernity and the Harlem Renaissance (see Gates and West 1996; by contrast, see James 1996). He criticizes the general poverty of a self-sustaining support system for black academic intellectuals—a lack of interdisciplinary journals and magazines, for instance, critically analyzing black culture and its relation to American society (41–42). While the contributions of independent black intellectuals and support systems may offer less for structural reasons than one would wish, West unfortunately and reductively paints with a single stripe a large body of people along with some important and fascinating critical work. He may be right in bemoaning the failure of "black" capital to furnish material support for critical black intellectual projects (sometimes capital represents just capital's narrow interests, period). Nevertheless, this is a dire circumstance generally faced by the Left. Contrast the number and nature of magazines and journals on any library or store shelf funded by neoconservative foundations with those financially supported by critical concerns.

The conclusion to this line of analysis is marked by a further tension. West insists that both political and intellectual leadership need to be prophetic and race-transcending rather than race-distancing or race-embracing. Race-denying or race-distancing political managers and academics avoid representing black political or intellectual interests in the name of neutral political or academic representation (Tom Bradley, Wilson Goode, and the "mean-spirited" Adolph Reed are cited). The dialectically opposed race-identifying or race-embracing protesters (Farrakhan and Marion Barry, and much of Afrocentric thought) rhetorically reproduce the sort of racist hierarchical categories they so vociferously object to. By contrast, the race-transcending leadership of a Harold Washington or Jesse Jackson circa 1988, and of James Baldwin and Toni Morrison embody the virtues necessary to prophesy deliverance.

This tripartite typology (denying, embracing, or transcending racial appeal) is useful as a critical heuristic in the domain of social critique. West's commitment to race-transcendence is both morally and politically appealing, even if he does little more in filling out its content than mention some necessary components, a point to which I will return later. However, it may be misleading, and in a nontrivial way, to map a critique of intellectuals onto political leaders. For one, problems of political economy facing blacks today are significantly more complex than they were, say, even during the civil rights struggles. Perhaps the failure of leadership noted by West is a product not so much of class but of an insistence that the issues are singular, discrete, and homogeneous when they are disparate, heterogeneous, and irreducible. Moreover, once a resounding critical voice emerges these days, like that of a Cornel West, it gets corporatized. Agents take over and charge exorbitant fees, contractual conditions mediate critical engagement and relations, rights are sold or withheld. The critical voice begins to quaver beneath the weight.

These demands necessitate that intellectual representation and critique be significantly more nuanced, and in many ways the record is more complex than West acknowledges here. It follows that West's somewhat snide slighting of black intellectuals, independent and academic alike, is not simply silly but counterproductive. It indiscriminately (and perhaps all too discriminatingly) undermines important critical work otherwise unavailable; it inadvertently reifies the judgment of the Right that there, but for affirmative action, would go white males; and it sounds distinctly self-serving, even if unintentionally so. In short, though West's line of criticism seems designed to promote the independence—the racial transcendence, as the argument would have it—of his own critical voice, a reader unfamiliar with his earlier work may wonder what he thinks about the views generally represented as black neoconservative. It is with more than passing interest, then, that I turn to what West has to say about this subject, and about the related matter of affirmative action.

Race Matters gives a candid critical reading of blacks' generally uncritical support of Clarence Thomas and of the dramatic failure of black leadership in resorting to a bald racial (and blatantly sexist) appeal in promoting for Supreme Court justice a person whose expressed commitments were generally antithetical to the interests of blacks.[8] West succinctly pinpoints the vulgar racial reasoning upon which Thomas's campaign ultimately succeeded: the appeal to black (racial) authenticity (to which one might also add white guilt). This appeal effected the closing of black ranks behind Thomas's nomination by way of black male subordination of black women in the putative interests of the black community facing a hostile white environment (23–25).

This appeal to the rationale of black authenticity presumes a fixed essentialist conception of blackness, of who is really black. West contrasts this with a dramatically more appealing, historically based conception. Blackness consists in being the subject of white supremacist abuse *and* part of a rich culture and community struggling against this abuse (25–26). This raises a crucial question, namely, whether blackness can and does have any self-defined meaning beyond that crafted in response to white abuse. The conception of blackness as constructed rather than given is understandably reactive, for it is predicated largely upon the pervasive presumption of victimization. Elsewhere in the book, however, West suggests more affirmatively at least the potential for fuller black self-definition in extolling the virtues of, and need for, black self-respect and self-love. If the investment in struggle is what West means by blackness as a political category, then perhaps this imperative to promote and sustain black self-respect and self-love is what he intends by his repeated affirmation of blackness as an ethical conception.

Against this background, West identifies some acceptable features of black neoconservative critique: the rejection of victimization status for blacks, and especially identification of the breakdown of moral fabric and values among younger blacks. Nevertheless, he is generally critical of the poverty of neoconservatives' oversimplified and truncated discourse. Thus, West notes the substitution by black neoconservatives of the appeal to nation for the appeal to race, of their appeal to their own victimization at the hands of liberals for liberals' appeal to racial victimization, and most important the failure of neoconservatives to acknowledge the crucial structural features of poor blacks' socioeconomic conditions. Accordingly, West identifies the eclipse of U.S. economic predominance and the structural transformation of the U.S. economy as factors underpinning what he characterizes as the moral disintegration especially of poor black and working poor communities throughout the country.[9]

In addition, West allows himself a series of questionable analytical reductions. He attributes the poverty of black neoconservative analysis to its being predicated narrowly upon a critical response to liberalism. In turn, he argues that liberalism restricts the cause of black poverty to racial discrimination. Moreover, West reduces the logic producing conservatives' own xenophobia, sexism, and homophobia to a psychologism, that is, to conservatives' quest for order. He is correct to consider neoconservative analysis to be little more than reactions to its reconstruction of liberalism. Nevertheless, we cannot here fail to notice another tension in West's own analysis. He opens his book by bemoaning liberalism's economistic commitments in responding to racial discrimination. Thus, he rightly picks up on the ambivalence in liberalism between appeals to racial discrimination and appeals to structural conditions such as class in accounting for the contemporary black condition (William Julius Wilson's vacillation over the last fifteen years or so being a case in point). West himself attempts to combine these explanatory elements in a complex mix, tempered by the addition of such cultural considerations as the repeatedly noted flight of traditional morality. But, it must be asked, what's so great about "traditional morality"? This seems, as the slogan goes, as much a part of the problem as the solution. West suggests that traditional morality is instrumental to warding off "self-hatred and self-contempt" (17). Yet traditional morality, recall, is as tied to racist, sexist, and homophobic commitments as it is to love and respect (Goldberg 1993, ch. 2). Finally, West's psychologizing of neoconservative bigotry as an appeal to order fashions a further form of reductionism by attributing a singular logic to a broad set of expressions with complex motivations and reasons.

Moreover, West defends affirmative action programs against neoconservative attack, even as he notes their limited value and effects. Far from reducing black self-respect, West argues, affirmative action has furnished a redistributive mechanism insufficient to do away with poverty or to effect equality. He recognizes that the mechanism has benefited middle-class Americans disproportionately (accordingly, he affirms his own commitment to a class-based policy of affirmative action); and though he recognizes the importance of affirmative action's role, he considers it largely to have been a reactive one. That is, affirmative action has worked mainly to inhibit discriminatory practices against women and people of color (64).

The swiftness of West's analysis here not only leaves him silent about the moral arguments sustaining affirmative action; it also renders him less than careful in places. Though affirmative action may be contextually necessary to diminish discrimination (West insists that were it absent, racial and sexist discrimination would return with a vengeance), discrimination nevertheless continues despite such programs. West also insists, again rightly, that elimination of black poverty is a *necessary* condition of black progress, but adds, oddly, that affirmation of black humanity is but a *sufficient* condition for black advancement (65). Of course, West may be suggesting, contrary to neoconservatives, that affirmative action has had more to do with affirming black humanity than eliminating black poverty; if so, I think he is largely correct. But, obviously, black progress can be absent despite black (self-)affirmation, for black persons may lose out in the competition for jobs and resources despite equality of regard for them. After all, racist exclusion, or at least its legacy, may assume various forms. Black (self-) affirmation more likely serves rather as another necessary condition for black progress, one without which such progress cannot materialize but the presence of which does not guarantee (self-)advancement.

Despite these gaps, silences, rhetorical overextensions, and miscues, the first five articles in West's book do hang together. They offer a provocative and critical, if in places rocky, excavation of the contemporary state of black America. They explore the conditions of its emergence and problems, its poverty and the possibilities of political leadership, and probe its occasional moral lapses and suspensions. The final three articles perceptively and in places challengingly spell out some pressing cultural problematics confronting blacks in their relations with nonblack Americans. Here, West develops three discrete, though sometimes related, analyses. First, he analyzes contemporary tensions between black and Jewish Americans, especially in the face of some current black anti-Semitism and Jewish antagonism to black interests. Second, he confronts the silence of blacks and whites alike about black sexuality, and the implications of this silence in and for racialized relations. Finally, West gives analytical voice to the youthful black rage expressed in response to the "absurd" conditions faced today by young blacks, and the importance of the figure of Malcolm X in articulating this rage. He insightfully interprets the analytical importance of Malcolm as encapsulated in the relations among black self-affirmation, desire for emancipation, deep-seated anger against a society seemingly designed to shut blacks out, and the looming probability of an early death.

Thus, *Race Matters* touches analytically upon virtually all the primary problematics pertaining to matters of race in contemporary America. Its shortness and breezy style all too luringly invite a quick and cursory reading. This is unfortunate, for such a reading would have one cast too quickly over and dismiss too readily some thoughtful, sometimes complex, and usually thought-provoking contributions. To address what West's account has to commend it as a pedagogy about race and the production of the public intellectual and social critic, one must bring into sharper relief some assumptions that frame his analysis.

Two fundamental assumptions structure Cornel West's analysis in *Race Matters*. Having rejected early on the deterministic structuralism of political economy and the finger-pointing moralism of cultural conservativism, West is left to rest his critique on a contrasting background communitarianism. Thus, he speaks of the "breakdown of family and neighborhood bonds" and of the "collapse of spiritual communities" which have "created rootless, dangling people" (5); and of the lack of "vital communities to hold up precious ethical and religious ideals" (37).

This failure of community ties lies at the heart of West's attack on the black middle class, on the poverty of contemporary black leadership, and on the perceived absence of moral commitment, which he thinks has been swallowed by the unmitigated drive for personal achievement, egoistic self-advancement, and self-serving interests.

Philosophical liberalism is wedded strongly to a conception of sovereign yet atomistic and isolated individuals freely choosing their own commitments, endeavors, and actions. The space of the sovereign individual is taken to be protected by rights delimiting incursion by others, institutions, and the state. Communitarianism defines itself in terms of a critique of this liberal view of the self, holding that human beings acquire an identity through the historically defined communities to which we belong. Individuals' conceptions of the good—of what ought to be pursued as a matter of morality or value—are not self-defined so much as they are acquired by way of our necessary socialization in a community. Persons are situated in specific social contexts, sharing moral values, a common conception of the good, and mutual goals acquired in and through community membership.

Cornel West's critique of the state of black America, and of America more generally, then, is aimed largely at the failings of the liberal model and its political implications. The radical egoistic individualism of the black middle class, as of the middle class more generally, is cited as the prevailing cause and symptom of disintegration of a vital black community. This failure of community is considered in turn to underscore the dissolution of moral habits, virtuous relations, political resistance, and leadership. In short, the crisis in black America is part of the moral crisis of America more generally, its malaise a function of the economic advance of a few black middle-class *individuals* and the almost inevitable attendant moral, social, and political failures.

The second, though more silent, frame of West's analysis is derived from his repeated emphasis on self-love and love of others. The need for more love of self and others is called for as a contrast to the contemporary overemphasis on liberal self-interest and the absence of community that is the object of West's communitarian critique. What West means by this, as he sometimes says, is the Kantian imperative enjoining greater self-respect and respect of others. But this commitment to the language of love in racial matters carries with it another, more reductive implication, for it suggests that racist exclusion, invisibility, discrimination, and bigotry can be understood best in terms of the existential experience of hate. Racist expression is reduced to the offense of hate speech, racist violence to hate crimes. The power that is at the heart of any racist expression is reduced to the realm of offensive ideas, institutional exclusions are reduced to existential experiences such as angst and psychological alienation, and resistance is reduced to a stress on significance, hope, and the spirituality of psychic conversion.

These two framing ideas—communitarianism and a call for love—draw West away from a more radical focus on political economy and the continuing legacy of racist discourse. I don't mean to deny the necessity of community ties and psychological well-being, of communal regeneration and the defeat of the nihilistic threat, such as it is. Yet, as analytical frames they are reductive, and misleadingly so. Response to racism requires, minimally, not that my neighbors love me but that they treat me fairly and, as Bill Cosby put it, that they leave me alone. The socioeconomic plight of most black people in America today needs to be addressed not simply in terms of an antinihilistic need for community but, as West himself acknowledges, though all too fleetingly, in terms of radically redistributive measures.

The radical critical voice of Cornel West we have heard over the past decade is still there, but it has become muted. Thus, his appealing identification of morally grounded multiracial alliances and coalition strategies is understressed. Thus, he quietly mentions, without elaborating, the importance of black cultural democracy and transracial relations, of grass-roots organization and organic leadership, of public space and resource equality. These are central features of transformation, as are hybrid postracial identities and pragmatic politics. Indeed, so much does West understress these considerations that he is almost completely silent about the content of these key modes of resistance and transformation. Just as he is virtually silent about the central matter of racialized power, so he says close to nothing about the scope, methods, and content of his prophetic framework;[10] about what antiracist coalition strategies might be effectively adopted; about the moral content of Jewish and black identities that would promote their alliance; about the political leadership needed (as opposed to the kind that is not); and most important, about the ends toward which cross-racial alliances and racially transcendent coalitions ought to work. Indeed, were he to stress throughout the radical, and radically antiessentialist implications of hybridity that he mentions in conclusion, it would likely undermine the essentialist tug of the language West seems compelled, if only for populist reasons, to adopt.

I mention these silences because one gets from *Race Matters* the overwhelming sense that the silences are pregnant with significance. Confronted with a unique opportunity to speak to a very large audience about pressing racial matters all too usually swept aside in public discourse, Cornel West seems moved to adopt a set of terms widely circulating in the public domain even as he has critically rejected the presuppositions on which they are based. Caught between celebration (as of the second coming of the

New York intellectuals in Berube 1995; Boynton 1995) and dismissal (by a displaced wannabe in Wieseltier 1995), public intellectuals are made these days by giving in to the dominant nostalgic dreams or worst nightmares. West's critique is muted here precisely by assuming a framework of analytical concepts tied up intimately with the sort of philosophical liberalism he has criticized in the past, even as he has had the intellectual courage to identify its valuable elements. Thus, *Race Matters* teaches us all too clearly that the truths a public intellectual will speak to power are constrained, if not redirected, by the mediations power places before truth.

Today, when we so need critical public intellectuals—a Sojourner Truth or Frederick Douglass; a John Dewey, Ida B. Wells, or Antonio Gramsci; a W.E.B. Du Bois or a Philip Randolph—we create impossible demands: a public figure whose publicness is predicated on selling himself endlessly, rushing to speaking engagements literally every other day, and driving an elegant town car to a book cover photo session from the Platonic academy of Princeton (or more recently Harvard) to a rooftop high above the jazz streets of Harlem. That we have to be *told* the rooftop is in Harlem is hardly testimony to the power of the image in our culture, though it highlights a tension faced by West in representation. The book cover, read against the reiterated fact that the background is Harlem, encapsulates the dilemma of the successful public intellectual in our time: what gets foregrounded against a fading background—the indistinguishable, blurred image of racialized urban blight and the *wealth* of culture to which it is tied historically—is the figure of the public intellectual himself, the accessible persona, the face of a media star. Most observers recognize him without knowing what he stands for, or against (cf. Reed 1995), without any understanding of the problematic he is trying, in terms not quite his own because he has been divorced from those, to call our attention to and about which he often has interesting, complex, and challenging things to say.

Cornel West owes us nothing. What he owes himself only he can determine. So I do not want to add my voice to those who say that Cornel West owes us a more sustained critical analysis of matters racial. But in trying to gauge whether we should head West at the urgings of this most informed of public intellectuals, it would be welcome help.[11]

Notes

1. In surfing the Internet, I discovered West's "Toward a Socialist Theory of Racism," a paper published only in cyberspace. So his more radical work is being released to the relative anonymity of cyberspace, where electronic distance between text, author, and reader mutes the message. The euphoria over the public dimensions of Internet space has hidden from scrutiny the levels of ordering—of time, of engagement, of perception and conception, of knowledge—

that commercial, hence privatized, framing places upon consumption. At the same time, it deregulates the circulation of racist representation and rationalization, in old form and new.

2. I do not mean to leave the impression that a public intellectual is drawn inevitably, though often inadvertently, by the power of representation into the language of power and representation of power's interests. The measure of critical power and the power of the critical intellectual is furnished precisely by the capacity to undo power's command of language, to redirect significance and to signify redirection, to undo the web of power's meaning as one means to undo power's web, to shatter institutional disciplines as one fractures disciplinary institutions.

3. Parenthetical page numbers within the text refer to Cornel West (1993a).

4. The book consists of eight short chapters and an introduction. Only the penultimate chapter on black sexuality had not appeared before as a discrete article. Four of the remaining seven chapters critique the current impasse of black political and intellectual leadership. The especially thin chapter on affirmative action (all of five pages) discusses the sorts of policies West thinks black leaders should be pursuing.

5. Obviously, the existence of a black middle class, or various fractions of such a class, long precedes this period. See E. Frazier (1965).

6. West makes a number of disparaging remarks about the clothing styles of black politicians and intellectuals, which, he says, symbolize their critical distance from the real concerns and experiences of the bulk of black people. Though he probably had Ron Brown in mind, the counterexample he offers namely, Adam Clayton Powell—demonstrates that expensive tastes need not compromise representation of blacks' political interests. And though West wishes to render black academics more self-conscious about their dress so that they might be taken more seriously when addressing black church and community groups, this hardly commands that they dress like DuBois—or look like West, for that matter. In contrast to West's aesthetic privileging of DuBois's dress, Paul Gilroy (1993, 17) provocatively notes that DuBois invested considerable personal capital in modeling his clothes and mustache on those of Kaiser Wilhelm II. A critique of the aesthetics of contemporary fashion needs to be more evenhanded than West's seemingly self-serving moralizing allows.

7. He includes in this litany, as I do not, the marginalization of humanistic studies, though this strikes me as less true than the others. The influence of humanistic studies has altered in kind, rather than diminished, and this may have to do with their transformed content, styles, and methods. But West's inclusion of humanistic stories implicitly, and uncritically, lauds its past effects. This romanticizes some questionable assumptions and practices in the history of the humanities.

8. For a sustained critical reading of the Thomas affair, see Toni Morrison (1992), in which West's chapter first appeared.

9. West commits two related errors in this account, however, one empirical, the other causal. First, he overstates the levels of black youth employed in Southern agriculture in the 1950s. He claims that 50 percent of all black youth were employed in agriculture, overwhelmingly in the South. Census reports for 1950 put this figure at more like one-third. Second, he directly links the disappearance of these agricultural jobs to urban unemployment of black youth shortly thereafter (1993a, 54). The causal chain suggested here is misdirected: unemployment levels for black youth in northern cities by the mid-1960s was a function not so much of black youth migrating in large numbers from rural areas as it was of massive loss of blue-collar manufacturing jobs from the mid-1950s on. The transformation in the U.S. economy that West notes (54) was already well under way much earlier than he acknowledges.

10. All he says here is that the prophetic framework involves moral assessment of the various perspectives held by black people, particularly of the responses to white supremacism,

though the criteria for moral assessment are never specified other than to add that views will be chosen based on the appeal to black dignity, self-love, decency, and the rejection of any claims to cultural hierarchy (1993a, 30). West discusses at only slightly greater length the related conditions for "psychic conversion" in the closing chapter on Malcolm X.

11. I owe a great deal to insightful discussions about *Race Matters* with Howard McGary (who convinced me that it is a more complex book than a quick cursory read would have it), Tommy Lott, Paul Gilroy, Bill Lawson, Henry Giroux, and especially with my colleague Pat Lauderdale.

References

Becker, Carol (1995). "The Artist as Public Intellectual." *Review of Education/ Pedagogy/Cultural Studies* 17, 4: 385–96.

Berube, Michael (1995). "Public Academy." *The New Yorker*, January 9.

Black Public Sphere Collective, eds. (1995). *The Black Public Sphere*. Chicago: University of Chicago Press.

Boynton, Robert (1995). "The New Intellectuals." *Atlantic Monthly*, March.

Brenkman, John (1995). "Race Publics." *Transition* 66, 8 no. 2: 4–37.

Frazier, E. Franklin (1965). *Black Bourgeoisie*. New York: Free Press.

Gilroy, Paul (1993). *The Black Atlantic: Modernity and Double Consciousness*. Cambridge: Harvard University Press.

Giroux, Henry (1997). "In Living Color: Public Intellectuals and the Politics of Race." *Channel Surfing*. New York: St. Martin's.

Goldberg, David Theo (1993). *Racist Culture: Philosophy and the Politics of Meaning*. Oxford: Basil Blackwell.

Habermas, Jurgen (1989). *The Structural Transformation of the Public Sphere*. Trans. Thomas Burger, with Frederick Lawrence. Cambridge: M.I.T. Press.

James, Joy (1996). *Resisting State Violence*. Minneapolis: University of Minnesota Press.

Morrison, Toni (1992). *Playing in the Dark*. Cambridge: Harvard University Press.

Reed, Adolph (1995). "What Are the Drums Saying, Booker?" *The Village Voice* 40:15, April 11, 31–36.

Said, Edward (1993). *Representations of the Intellectual: The 1993 Reith Lectures*. New York: Pantheon.

West, Cornel (1993a). *Race Matters*. Boston: Beacon.

West, Cornel and Gates, Henry Louis, Jr. (1996). *The Future of the Race*. New York: Knopf.

——— (1993b). "The Dilemma of the Black Intellectual." In *Keeping Faith: Essays on Religion, Philosophy and Politics*. New York: Routledge.

Wieseltier, Leon (1995). "All and Nothing at All." *New Republic*, March 6.

Williams, Patricia (1995). *The Rooster's Egg: The Persistence of Prejudice*. Cambridge: Harvard University Press.

4

The Romance of the Intellectual
and the Question of Profession

Jeffrey Williams

In the current hagiography of intellectuals, Edward Said, or rather the image projected of Said and his career, has taken an exemplary cast. Of late, Said has been widely accorded pantheon status, grouped with other larger-than-life, contemporary intellectual figures such as Noam Chomsky, Susan Sontag, or Michel Foucault, and he anticipates and provides a model for the recent apotheosis of the public intellectual.[1] He was there long before Cornel West.[2] His reputation has in part been built from his work in literary criticism and critical theory, of course, which has been prodigious and influential. His early book *Beginnings*, a long meditation on inaugural moments in literary texts and in some ways a response to Frank Kermode's influential *The Sense of an Ending*, infused the American scene with a learned and nuanced account of Continental theory and provided a pivotal bridge between the humanist tradition (of Auerbach and Curtius, as well as Blackmur in this country, for whom Said expresses admiration) and the new theoretical canon (of Derrida and Foucault, whom Said compares).[3] If *Beginnings* concretized Said's reputation as a central figure in the advent of literary theory, his next book, *Orientalism*, expanded his reputation beyond the confines of literary studies to the larger academic-intellectual community, influencing a range of other academic disciplines, such as anthropology, Oriental studies, international studies, and postcolonial studies (which his work helped establish), as well as to a general (educated) public.[4] After that, *The World, the Text, and the Critic*, a collection of important pieces on theory, further cemented Said's reputation and position in the new discourse of theory, arguing powerfully for attention to worldly concerns as opposed to the narrowly textualist focus of most contemporary theory.[5] Most recently, *Culture and Imperialism*, capping off Said's analysis of the resonances of imperialism in much European literature, has been hailed as a magnum opus (as its dust jacket full of grandly laudatory blurbs asserts), functioning as the icing, as it were, on Said's literary-intellectual reputation, in effect testifying to his now monumental status.[6]

Along with this substantial body of work have come various accolades, honors, and testimonials assuring Said's pre-eminence in the academic-intellectual field: an endowed chair at Columbia and recently a University Professorship there; the Gauss lectures and other such honors for leading critics;[7] conferences, convention sessions, and special issues of journals devoted to his work, including a recent event at Columbia, "After Orientalism: Around the Work of Edward Said," feting his career;[8] a recent book collection addressing his work in the new series from Blackwell's on landmark figures;[9] and on and on. In short, his career has been marked by all the signposts of prominence and recognized by a plethora of elite "legitimating bodies," as Anna Boschetti puts it in the field. "Legitimacy," Boschetti writes in *The Intellectual Enterprise*, "is a result of recognition by already established legitimating bodies: the narrow circle of producers, critics, editors, and journals which has the power to consecrate others because it is itself consecrated."[10] Beyond the specific terms and merit of his work, the accumulation of these honors signals the circulation of Said's reputation and consecration of his position within the academic-intellectual field.

Beyond his estimable academic purchase, though, what has served to catapult Said from academic eminence, from being what James Sosnoski calls a Master Critic[11]—similar to other notable contemporaneous literary figures, such as Stanley Fish or Harold Bloom—to the pantheon has been his political work and profile *in conjunction with* his academic reputation. A Palestinian by birth, he has been a longstanding spokesman for Palestinian and other oppositional political causes, serving on the Palestine National Council and frequently representing those causes in highbrow mainstream media, such as the *New York Times* or Ted Koppel's *Nightline*, eloquently and urbanely pointing out injustices done to Palestinians, particularly under the auspices of Zionism. Further, his writing, especially since *Orientalism*, has dealt more directly with the systematic disparagement of the "Orient"—not only textually, but also in its material consequences—as a self-defining projection of the West. He has done this in a series of non-fiction trade books, such as *The Question of Palestine, Covering Islam, After the Last Sky*, a coedited collection, *Blaming the Victims*, and, finally, the recently published *The Politics of Dispossession*.[12] These books, taken together, serve as a corrective to standard western views of Palestine and the Arab world, and powerfully critique not only literary representations of the Middle East but also the way the Arab world is represented in media (*Covering Islam*) and its consequent play in actual politics (*The Question of Palestine, Blaming the Victims*, etc.).

What is taken as exemplary about Said's work is that it bridges the normally separated zones of academe—the specific if not rarefied world of literary criticism and critical theory—and contemporary politics and larger world affairs. In this regard, his only peer on the scorecard of contemporary American intellectuals is Chomsky, because both have made notable scholarly as well as political contributions.[13] Though Chomsky has been indefatigable in speaking and writing about the way in which consent is manufactured by an essentially repressive postindustrial state, his groundbreaking work in linguistics bears indirectly at best on his political interventions. Said's project, while more narrowly focused politically, seems to have a more organic consistency, conjoining both academic-theoretical and practical-political dimensions and thus projecting a relatively unified narrative trajectory of career. In his occupying these multiple zones of intellectual life—academic and public, literature and politics, theory and journalism, classroom and television—Said is sometimes cast as a latter-day, Sartrean-engaged intellectual.[14] Anna Boschetti observes of Sartre something that I believe applies to Said as well: "His success is essentially a result of his having occupied several positions at the same time."[15]

As should be clear, I detail all of this not simply to march out Said's credentials—either to augment or for that matter to detract from his reputation—but rather to underscore how the image of his intellectual career has been constructed and projected within the intellectual field. Though his achievement is undeniable, the general position Said takes on the current scene—the nearly unequivocally laudatory charge his name carries[16]—speaks to various factors of the economy of the extant intellectual field and the symbolic profits that accrue therein. Said fills a particular position within that field, or a series of related positions: he offers a solution to the embarrassment of the political irrelevance of academic-intellectual life, a kind of marquee of relevance against the ivory tower syndrome (he performs elegantly on *Nightline*); he serves as a self-abasing reminder of professional guilt over the usual perception of academic irrelevance and impotence;[17] he negotiates the tensions of professionalism, simultaneously appearing as a consummate professional—elegant, urbane, eloquently speaking as a humanist—and as a participant in or even quasi-statesman for "real world" political causes that presumably are "outside" the profession;[18] he provides an example of an organic intellectual, speaking for his people and homeland, but with an accredited, traditional East Coast elite purchase, in the Brahmin tones of the Ivy League;[19] and he straddles political poles, offering a specular image of the grand humanist, in the legacy of his teachers, R.P. Blackmur and Henry Levin, and writing on canonical cultural issues, at the same time that he carries moderate Left credentials.[20] In short, rather than encumbering or isolating him, Said's academic reputation and position—not least of which is his accession to Lionel Trilling as Columbia's and New York's great cosmopolitan man of letters—grant him a privileged position from which to make his political interventions and a cache of credibility in his public appearances, counterbalancing anti-Arab sentiment through his urbane and polished persona. Conversely, his political statements and performances yield a great deal of symbolic capital to his position as a man of letters and a cosmopolitan intellectual. His position as an exemplary intellectual is built precisely on his negotiation of this series of contradictory positions, lending his name optimum symbolic capital.

Given the substantial persona of intellectual engagement that Said projects, it should carry some weight when he explicitly addresses the question of the intellectual and the intellectual vocation, as he does in his recent book, *Representations of the Intellectual*.[21] Further, the book sketches out a project that Said has been planning for some time, building on his earlier work on modern institutions—in the several senses of that term—of knowledge and the roles intellectuals play in those institutions. One might suppose that any oppositional intellectual worth her or his salt would buy it, pick up a pencil, and take notes.

Taken by itself, *Representations of the Intellectual* is a compact book—barely 120 pages—that collects six lectures originally commissioned for and delivered on the BBC in 1993, so it does not give a fully elaborated account of the history of the intellectual or a lengthy meditation on the theoretical and political issues involved, the kind of dense and nuanced work one might expect in the wake of *Beginnings* or *Culture and Imperialism*. I do not cite this as a detraction, but as a generic qualification. For the most part, I take this brevity as a virtue, because it presents Said's essential mandates for being an intellectual synoptically, providing a kind of elegant guidebook on the question of intellectuals in a way that is easy to read and, I would imagine, easy to teach. In its directness and force, it is reminiscent of such polemically charged statements as Sartre's *What Is Literature?* or Orwell's "Why I Write." In accessible and felicitous prose, learned without being ponderous, Said briskly outlines the ways in which intellectuals have represented their tasks and vocation and how they have defined themselves, arguing for one particular version of what he believes an intellectual should do.

In a short introduction, he hits the key notes of his prescription: intellectuals should speak to a wide public; eschew nationalism, party orthodoxy, professionalism, or any other kind of "insider" thinking; uphold a universal standard; and, what seems to me bracing but somewhat cryptic, speak the truth to power. In some ways, a synonym for his definition of an intellectual would most succinctly be a dissenter, as indicated by the two examples he names, Noam Chomsky and Gore Vidal (xviii). This dissenting cast takes on a distinctly romantic character: he stresses the lonely independence, exile, and self-imposed marginality of the intellectual (xvi). I take this point—the essentially literary portrait and romanticization of the life and work of an intellectual—as the crux of his definition of the intellectual, and will return to it shortly.

In the first chapter, Said starts out with a survey of standard views of the intellectual, from Julien Benda (as an unworldly clerisy), Gramsci (organic vs. traditional), Foucault (specific vs. universal), and Alvin Gouldner (as a specialized new class). Said sorts through each of these, discarding what he finds debilitating, to make up his composite intellectual ideal: independent and not beholden to interests of the world (thereby reconstituting the otherwise conservative Benda and his attack on intellectuals), pivotal to the functioning—for good or ill—of modern society (from Gramsci, the necessity of intellectuals, but without the determinism of class), acting "on the basis of universal principles" (counter to Foucault's typifying modern intellectuals as specific, within local fields and having local effects), and precisely against the interests of specialization (against Gouldner's portrait of the new intellectual expert). For Said, the task of the intellectual is "a vocation for the art of representing" (13), representing a standpoint, however quixotic and regardless of cost, to a public. Said goes on to fill out the chapter by rehearsing three literary portraits of intellectuals, from Turgenev's *Fathers and Sons*, Flaubert's *Sentimental Education*, and Joyce's *Portrait of the Artist As a Young Man*. He takes Stephen Dedalus's manifesto of "silence, exile, and cunning" as an exemplary "affirmation of intellectual freedom" (17).

In the next two chapters, Said takes up the question of societal pressures or constraints, particularly nationalism and religious tradition. An intellectual should appropriately not sign on with or accommodate narrow nationalist or similar causes, but rather stay free to dispute their prevailing norms—as he has done most recently in critiques in the *Nation* and elsewhere of Arafat and the new peace.[22] This position has two poles: first, that of remaining an inveterate individualist against "prevailing norms"; and second, that of embracing a universalist vision to understand what other nations or religious groups are suffering. As a corollary to this antiorthodoxy, in chapter 3 Said talks about the necessarily exiled or outsider position of the intellectual. For him, exile is the prime "metaphorical" if not actual condition of an intellectual, and he takes Adorno as his key example.

In chapter 4, Said continues his list of dangers to intellectual integrity, shifting from external dangers (nationalism and societal pressures) to more internal disciplinary pressures that he groups under the term professionalism. He brings up Regis Debray's striking genealogy of intellectuals—as Debray puts it, the model of intellectual life has gone from teacher to writer to celebrity—and Russell Jacoby's condemnation of the American scene, although, surprisingly, Said defends the academic positioning of contemporary intellectuals against Jacoby's facile narrative of their fall (72). In this chapter, Said details several aspects of professional life that he finds damningly harmful: the present mode of specialization, which shuts out other pursuits and cuts one off from larger concerns; the cult of expertise, which further limits and controls intellectuals; the drift to power and authority, to those who fund experts; and, in general, conformity to prevailing ideas and power relations. Against the narrowness of specialization and the complicit interestedness of expertise, Said argues for amateurism. This move, while obviously motivated to break the circuit of compromised professionalism, seems an overdetermined concept at best, carrying a belletristic residue that hardly accords with Said's view of engagement, and contradicting what would seem to be Said's actual position in the university and as a professional literary figure. But more on that in a moment.

These chapters are basically cautionary, meting out prohibitions to legitimate intellectual activity, whereas the next chapter builds to a kind of crescendo, offering a more positive vista for what an intellectual should do: speak the truth to power, question authority, and argue for universal principles—to as large a public audience as possible. He unabashedly espouses grand humanist values, such as universal justice, and again the enemy is sectarianism; as he puts it, "if you wish to uphold basic human justice you must do so for everyone, not just selectively for the people that your side, your culture, your nation designates as okay" (93). The sixth and last chapter, "Gods That Always Fail," reinforces this point with a cautionary anecdote, describing an unnamed "brilliantly eloquent and charismatic Iranian intellectual" who spoke actively and forcefully for the Iranian revolution in the late 1970s until 1981, when Bani Sadr was forced into exile. Later, Said tells of encountering him speaking actively and forcefully *against* the Imam and the excesses of his regime. For Said, the failing here is that this person did not retain his intellectual autonomy, but was a true believer and therefore played out a cycle of conversion and recantation (113). This closing exemplum picks up Said's longtime stress on secular values, against the excesses done in the name of religion, nations, parties, professions, and methods, and lends *Representations of the Intellectual* an almost wistfully elegiac as well as cautionary note.

There is finally a certain uplifting quality to *Representations of the Intellectual*, even a headiness, in its model of an independent intellectual staunchly speaking truth to power, doing for intellectuals, academic or otherwise, what *All the President's Men* did for journalists. In this, Said's definition of intellectual activity relies on what I take to be an essentially literary myth, fashioning the intellectual as a kind of existential hero who stands by her- or himself, alone, warding off power, without any social ties but simply drawn on by truth. Generically, then, *Representations of the Intellectual* constitutes a pseudo-romance of intellectual activity, the intellectual as lonely knight (isolated, exiled, uncorrupted by business concerns, etc.), crusading against lies and hypocrisy.[23]

This depiction, despite its attractiveness, complicates any vista of political engagement. Said's choice of Joyce's *Portrait of the Artist As a Young Man* as an intellectual profile is revealing here: Dedalus's motto of "silence, exile, cunning" taps into the strand of the forlorn, alienated romantic artist/ modernist intellectual, a variant on the literary scheme mentioned above— hardly a model for genuine political engagement, one would think. Dedalus himself is decidedly antipolitical and disdains the anticolonial, nationalist politics of his schoolmates, such as McCann and Cranly.[24] That Said takes this as an exemplary case is particularly strange because it obviously runs against the grain of his own example: he has not been silent, and although he was born in Egypt, his relation to exile is complicated.[25] Further, his image is residually tied to the political interests of Palestine, to a dispossessed nation and its people. Dedalus, if anything, portrays a disaffected intellectual, self-absorbed and self-interested.

A significant component of this depiction of intellectual life is Said's stress on individualism, his insistence that the intellectual stand alone, autonomous, outside any group affiliation, representing his or her own individual views and interests. That is the quality that Said finds Dedalus to exemplify. This prescription of individualism is troublesome, though, because it detaches intellectuality from *collective* action—politics, after all, consists of the concerted actions of people amid groups of people—and displaces politics to a question of individual ethics, to issues of individual choice and responsibility. As Said puts it, an intellectual is "an individual . . . with a faculty for . . . articulating a message." The trouble with this view is that it might well apply to David Duke, Rush Limbaugh, or Pat Buchanan, as well as to Said himself. Further, Said ascribes a free-floating quality to an intellectual who by his definition speaks to a public sphere, but he fails to account for the channels through which one might gain access to that public sphere. Not everyone can publish with Pantheon or Knopf, regardless of intellectual merit and integrity, not to mention appear on *Nightline* or in the pages of the *New York Times*. The public channels of information are controlled by prevailing interests (as Noam Chomsky and others have frequently pointed out and detailed), although that is not to say that someone like Said is irredeemably compromised, since there are various contradictions in that control. It is to say, however, that the intellectual is never independent or solitary, but valuable insofar as he or she speaks for and represents collective concerns, within a collective economy or institution.[26]

A related component of Said's romance of the intellectual is his call for amateurism. This also draws on the network of the Romantic loner and individualist, unbeholden to more worldly concerns, particularly to the world of money and business, picking up a strand of romantic ideology or nostalgia for premechanistic, preprofessional days, the halcyon time before the divisions of modern capitalism. At the same time, though, it is a distinctly capitalist notion, precluding a degree of financial security, of the gentleman of leisure who has the resources to pursue his hobbies, from collecting butterflies to commenting on politics. The ideology of the amateur is powerful and common in literary studies, and taps into the humanistic construction of the critic, exemplified in R.P. Blackmur's "The Critic's Job of Work," which begins "Criticism, I take it, is the formal discourse of an amateur."[27] The advantage of this view, for Said, is that it casts the intellectual outside the pull and influence of professional concerns, thus ensuring the critic's integrity. However, this view seems strangely contradictory, because Said's position as an exemplary professional is what provides validation and legitimation for his political views and gives him a privileged public location from which to make his political interventions. Further, Said himself urges that criticism take up worldly or secular concerns, beyond narrow "textual" concerns, whereas amateurism casts itself against the dirt of worldliness.[28] And, in general, though amateurism escapes the parochial limitations of professionalism, it is predicated on and imbricated in the general configuration of capitalism, the workings of wealth and power that foster a leisure class to pursue the arts and mindly interests.

Given these manifest contradictions and seeming ideological swerves, why then does Said propose this definition of the intellectual? Rather than simply ascribing it to an unregenerate humanism—in the line of Auerbach and the direct descendant of Blackmur, a line he has praised and defended—or to his uncritical subscription to a powerful but mystified literary image, I would pose two explanations, one bespeaking his theoretical coordinates and the other his specific situation. First, his definition of an independent, free-floating intellectual places him or her beyond interest, professional, national, religious, or even personal. Oddly enough, despite his frequently expressed animus toward organized religion of any kind, this casts the intellectual as a kind of latter-day prophet, speaking truth wherever he or she may go, despite resistance and threats as well as rewards—the intellectual as Joan of Arc. The gain here is that the intellectual is incorruptible. Put in more neutral philosophical terms, a salient characteristic of Said's portrait is *disinterestedness*. In addition, the intellectual stands up for universal values, without purposeful gain, and he or she has an obligation to make necessary statements, despite costs or hesitations. These attributes in large part mirror those of the aesthetic that Kant delineates in the *Critique of Judgement*—disinterest, universality, purposiveness without purpose, and necessity—to determine whether an aesthetic judgement, a judgement of taste, is reliable or valid.[29]

In other words, Said's definition of political engagement and the intellectual's purchase on politics is finally based on *aesthetic* criteria. Throughout *Representations of the Intellectual*, a decided ambivalence emerges toward the *messiness* of politics, toward the messiness of coalition and affiliation and the complication of representing actual interests. The aestheticized intellectual transcends the mire of worldly interest, in profession or state. This explains the otherwise retro-turn to amateurism: the category of the amateur is purportedly disinterested, without the affiliation or sheer economic need of the professional. That the category of the amateur is inextricably bound with ruling-class privilege is a question that Said never broaches.

Second, *Representations of the Intellectual* functions in a way as an apologia, offering an explanation for Said's career, for the way he has cut his intellectual course and his navigations through the various institutions and political terrain of the past thirty years. It generalizes a rationale for the specific historical positions that he occupies and straddles: as an expositor of western culture (from the *Iliad* to *Aida*) and defender of the values of humanistic study, but also as someone who translated Arafat's speeches when Arafat first visited the United Nations; as a traditional intellectual, an endowed professor at an old and ivied university known for its Great Books curriculum, who also effectively and organically presents the case of Palestinians and other Arab peoples who are typically unrepresented or negatively drawn in western media; as an independent and autonomous intellectual who has also participated in the Palestine National Council and served the Palestinian cause in various ways; as someone who claims an amateur status, as a scholar and political figure, who meanwhile appears as an extraordinarily erudite and urbane professional literary figure, and who has access to various public venues, such as the *New York Times* and television.

As Said puts it himself, he very keenly has the sense of being a double agent, of being in both camps: of teaching literature at Columbia and of having had an office across the hall from his elder colleague and friend Lionel Trilling, and yet participating actively in anti-Zionist, Arab-American politics.[30] In this sense, then, the qualities that Said prescribes—autonomy, independence, amateurism, and so forth—legitimate his particular and otherwise unique position, giving him a credibility that would not otherwise be available to a spokesman for Arab causes because they distance him from those causes. He is granted a position to speak for Palestine by virtue of his cosmopolitan, western persona—by virtue of *not* being an Oriental but rather a leading western man of letters and professor.[31] Conversely, he represents Palestine by being detached from Palestine, by being an exile and not being attached to a particular location. And his espousal of amateurism detaches him from the weight of being a part of a western institution, of being complicit in or restricted by the knowledge production and social circulation of an elite university. Said's attribution of autonomy gives him a medial position, simultaneously representing and also denying status quo western values (and oppression) and extreme political opposition (i.e., the aspersion of terrorism).[32] In short, Said evacuates the political position he locates in order to legitimate that position.

Overall, then, as a guidebook or how-to, *Representations of the Intellectual* has limited utility. It primarily serves a literary function, to project a romance of intellectual life as well as to legitimate Said's atypical and complicated position. Still, the one salutary vista that I would take away from *Representations of the Intellectual* is its persistent call for *engagement*, Said's citing the obligation of intellectuals to be politically committed and to represent oppositional and otherwise unrepresented positions. Rather than evacuating the concept of professionalism as Said does, however, I would reclaim it more neutrally, as simply a description of the predominant location of contemporary intellectual life, offering a potential zone of opposition as well as of complicity and conformity.

For Said, on the one hand professionalism is constituted by specialization, by the parochial limiting of its object of study, its modes and methods, and its boundaries. Said argues against the disciplinary self-quarantining implicit in specialization, which removes that discipline from the public sphere and more general relevance. In short, those specialized professionals are self- or profession-interested, and thus closed off from interdisciplinary as well as larger world concerns. On the other hand, professionalism implies a cult of expertise, a cadre of experts who consult for business and government, and Said eschews this version of professionalism as well, because it serves the interests of power and authority (80). This species of the professional is again self-interested, presumably for gain and the favors and spoils of power. The first of these I would identify as an *insular or parochial professionalism*, and the second an *accommodationist* or *consultant professionalism*.[33] In Said's scheme of things, amateurism skirts both these wayward paths: it moves the intellectual out of the insular zone of normal professional work, presumably to more worldly concerns, and from the opposite direction it pulls professionals back from the taint of worldly concerns. The professional position is both not worldly enough and too worldly, too clerical and not clerical enough; this version of professionalism carries a constitutive antigen of antiprofessionalism, a dilemma that Bruce Robbins underscores throughout his recent *Secular Vocations*.[34]

In light of these two versions of professionalism, it is not hard to see why Said attempts to shun them in staking a political vista. However, a different way of seeing the vista of professional location exists beyond the cautionary and schematic nature of these two negative poles. I would mark this alternative, in part borrowing from Said himself, as a *secular professionalism*. This takes up Said's polemic in *The World, the Text, and the Critic* for a worldly, secular, and oppositional criticism, rather than the narrow textualism that prevailed through the 1980s under the sign of deconstruction and the predominance of literary theory generally.[35] And it also draws on the example of Said himself, on his work and his public profile and statements, which in their best aspect combine an impeccable professionalism *and* a secular political purview. I find this version of professionalism far preferable to Said's opting for amateurism because, as I've said, amateurism at best carries the connotation of fanciful or belletristic interest, and at worst a history of wealth and privilege that is obscured in its purported disinterest, and further because it is strategically more efficacious, stressing the political potential inherent in the largely academic location of contemporary intellectuals. It moves the definition of intellectual activity away from that of an arcane hobby to that of engagement, albeit negotiating various institutional channels.

This use of professionalism provides a medial term of negotiation between the intellectual field and the larger world, between guild and public interest, rather than a caution against one or the other. Professionalism is a crucial mode of representation of the intellectual field in the public realm. Seen in this way, the university provides a home base that can enable the kind of intellectual activity and engagement that Said argues for, offering a relative degree of leisure and opportunity to conduct critical projects, and access to research materials, a fixed income for a degree of material security, and a platform of validation from which to speak. As Noam Chomsky extols in "The Responsibility of Intellectuals,"

> Intellectuals are in a position to expose the lies of governments, to analyze actions according to their causes and motives and often hidden intentions. In the Western world at least, they have the power that comes from political liberty, from access to information and freedom of expression. For a privileged minority, Western democracy provides the leisure, the facilities, and the training to seek the truth lying hidden behind the veil of distortion and misrepresentation, ideology, and class interest through which the events of current history are presented to us.[36]

That leisure and training is largely fostered by the university. Although there are many different strata in universities and different kinds of privilege—very few of us are fortunate enough to hold an endowed chair at Columbia, and a university position is not by any means a sinecure—I would maintain that the academic-professional zone of intellectual work offers distinct possibilities and advantages. Beyond granting gainful employment and access to resources, it represents a public sphere, one of the few to remain in the post-Fordist moment, in which many citizens can address and debate public issues. As Said himself puts it in an interview, "[T]here's no question that, in some ways, neither Chomsky nor myself would have had the audiences we've had without the university. A lot of the people who listen to us when we speak—it's certainly true in his case—are university students. The university provides one with a forum."[37] Further, it offers a zone of accreditation or credibility from which one can intervene in debates in other and larger slices of the public sphere. Rather than having a bad conscience about it, or for that matter rather than celebrating it as idyllic, I would stress that professionalism is neither a fall nor a benefit, but a pivotal term of negotiation of intellectual life in the context of late twentieth-century institution. The imperative is to mobilize it for oppositional uses that might otherwise be suppressed or voiceless, rather than to abandon or disdain it.

Notes

1. As Cornel West declares, "Said stands now as the towering figure among left humanistic intellectuals" (*Keeping Faith: Philosophy and Race in America* [New York: Routledge, 1993], 100). I take the hyperbole here, regardless of merit, to indicate that it has become something of a commonplace that Said is regarded as "our" exemplary intellectual.

2. The figure of the public intellectual has been announced with much fanfare of late, typified by the front-page *New York Times* feature "Journeys from Ivory Tower: Public Intellectual Is Reborn," by Janny Scott (9 August 1994, A1, B4). Scott sidesteps the example of

Said. West has recently been lauded as the great new public intellectual hope in many places; significantly, Michael Bérubé's review-essay in the *New Yorker*, "Public Academy" (9 January 1995, 73–80), casts the new group of black intellectuals, such as West, bell hooks, and Derrick Bell, as taking the place of New York Intellectuals. See also Robert S. Boynton, "The New Intellectuals," *Atlantic Monthly*, March 1995, 53–70.

3. Although Said's first book was *Joseph Conrad and the Fiction of Autobiography* (Cambridge: Harvard University Press, 1966), *Beginnings: Intention and Method* (New York: Basic Books, 1975) was his breakthrough book, given the imprimatur of Hillis Miller as a "major event for literary criticism and for humanistic study generally" (back cover blurb). See also Miller's essay "Beginning with a Text," originally published as part of a special issue of diacritics (6, No. 3, Fall 1976) devoted to Said's work and reprinted in Miller, *Theory Now and Then* (Durham, NC: Duke University Press), 133–42.

4. *Orientalism* (New York: Pantheon, 1978) provoked a great deal of debate; for some sense of its reception, see Dennis Porter, "*Orientalism* and Its Problems," in *The Politics of Theory: Proceedings of the Essex Conference on the Sociology of Literature, July 1982*, ed. Francis Barker et al. (Colchester, UK: University of Essex, 1983), 179–93; in anthropology, James Clifford, "On *Orientalism*," in *The Predicament of Culture: Twentieth-Century Ethnography, Literature, and Art* (Cambridge: Harvard University Press, 1988); and Said's "Orientalism Reconsidered," in *Literature, Politics, and Theory: Papers from the Essex Conference 1976–84*, ed. Francis Barker et al. (London: Methuen, 1986), 210–29.

5. *The World, the Text, and the Critic* (Cambridge: Harvard University Press, 1983) includes well-known and oft-cited Said pieces, such as the introduction, "Secular Criticism," "Reflections on American 'Left' Literary Criticism," "Traveling Theory," and "Criticism Between Culture and System." Some commentators mark this book and *Orientalism* as a turn for Said from the concerns of high theory, whereas other critics see them as consistent developments. For the former view, see Daniel O'Hara, "Criticism Worldly and Otherworldly: Edward W. Said and the Cult of Theory," *boundary 2* 12, No. 3, and 13, No. 1 (Spring/Fall 1984), 382; for the latter, see Tim Brennan's "Places of Mind, Occupied Lands: Edward Said and Philology," which traces the place of philology and traditional, high humanist concerns through Said's work, in *Edward Said: A Critical Reader*, ed. Michael Sprinker (Cambridge, MA: Blackwell, 1992), 74–95.

6. *Culture and Imperialism* (New York: Knopf, 1993) includes back-cover blurbs by luminaries such as Frank Kermode, Henry Louis Gates Jr., Noam Chomsky, Cornel West, and others; though such markers are ephemeral and typically hyperbolic, they function symbolically to affirm Said's exemplary image and position.

7. Other such honors include the Eliot lectures, the Reith lectures, a fellowship at the Center for Advanced Study at Stanford, a visiting professorship at and courtship by Harvard, to name a few. At random, a contributor's note—again, like blurbs, ephemeral, but a telling venue for the attribution and circulation of intellectual reputation—in *boundary 2* testifies to Said's place in the intellectual field: "Long considered among the foremost literary, political, and historical intellectuals in the world, he is the author of many books and innumerable articles" (*boundary 2* 21, No. 3 [Fall, 1994], 272]).

8. Held 18–19 October 1996. *Social Text* 40 (1994) carries a special section on Said, drawn from an MLA panel and largely on the occasion of the publication of *Culture and Imperialism*, and, as noted above, *Beginnings* was met with a special issue of *diacritics* devoted to it. To give one further instance, Said's *Critical Inquiry* article "Representing the Colonized: Anthropology's Interlocutors" carries the note, "This paper was originally delivered at an invited session of the 86th annual meeting of the American Anthropological Association in Chicago, 21 November 1987. . . . The session was entitled "Anthropology's Interlocutors:

Edward Said and Representations of the Colonized," and drew the comments of well-known anthropologists such as Talal Asad, Richard Fox, Renato Rosaldo, and Paul Rabinow." (*Critical Inquiry* 15, No. 2 [Winter 1989], 205).

9. Sprinker, *Edward Said.* The series also includes volumes on Derrida, Foucault, Habermas, and Althusser—in other words, a kind of "Superstars of Theory."

10. Anna Boschetti, *The Intellectual Enterprise: Sartre and* Les Temps Modernes, trans. Richard C. McCleary (Evanston, IL: Northwestern University Press, 1988), 3. Boschetti draws conspicuously on the influential sociological work of Pierre Bourdieu, particularly on the concept of field and how social fields operate.

11. See James Sosnoski, *Token Professionals and Master Critics: A Critique of Orthodoxy in Literary Studies* (Albany: State University of New York Press, 1993).

12. *The Question of Palestine* (New York: Times Books, 1979); *Covering Islam: How the Media and the Experts Determine How We See the Rest of the World* (New York: Pantheon, 1981); *After the Last Sky: Palestinian Lives,* photographs by Jean Mohr (New York: Pantheon, 1986); *Blaming the Victims; Spurious Scholarship and the Palestinian Question* (London and New York: Verso, 1988; coedited with Christopher Hitchens); and *The Politics of Dispossession: The Struggle for Palestinian Self-Determination, 1969–1993* (New York: Pantheon, 1994). All published by trade presses, these books speak to a different and wider zone of readers than standard academic fare.

13. In *The Political Responsibility of the Critic* (Ithaca, NY: Cornell University Press, 1987), Jim Merod lionizes both Said and Chomsky precisely for their actual political engagement alongside their theoretical work. The other critics he reports on—such as Fredric Jameson—fall short of that standard.

14. O'Hara takes it this way, dividing intellectuals into two camps, those represented by Heidegger (complicity) and those by Sartre (social criticism and self-revision), placing Said in this second camp. See "Criticism Worldly and Otherworldly," 381.

15. Boschetti, *Intellectual Enterprise,* 5. Cf. Barbara Harlow, who celebrates Said for his work for "multiple constituencies, both literary-critical and political" ("The Palestinian Intellectual and the Liberation of the Academy," in Sprinker, *Edward Said,* 173).

16. Though Said is denigrated and even demonized by those affiliated with Israeli causes (see, for instance, Edward Alexander, "Professor of Terror," *Commentary* 88 [1989], 49–50), recognition of his reputation and position in the intellectual field is unanimous.

17. Stanley Fish points out a tendency in academics to self-abnegation in "The Unbearable Ugliness of Volvos," *English Inside and Out: The Places of Literary Criticism,* ed. Susan Gubar and Jonathan Kamholz (New York: Routledge, 1993), 102–108.

18. In *Secular Vocations: Intellectuals, Professionalism, Culture* (New York: Verso, 1993), Bruce Robbins underscores the constitutive ambivalence and ambiguity of professional location; see especially "The East Is a Career: Edward Said," 152–79.

19. As Imre Salusinszky puts it: "The first time I met you, in a class at Yale, I anticipated that you'd speak with a colorful accent, like mine. . . . But I was surprised at this New York persona: urbane and rather assimilated" (Edward Said, Interview, Imre Salusinszky, *Criticism in Society: Interviews with Jacques Derrida, Northrop Frye, Harold Bloom, Geoffrey Hartman, Frank Kermode, Edward Said, Barbara Johnson, Frank Lentricchia, and J. Hillis Miller* [New York and London: Methuen, 1987], 127). As Tim Brennan notes, "While still talking in the persuasive, coaxing tones of a professional literary person, he keeps declaring himself in a way he knows will trouble many of his more traditional readers" ("Places of Mind," 89; see also 92).

20. R.P. Blackmur was his mentor at Princeton, Levin at Harvard; see Michael Sprinker, "Introduction," *Edward Said,* 2. See also Said's tribute to Blackmur, "The Horizon of R.P. Blackmur," *Raritan* 6, No. 2 (Fall 1986), 29–50.

Though Said has an ambivalent relation to Marxism—he avows the influence of Marxist writers on his work, but disavows systems that prescribe criticism in advance (see *The World, the Text, and the Critic*, 28–29, and Sprinker, *Edward Said*, 261–62)—many of the Left critics in *Edward Said: A Critical Reader* induct Said into a Left hall of fame. See especially Tim Brennan, "Places of Mind," and Barbara Harlow, "The Palestinian Intellectual." For a less celebratory but attentive critique of Said's political ambivalence and his eschewal of Marxism, see Aijaz Ahmad, *In Theory: Classes, Nations, Literatures* (New York and London: Verso, 1992), esp. 203–19.

21. Edward Said, *Representations of the Intellectual: The 1993 Reith Lectures* (New York: Pantheon, 1994).

22. See "Oslo I to Oslo II: The Mirage of Peace," *The Nation*, 16 October 1995: 413–20; "Bookless in Gaza," *The Nation*, 23 September 1996: 6–7.

23. As Said puts it, "I find myself to a certain degree in sympathy with Chomsky's position, a kind of anarcho-syndicalist position, *which has great romantic appeal*" (my emphasis; Jennifer Wicke and Michael Sprinker, "Interview with Edward Said," in Sprinker, *Edward Said*, 261–62). For a relevant review of *Representations of the Intellectual* that underscores Said's "romantic pose" and finally solipsism (the lone intellectual hero), see Michael Walzer, "The Solipsist as Hero," *The New Republic*, 7 November 1994, 38–40.

24. The Irish situation is one that Said himself has identified as demonstrating postcolonial politics; see "Yeats and Decolonization," Terry Eagleton, Fredric Jameson, and Edward Said, *Nationalism, Colonialism, and Literature* (Minneapolis: University of Minnesota Press, 1990), 69–95.

25. As he notes in a recent essay, "Now let me speak personally and even politically if I may. Like so many others, I belong to more than one world. I am a Palestinian Arab, and I am also an American" ("Identity, Authority, and Freedom," *boundary 2* 21, No. 3 [Fall 1994], 11).

26. For a counterpoint to Said's imperative for autonomy in intellectual life, see Michael Walzer, "Introduction: The Practice of Social Criticism," *The Company of Critics: Social Criticism and Political Commitment in the Twentieth Century* (New York: Basic Books, 1988), 3–28. Walzer stresses the connectedness of the critic-intellectual, stipulating that "criticism follows from connection" (23) and reasoning that "if he [the critic] were a stranger, really disinterested, it is hard to see why he would involve himself in [social] affairs" (20).

27. R.P. Blackmur, "The Critic's Job of Work," *Form and Value in Modern Poetry* (Garden City, NY: Doubleday, 1957), 339.

28. This is the motif of *The World, the Text, and the Critic*, articulated in the introduction, "Secular Criticism," 1–30.

29. See Immanuel Kant, *Critique of Judgement*, trans. J.H. Bernard (New York: Hafner Press, 1951), especially "Analytic of the Beautiful," 37–81.

30. Said describes his situation like this:

> A great deal of what I consider to be interesting and valuable experience autobiographically, had to be kept away professionally. It was certainly the case that when I was beginning to teach at Columbia that I was really considered two people—there was the person who was the teacher of literature and there was this other person, like Dorian Grey, who did these quite unspeakable things. If I could give an example: I was very friendly with Lionel Trilling, who had his office across the way from mine, and he was very kind and solicitous, and I have always liked him a great deal, but we never once, in the fifteen years that we were friendly, let these other matters come up; and I trained myself to live that way. (Raymond Williams and Edward Said, Interview, "Media, Margins, and Modernity," Raymond Williams, *The Politics of Modernism: Against the New Conformists*, ed. Tony Pinkney [London and New York: Verso, 1989], 187)

He also talks about his "leading a schizophrenic life" between the academic study of literature and larger social concerns (Salusinszky, *Criticism in Society*, 133). See also Edward W. Said, Interview, *diacritics* 6, No. 3 (1976), 35, for an early discussion of his leading two different lives, a situation he analogizes to Conrad's *Secret Sharer*.

31. Said makes this remark about Arafat and Arafat's reception in the West: "There's a kind of stubborn and somehow uninformed refusal on the part of the Palestinians to accommodate easily. . . . It's almost epitomized in the appearance of Arafat; he doesn't correspond to any known notion of what a national leader should look like" (Edward W. Said, "U.S. Intellectuals and Middle East Politics," interview conducted by Bruce Robbins, *Intellectuals: Aesthetics, Politics, Academics*, ed. Bruce Robbins [Minneapolis: University of Minnesota Press, 1990], 139). Said himself doesn't dress or look like Arafat, but exactly how one might expect an elegant humanities professor to look.

32. For an example of the knee-jerk charge of terrorism—and why Said needs to distance himself from such aspersions—see Alexander, "The Professor of Terror."

33. See my "The Life of the Mind and the Academic Situation," *College Literature* 23, No. 3 (1996), 128–46.

34. For a relevant response, see Catherine Gallagher, "Politics, the Profession, and the Critic," *diacritics* 15, No. 2 (1985), 37–43.

35. See "Secular Criticism," esp. 28–30.

36. *The Chomsky Reader*, ed. James Peck (New York: Pantheon, 1987), 60.

37. *Criticism in Society*, 133.

Gendering Identities

5

Psychoanalytic Questions, Pedagogical Possibilities, and Authority

Encountering the "And"

Sharon Todd

My first encounter with *Feminisms and Critical Pedagogy* was unsettling. Editors Carmen Luke and Jennifer Gore situate the essays collected here in overarching yet specifically differentiated positions of poststructuralist feminisms. When I glanced at the title, I had assumed the book would address the relations and the dissonances between feminisms and critical pedagogy—discursive, practical, political, philosophical, and otherwise. This assumption was based upon a (mis?)reading of the signifier "and," a reading that dissolved when I discovered on the back of the book a description of some of the essays as outlining "the current stand-off between feminist educators and critical theorists." That feminists were labeled "educators," while critical pedagogues were "theorists" was not without its effects. That both these terms were engaged in a standoff conjured up images of the Oka crisis, in which Mohawks were engaged in a life struggle over ancestral lands, while the white-right issue was golf.[1] In casting the discursive and academic relationship in the light of a standoff, the book has made it impossible for me to "stand outside" the imbroglio. I must "take a stand" on the issues, the arguments, and the assumptions. Thus what I hoped would be a fluid encounter turned out to be one marked by untransgressed borders.

This essay is an attempt to cross those borders established by the stand-off, remembering that these are shifting discursive and academic terrains and not the bloody fields of North America where losing a (way of) life for some is par for the course for others. While I am sympathetic to the book's aim of critique and displacement of phallocentric knowledges in critical and other pedagogies, I nevertheless find myself in an "uneasy" relation-ship (to echo the editors' own relationship to critical pedagogical theory and practice) to the kinds of arguments presented there, which situate fem-inisms *and* critical pedagogy as oppositional discourses whose attentions to notions of authority and power (among others) are necessarily always at odds, always already unreconcilable.[2] What I hope to do here is offer a cri-tique of the book in the spirit of displacing the "and" (Felman 1982a) through a psychoanalytic intervention, displacing the borders that delimit the territories of critical pedagogy and poststructural feminisms.

A Possible Encounter?

The subtitle of this essay concerns the possible encounter between psycho-analysis and pedagogy, particularly feminist pedagogy, over the notion of authority. I intend to demonstrate that claims to decentering authority from those poststructuralist-feminist positions advocated in *Feminisms and Critical Pedagogy* do not consider the dynamic of authority in specifically poststructural *psychoanalytic* terms. Instead, many of the authors adhere to a concept of authority that is not dynamic, but always already patriarchal.[3] This suggests to me that there is a foreclosing of the pedagogical dynamic as a movement of fantasy and of the imaginary identifications that constitute, subvert, and transform that dynamic. By this I mean that these theorists have elided the ways authority operates as reality in illusion and fantasy, as well in the social and discursive practices of the classroom. This psychic reality, however, once theorized, can act heuristically to help explain *how* the political becomes personal, *how* teacher authority operates internally, *how* this authority is contested, *how* this authority is often reinvested despite professed nonauthoritarian practices. The critical intervention of psycho-analysis into pedagogy renders "psychoanalysis . . . [as] first and foremost *a critique of pedagogy*" (Felman 1982b, 23). Not because psychoanalysis is prior or superior to what we conventionally mean by pedagogy (as that which occurs in a classroom), but because psychoanalysis is itself a form of pedagogy, a learning encounter constituted by intersubjective utterances and gestures, and by the meanings, desires, and fantasies that both underlie and are themselves reconstituted by the context of the analytic interaction. This paper, then, works in the spirit of reflecting upon the encounter between psychoanalysis and education "not as an answer, but as a question, questioning at once its possibilities and its limits" (Felman 1982a, 10).

A Psychoanalytic Encounter

My reading of *Feminisms and Critical Pedagogy* is based on an understanding of the student-teacher relationship as that which revolves around what Lacan (1981) has called the "subject who is supposed to know." The "subject who is supposed to know" is constituted through an intersubjective encounter with another person. In the educational setting, the teacher is this all-knowing subject who has all the answers, who, as teacher, *exists* in relation to the student, exists for the student, and exists, one might say, because of the student. For Lacan, "as soon as the subject who is supposed to know exists somewhere . . . there is transference" (232). The transference is the process through which unconscious wishes get projected onto this all-knowing subject. Thus, the teacher, like the analyst, becomes, among other things, an authority figure for the student, perhaps going against that which the teacher perceives herself to be. Jay (1987) explains that the demand to be the subject who is supposed to know "is the most exacting and intractable imposition that teaching and its institutions put upon an instructor, and the one which must be analyzed and resisted if education is to be something more than socialization or consumption" (785). Simultaneously, the teacher is caught up in a countertransference, responding to her students' demands, completing the intersubjective circle. Penley (1989) observes:

> In addition to the fact that education cannot take place without transference, the teacher has another reason for not wanting to give up this identificatory power over the students, and that is his or her own narcissistic satisfaction in seeing the students gradually coming to want what he or she wants "for" them. Seen in this light, education is on the side of narcissism and the imaginary, the ideal and "illusion." (168)

Seen in this light, the authority the teacher holds operates as both real and imagined. Indeed, what is imagined has very real effects on classroom dynamics themselves.

Textual Encounters: *Feminisms and Critical Pedagogy*

Feminist pedagogy, as a diverse, nonstatic discourse has directed its concerns to many fronts over the last decade, or so. In the past, many theorists (e.g., Clarricoates 1981; Walkerdine 1981; Wolpe 1978) looked at the sexual division of labor, and the specific ways gender relations were reproduced in the process of schooling. Gender was made a central category of analysis, which enabled a much-needed expansion of the theories of reproduction that class-based analyses of schooling provided (e.g., Anyon 1980, 1981; Bourdieu and Passeron 1977; Bowles and Gintis 1976). Though gender is still a major, if no longer the only, category of analysis in feminist pedagogical literature, feminist pedagogy has become increasingly diasporic. Some theorists provide a sociological gloss examining the intersections of race, class, and gender in classroom dynamics (Gardner, Dean, and McKaig 1989; Luttrell 1989); others offer more individualistic accounts of feminist teaching, drawing on "women's" ways of knowing and relating (Noddings 1984; Belenky et al. 1986); others draw from postcolonial theory (hooks 1989; Mohanty 1990/93); while still others draw on the body of critical pedagogy to elaborate more fully a feminist pedagogical theory (Maher 1987; Weiler 1988).[4]

Theory in many fields, including feminism and education, has had to contend with the importation, appropriation, and development of postmodern and poststructuralist thought. However, a precarious relationship exists between poststructuralism's antifoundationalism and feminism's grounding in a politics of location, difference, and identity. A number of feminist authors (Bordo 1990; Felski 1989; Fraser 1992; Fraser and Nicholson 1990; Leland 1992) have highlighted the instabilities of this theoretical relationship and have posited various ways of keeping a feminist politics alive within the apolitical posturing of poststructuralism. Bordo, Felski, and Fraser and Nicholson suggest that feminists need not dispense with large narratives in paying attention to the politics of the local, particularly those narratives that focus on unequal power relations. Because of its focus on power, Foucault's work has been central to feminism, especially with regard to education theory (Gore 1993; Lather 1991). Recently, there has been a proliferation of intertextual readings between postmodernism/poststructuralism on the one hand and the "text" of both the classroom and education theory on the other (Ellsworth 1989; Gore 1993; Lather 1991; Nicholson 1989). Also, what I see as stemming from the importance of discursive analysis in poststructuralist theory is the challenge feminists pose to perceived Enlightenment assumptions of "emancipatory" pedagogical discourse and practice, specifically referred to as critical pedagogy. For instance, Weiler has questioned the singular experience of oppression that has seemingly foregrounded the emancipatory project of Paulo Freire's educational theory. Elizabeth Ellsworth has attempted to illustrate that critical pedagogy is founded on what she interprets as a "myth" of empowerment that does not translate into actual empowerment. Similarly, Patti Lather has articulated the need to decenter the "false consciousness" model allegedly still upheld by critical pedagogical theory. Thus these critiques are levied on three fronts: on the institutional practice of teaching, on the discourse of critical pedagogy, and on the educational practice resulting from this discourse.

The essays in *Feminisms and Critical Pedagogy* range from Valerie Walkerdine's incisive critique of the progressivism of the sixties (the only essay not to address critical or feminist pedagogical literature) to Patti Lather's advocacy of constructing a "postcritical" pedagogy. In what is definitely not a postcritical book, however, the essays ostensibly challenge the assumptions underlying critical pedagogy's development of the concepts of student voice and dialogue, to name but two. However, it is my contention that by positioning poststructuralist feminism(s) "outside" the discourse it aims to be critiquing, and by not theorizing its own imaginary construction in its poststructural critiques, it runs the risk of leaving the effects of authority intact, both at the levels of discourse and of classroom practice.

But not all of the essays engage in such practices. Those by Jennifer Gore, Magda Lewis, and Jane Kenway and Helen Modra focus on an assessment of the theory and practice of *feminist* education. Though all of the essays offer something of value to the enterprise of reconfiguring pedagogy along lines of difference and subjectivity—particularly the essays by Gore and Lewis that do take up the issue of authority—Luke and Gore (Introduction) appear to be encouraging an oppositional discourse that focuses more on the assessment of critical pedagogy discourse than on the re-visioning of pedagogy from a poststructural feminist standpoint. This assessment takes energy away from the important issues surrounding the development of poststructural feminist positions for educational practice. Furthermore, many of the readings of critical pedagogy, unlike those of feminist pedagogy, do not take into consideration the variety within the discourse itself (Orner, Ellsworth, Luke). Rather than positing a differential discourse, they erect a phallocratic boundary that marks a hierarchical position between feminisms and critical pedagogy. On a textual level, for instance, the editors acknowledge on 9 that although the essays in the volume are based upon critical pedagogy discourse from the 1980s, critical pedagogy has "incorporated" poststructuralist and postmodern theory in recent years. However, three pages earlier, the editors charged that the "male authors" of critical pedagogy "speak a good postmodernist game of 'multiple narratives' and 'border crossings' " (6). Signifying the changes in critical pedagogy as a *game* precludes the possibility that the incorporation of poststructuralism/postmodernism should ever be anything more than a masquerade, an act, and should not, therefore, be taken seriously. Moreover, in bringing to bear the sex/gender of the authors without explaining its relationship to the discourse, the signifier "male" here is ill placed. Nowhere in this book, which relies so heavily on the *male* author Michel Foucault's analysis of disciplinary power, is the question of sex/gender of the author ever raised or put into an appropriate framework. Somehow, in the context of critical pedagogy discourse, we are to read *male* as authority, as patriarchal law. This is not to say that neither critical pedagogy nor Foucault's discourse analysis are free of the effects of male subjectivity or patriarchal law; I agree with Luke and Gore's borrowing from Donna Haraway (1988) that all knowledges are situated (9) and hence ultimately tied to subjectivity. However, what I object to are the kinds of rhetorical strategies that preclude the taking up of issues, which foreclose on explanations of how maleness plays into certain theories while not in others, and which leads Luke, in her essay ("Feminist Politics and Radical Pedagogy"), to construct a neobinarism of male/feminist (46). To label, to categorize, to explain away the assumptions under the signifier "male" does not push anyone's thought about authority beyond patriarchal limits. Exactly what kind of textual authority is being constituted here? What room does it leave for poststructural feminists who wish to use critical pedagogical discourse without succumbing to the temptation of pigeonholing?

In deploying a cautionary postmodernism, Luke in her essay asserts that an educator's position "can only be emancipatory if our attention to the politics of the local (of struggles, identities) are [sic] tied to dedicated engagement with and teachings of the politics of global structures and justifying narratives of oppression" (49). These aspects of her position are echoed throughout the book, which attempts to eke out a theoretical space between feminism and poststructuralism around the notions of "multiplicity" and "specificity."

Orner, for instance, in "Interrupting the Calls for Student Voice in 'Liberatory' Education: A Feminist Poststructuralist Perspective," posits poststructural feminism as a solution to the problematic conception of student voice in critical and feminist pedagogy. "It seems impossibly naive to think that there can be anything like a genuine sharing of voices in the classroom" (81). She suggests that the teacher's voice has often been left unchallenged, untheorized, and caught up in monarchical forms of power. Thus, counter to critical and feminist pedagogical claims, poststructuralism offers a theoretical tool with which "to recognize the power differentials present and to understand how they impinge upon what is sayable and doable in that specific context" (81). Orner further suggests that "an analysis of whose interests are served when students speak is needed" (87). Moreover, she claims that the interrogation of student voices Henry Giroux advocates leads her to ask, "Who interrogates whom and why?" (87). However, though Orner seems to recognize the inequalities present in the classroom, in "interrupting the calls for student voice," her view ultimately leads to an unreflexive voicing of opinion on the part of the students. Thus, my question is, whose interests are being served when students are *not* challenged to put their experience into an intellectual encounter? Exactly what are teachers supposed to do if not question, probe, and discuss with students their experiences in relation to the content of the course? What Orner fails to account for is how the displacement of authority in the classroom requires both teachers and students to speak, although, as Lewis (1993) has pointed out, silence also may put authority into question. Our utterances place our discourse in a public arena in which accountability and humility are a fundamental part of agency. It seems to me that it is not just voicing opinion but also the serious questioning of issues surrounding those opinions, and the self-reflection this enables, that can make all the difference.

Ellsworth's essay, "Why Doesn't This Feel Empowering? Working Through the Repressive Myths of Critical Pedagogy," echoes Orner's position. Occupying a central position in this volume, both figuratively and literally, it deserves some attention. Unlike Gore's essay, which encourages an engagement with authority, Ellsworth's essay tends toward an evasion of authority. In "working through the repressive myths of critical pedagogy," Ellsworth grounds her project in an interpretation of her experiences teaching a course titled "Media and Anti-racist Pedagogies." Her approach marks an important distinction between many feminist and critical theorists in education. Rather than construct an interpretation of critical pedagogy supported by analyses of concrete textual examples, she constructs an interpretation out of her own experience in the classroom. Let us examine this strategy more closely, for it raises important issues for all of us working in a critical mode.

In reading critical pedagogy as a static practice, Ellsworth blunts the dynamic edge that is the mark of all radical theory. One gets a sense that critical pedagogical discourse has remained virtually unchanged and the assumptions never questioned, thereby encouraging unself-reflexive teaching practices. She points out that the notion of dialogue in critical pedagogy is to make the classroom into a "public sphere" where "all members have equal opportunity to speak, all members respect other members' rights to speak and feel safe to speak, and all ideas are tolerated and subjected to rational critical assessment against fundamental judgments and moral principles" (106).[5] In relation to this notion of dialogue in critical pedagogy, she writes about her own experience: "*I expected* that we [her class] would be able to ensure all members a safe place to speak, equal opportunity to speak, and equal power in influencing decision-making" (107) [my emphasis]. For Ellsworth, however, engaging in dialogue in her class—because of the presence of "unequal privilege"—was both "impossible and undesirable" (106). Dialogue did not signify for Ellsworth a "safe" space in which students could speak (108).

A number of assumptions operate here to underline her oppositional stance to critical pedagogy, rather than to advance an engagement of the issues underlying her praxis. First, only by assuming that dialogue is *separate* from the engagement of unequal privilege can Ellsworth make the claim that dialogue is impossible. If dialogue is seen as the process through which trust and sharing of ideas (which she interprets as prerequisite to and not coterminous with dialogue in critical pedagogy) are striven for, how can dialogue ever be "impossible and undesirable" in a feminist classroom committed to developing trust and sharing?

Secondly, her *expectations* of what dialogue should offer, and of the equality it presupposes, are more indicative of *her* desire than of critical pedagogy's theoretical rendering of dialogue. In offering her interpretation of critical pedagogy's notion of dialogue, the subtext of her desire is left out. As teachers, we all have a psychic investment in the pedagogical relations of the class. In assuming "equal power in influencing decision-making," Ellsworth is conflating critical pedagogy's notion of dialogue with her own—dare I say "liberal"—egalitarian position; a position that, as Laurie Finke (1993) points out, may mystify "psychic investments" (8). What often operates in feminist pedagogies is the "fiction of the teacherless classroom" (Finke 1993, 17), where the teacher's voice is one among many in the class. However, it is impossible to ignore that "the process feminist pedagogy seeks to describe is not the student's *discovering* a voice that is already there, but her *fashioning* of one from the discursive environment through and in which the feminist subject emerges" (14). Moreover, as Penley (1989) asserts, to be effective, the teacher "must fully assume the mantle of the subject who is supposed to know. To relinquish that imaginary position would be to lose the most important pedagogical tool of all" (168). Similarly, Giroux and Simon (1989) encourage teachers not "to suppress or abandon what and how they know. Indeed, the pedagogical struggle is lessened without such resources" (16). The feminist classroom is psychically invested with the desire for students to come to realizations about their own gendered subject positions and, in the case of Ellsworth's class, about their own racial positions as well. This does not mean that feminist classrooms should not encourage the "fashioning" of voice Finke describes (in fact, education is eminently *about* fashioning a certain type of subject position), but it needs to be reconfigured not only as a political and social goal but also as one subtended by the teacher's desire (Todd, in press). As Penley (1989) notes, feminist pedagogies aim

> toward a dispersal or even elimination of authority. The risk, of course, in aiming at or claiming the eradication of power relations is that the force and pervasiveness of those relations may be overlooked, "out of sight, out of

mind." But can the feminist classroom afford to lose sight of the extreme power of the transferential relation, of the narcissism underlying the demands of both students and teachers, or the basically eroticized nature of learning (the constant appeal for recognition)? (173–74).

Basically, nonauthority is untenable in an educational situation in which the teacher is the one who *sets out* curriculum, *plans* activities, *decides* to construct an ostensibly nonauthoritative environment, and *encourages* discussion. The decision to proceed or not to proceed, to intervene or not to intervene, to take up issues or to leave them unchallenged are decisions the teacher is compelled to make as an authority—both real and imagined—in the class. This is not to say that students cannot intervene or challenge, but that students' actions have very different consequences because of their differential relation to power. And, as we all know from being students as well as teachers, power can be felt acutely through evaluation. As I see it, the challenge is to develop (a notion of) dialogue that confronts the impossibility of nonauthority, not to claim that dialogue is "impossible and undesirable" because authority is present. Ellsworth assumes that her "ought" of nonauthority is "possible and desirable" by implication. In my view, nonauthority is itself a "repressive myth" that confuses desire with the "reality" of the fields of identification and signification that constitute authority in the classroom.

Moreover, in the dubious adoption of ostensibly nonauthoritative practices to redress the inequalities of authority, three basic assumptions are made: (1) that teachers control authority and can simply forge new classroom relations if the will is present; (2) that a change in classroom structures is directly correlated to a change in the students' attitudes, ideas, and sense of voice (e.g., that a circular seating arrangement will lead to more openness in the class); and (3) that students will interpret the teachers' actions the way teachers intend them. What this fails to realize, however, is that unconscious desire is an intervening moment between student and teacher relations. It ignores as well the real structural difference between teacher and student in terms of responsibility, evaluation, and accountability. Desire is not only a matter of "semiconscious" expectations but also of deeply felt demands on the part of the educator and of the student to work within the authoritative structures that are the very markers of difference between teacher and student. Recognizing desire as a structural dynamic highlights the need for us to understand that the relation of both feminism and psychoanalysis to knowledge and authority is central to any pedagogy (Penley 1989, 166).

On a final note, Ellsworth's essay serves more generally to highlight the unstable relation between poststructuralism and feminism as represented in the other essays edited by Luke and Gore. Lather's reading claims that

Ellsworth "intensifies differences" to create an "intertextual arena" (127). However, symptomatic of *Feminisms and Critical Pedagogy* in general, Ellsworth's essay reads more like the Roman Coliseum than an intertextual arena where reading critical pedagogical discourse through feminist practice may lead to effective reformulations of power and dialogue in critical pedagogy itself, as well as contribute to new forms of feminist poststructural educational theories. Instead, though the concluding chapter emphasizes the relation between the essays and the "subtext of women's academic careers which is fundamentally personal and private" (Luke and Gore 1992, 209), and which is structured by institutionalized patriarchal authority, the book as a whole fails to put forth new paradigms for engaging the real and imagined nature of authority in the classroom. Moreover, in promulgating the hierarchical positioning of the "and," *Feminisms and Critical Pedagogy* constructs the very binarisms it attempts to displace, with the result that the dynamic of authority is left largely unaddressed.

Notes

1. In the summer of 1990, members of the Kahnesatake reserve at Oka were in an armed standoff with the Sûreté du Québec (the Québec provincial police force) and later the Canadian Army. Originally, the Mohawks had erected a barricade in response to a plan to turn some of their ancestral lands into a golf course, as well as in response to the failure of the federal government to make a land claim settlement. The word "standoff" marked the determination of the Mohawks to persist in their cause while Kahnesatake was held in a state of siege.

2. "Oppositional" as I mean it here refers to a stance that implies a hierarchical positioning of one discourse over another, a stance that I find especially problematic given that these feminists are writing from *poststructural* feminist perspectives.

3. I agree with Henry Giroux's (1988) view: "The concept of authority can best be understood as a historical construction shaped by diverse, competing traditions which contain their own values and views of the world" (74). Hence authority is not simply patriarchal, but is a movement that has patriarchy as one of its moments.

4. This list is by no means exhaustive. Kenway and Modra's essay in *Feminisms and Critical Pedagogy* provides a useful framework for understanding the two-pronged division in feminist pedagogy: the literature surrounding gender and schooling, and that centering on women's studies.

5. Note that these fundamental judgments are not true for everyone at all times, in all places. Critical pedagogy, like feminism, uses a political referent to assess what is "fundamental." I am not sure what Ellsworth would claim about her own "fundamental" of "equal power" for all.

References

Anyon J. (1980). Social Class and the Hidden Curriculum of Work. *Journal of Education,* 162 (Winter): 67–92.

———— (1981). Social Class and School Knowledge. *Curriculum Inquiry,* 11 (1): 3–42.

Belenky, M., McVicker, B., Goldberger, N., and Tarule, J. (1986). *Women's Ways of Knowing: The Development of Self, Voice, and Mind.* New York: Basic Books.

Bordo, S. (1990). Feminism, Postmodernism and Gender-scepticism. In ed. *Feminism/Postmodernism,* L. Nicholson, 133–56 New York: Routledge.

Bourdieu, P., and Passeron, J., C. (1977). *Reproduction in Education, Society and Culture.* London: Sage.

Bowles, S., and Gintis, H. (1976). *Schooling in Capitalist America.* New York: Basic Books.

Clarricoates, K. (1981). The Experience of Patriarchal Schooling. *Interchange* 12 (2–3): 185–203.

Ellsworth, E. (1989). Why Doesn't This Feel Empowering? Working Through the Repressive Myths of Critical Pedagogy. *Harvard Educational Review* 59 (3): 297–324.

Felman, S. (1982a). To Open the Question. In ed. *Literature and Psychoanalysis: The Question of Reading: Otherwise,* S. Felman, 5–10. Baltimore: Johns Hopkins University Press.

——— (1982b). Psychoanalysis and Education: Teaching Terminable and Interminable. *Yale French Studies* 63: 21–44.

Felski, R. (1989). Feminism, Postmodernism, and the Critique of Modernity. *Cultural Critique* 13 (Fall): 33–56.

Finke, L. (1993). Knowledge As Bait: Feminism, Voice and the Pedagogical Unconscious. *College English* 55 (1): 7–27.

Foucault, M. (1980). *Power/Knowledge.* New York: Pantheon.

——— (1979). *Discipline and Punish,* New York: Vintage.

Fraser, N. (1992). The Uses and Abuses of French Discourse Theories for Feminist Politics. In Ed. *Revaluing French Feminism: Critical Essays on Difference, Agency and Culture,* N. Fraser and S. L. Bartky, 177–94. Bloomington: Indiana University Press.

Fraser, N., and Nicholson, L.J. (1990). Social Criticism Without Philosophy: An Encounter Between Feminism and Postmodernism. In ed. *Feminism/ Postmodernism,* L. Nicholson, 19–40. New York: Routledge.

Gardner, S., Dean, C., and McKaig, D. (1989). Responding to Differences in the Classroom: The Politics of Knowledge, Class and Sexuality. *Sociology of Education,* 62 (January): 64–74.

Giroux, H. (1988). *Schooling and the Struggle for Public Life.* Minneapolis: University of Minnesota Press.

Giroux, H., and Simon, R.I. (1989). Schooling, Popular Culture, and a Pedagogy of Possibility. *Journal of Education* 170 (1): 9–26.

Gore, J. (1993). *The Struggle for Pedagogies: Critical and Feminist Discourses as Regimes of Truth.* New York: Routledge.

Haraway, D. (1988). Situated Knowledges: The Science Question in Feminism and the Privilege of Partial Perspective. *Feminist Studies* 14 (3): 575–99.

hooks, bell. (1989). *Talking Back.* Boston: South End Press.

Jay, G.S. (1987). The Subject of Pedagogy: Lessons in Psychoanalysis and Politics. *College English* 49 (7): 785–800.

Lacan, J. (1981). *Four Fundamental Concepts of Psychoanalysis.* Trans. A. Sheridan. New York: W.W. Norton.

Lather, P. (1991). *Getting Smart: Feminist Research and Pedagogy With/in the Postmodern.* New York: Routledge.

Leland, D. (1992). Lacanian Psychoanalysis and French Feminism: Toward an Adequate Political Psychology. In ed. *Revaluing French Feminism: Critical Essays on Difference, Agency and Culture,* N. Fraser and S.L. Bartky, 113–35. Bloomington: Indiana University Press.

Lewis, M. (1993). *Without a Word.* New York: Routledge.

Luke, C., and Gore, J. (1992). *Feminisms and Critical Pedagogy.* New York: Routledge.

Luttrell, W. (1989). Working-class Women's Ways of Knowing: Effects of Gender, Race, and Class. *Sociology of Education,* 62 (January): 33–46.

Maher, F. (1987). Toward a Richer Theory of Feminist Pedagogy: A Comparison of "Liberation" and "Gender" Models for Teaching and Learning. *Journal of Education* 169 (3): 91–100.

Mohanty, C.T. (1990). On Race and Voice: Challenges for Liberal Education in the 1990s. *Cultural Critique* 14 (Winter). Reprinted in H. Giroux and P. McLaren, eds., *Between Borders: Pedagogy and the Politics of Cultural Studies,* 145–66. New York: Routledge, 1993.

Nicholson, C. (1989). Postmodernism, Feminism, and Education: The Need for Solidarity. *Educational Theory* 39 (3): 197–205.

Noddings, N. (1984). *Caring: A Feminine Approach to Ethics and Moral Education.* Berkeley: University of California Press.

Penley, C. (1989). Teaching in Your Sleep: Feminism and Psychoanalysis. In *The Future of An Illusion: Film, Feminism, and Psychoanalysis,* 165–81. Minneapolis: University of Minnesota Press.

Todd, S. (in press). Looking at pedagogy in 3-D: Rethinking Difference, Disparity, and desire. In ed. *Learning Desire: Perspectives on Pedagogy, Culture and the Unsaid,* S. Todd New York: Routledge.

Walkerdine, V. (1981). Sex, Power and Pedagogy. *Screen Education* 38: 14–24.

Weiler, K. (1988). *Women Teaching for Change.* South Hadley, MA Bergin and Garvey.

——— (1991). Freire and a Feminist Pedagogy of Difference. *Harvard Educational Review* 61 (4): 449–74.

Wolpe, A.M. (1978). Education and the Sexual Division of Labor. In A. Kuhn and A.M. Wolpe, *Feminism and Materialism,* 290–328. Boston: Routledge and Kegan Paul, 1978.

6

Man Trouble

Douglas Kellner

In her 1989 study *The Remasculinization of America*, Susan Jeffords inter-preted key post-Vietnam films and literature as attempts to come to terms with the U.S. military defeat in Vietnam. For Jeffords, *The Deer Hunter, Rambo, Missing in Action*, and other "return to Vietnam" films, as well as key literary texts dealing with the Vietnam experience, articulated the sense of shame associated with defeat and in some cases provided compensation for U.S. humiliations with heroic fantasies of victory over the Vietnamese and their allies in the contemporary era à la *Rambo*. Conservative films and nov-els that dealt with the Vietnam debacle, in Jeffords's reading, presented ideals of remasculinization that would prevent future Vietnams. These overcom-ings of "the Vietnam syndrome" were closely connected to the conservative politics of Ronald Reagan and George Bush, which promoted militarism, virulent anticommunism, and traditional patriarchal-familial values.

In her subsequent 1994 book *Hard Bodies*, Jeffords continues her efforts to trace the destinies of masculinization in contemporary U.S. politics and culture through studies of the conjunction of Hollywood film and conserv-ative political discourses on the issue of masculinity. Jeffords argues that the "hard bodies" represented in the 1980s films such as *Rambo, Lethal Weapons,* and *Die Hard* presented cinematic representations of Reagan's conservative discourses in both the foreign policy and domestic arena. She also argues that a turn to more femininized and liberal men in the early 1990s represents a backlash against Reaganism and its conservative ideals, followed by a resurrection of more sensitive and domesticated hard bodies in films such as *Unforgiven* (1992). In the following review I will explicate Jeffords's readings of the politics of Hollywood film, will highlight her contributions, and will contest some of her readings and point to problems in her method of reading films politically.

Hard Bodies/Conservative Men

On Jeffords's account, the *Rambo* films (1982, 1985, 1988) articulated Reaganite foreign policy by championing militarism, anticommunism, interventionism, and the need for warrior heroes to promote U.S. interests. Rambo's rugged individualism and his hatred for big government, bureaucracy, and corrupt politicians also articulates Reaganite antistatist discourses, appropriating the trope of individualism for the conservative ideology of the present. *Rambo* and the other "return to Vietnam" films, which portrayed U.S. warriors returning to Vietnam to liberate American POWs, embodied the traumas of an era, including the emasculating of the American psyche in the military defeat in Vietnam, the shame of the Iranian and other "terrorist" hostage episodes, and the shocks of economic decline and the challenging of male privileges by women influenced by feminism.

Indeed, *Rambo* is shown dazed and out of work in the first film in the series, *First Blood* (1982), and must reconstitute himself as a resolute warrior in order to survive the humiliations visited upon him by a small-town sheriff and his deputies. The failure of the sheriff's men and the National Guard to capture him shows, in Jeffords's view, the consequences of weak and soft bodies and the degree of national deterioration that must be overcome in the contemporary era to resurrect American manhood. In the second *Rambo* film (1985), the warrior returns to Vietnam to free U.S. POWs and to overcome the shame of loss, also demonstrating what sort of bodies, action, and men will be needed to resurrect U.S. military and phallic power.

In all three *Rambo* films, the Stallone character is captured and tortured, evoking national humiliation and the pain suffered by the U.S. citizens and soldiers apprehended or defeated by military enemies and "terrorists." The pain and humiliation suffered is, arguably—though this is not Jeffords's point—symbolic punishment for U.S. loss of manhood and prestige, while the excessive violence used against those who captured and tortured "innocent Americans" can be seen as an appropriate payback for American humiliation and suffering (overlooking, of course, in the mythical mode, the pain inflicted on foreign "others" by U.S. policy).

Jeffords reads the torture scenes in the *Rambo* films as demonstrating that the national body can recover from wounds and reconstitute itself as dominant, as powerful, as in control. The Rambo body also provides the norm of the powerful body that can protect us from harm and against which soft and weak bodies can be differentiated and seen as lacking. She argues that *Rambo* and other conservative militarist films, such as *Missing in Action* or *Uncommon Valor*, work out the Reagan foreign policy agenda in cinematic terms that legitimate its emphasis on militarization and a strong military, its highly interventionist policies, and its patriotism and chauvinism, which believes that the United States is superior to the rest of the world.

Jeffords also claims that such films as *Terminator, Robocop, Lethal Weapon,* and *Die Hard* work out the Reaganite domestic policy by showing ordinary men becoming heros who are able to vanquish terrorists, drug lords, crime syndicates, and those who would threaten and challenge the domestic social order. In these films, average men transform themselves into action heros to solve intractable problems, using violence to eradicate "evil." Cumulatively, the men of hard-body films thus engage in heroic action to protect society from internal and external threats, justifying the use of violence against foreign and domestic threats by claims of "national security."

Such films are obviously myths and rewrite history, making the Vietnamese the villains in the U.S. war against Vietnam and overlooking the series of U.S. alliances with terrorists, drug smugglers, and lawless figures in the Iran/Contra affair, which most clearly embodied Reagan's foreign policy. Such mythical celebration of superheros also covers over the fact that Oliver North and other Reagan Rambos operated outside the law and the constraints of a constitutional system in pursuing their own policies and interests. But Jeffords claims that in the late 1980s and early 1990s, Hollywood contested the extreme masculism of the hard-bodied heros, reflecting the transition from Reagan to Bush and his pledge to produce "a kinder, gentler nation."

Feminized Men/Liberal Justice

Jeffords argues that the Bush administration and some Hollywood films of the era (1988–1992) realized the dangers of the excessive Reagan masculinization of politics and disdain for justice, and consequently revised images of masculinity to create models more concerned with justice. For Jeffords, films such as *Casualties of War* (1987), *Mississippi Burning* (1988), and *The Accused* (1989) show the need for morally strong men to stand up to abuses of the system and to struggle for justice, a theme notably missing in Reaganite political discourse and in the Hollywood films that articulated its ideologies. Jeffords also discusses films that attempt to present more sensitive images of men in the early 1990s. She reads such films as *Regarding Henry, City Slickers, One Good Cop, Kindergarten Cop*, and *Terminator 2* as reactions against the hard-bodies vision of masculinity in the Reagan era. Moreover, Jeffords interprets the 1991 Disney film *Beauty and the Beast* as a veritable course for men to become more sensitive, empathic, and loving.

In fact, many popular films represent a liberal backlash against the hegemonic conservativism. *A Few Good Men* (1992) shows the sort of Yuppie professionals needed in the society of the future in which there will be no longer room for the sort of conservative and macho militarist that Jack Nicholson plays. The Tom Cruise and Demi Moore characters represent the new liberal professionals, who are highly competent and motivated by a concern for justice. One sees a similar figure in the Tom Cruise character in *The Firm* (1993) and examples of honorable and competent professionals in *The Fugitive* (1993). Whereas in the original 1960s TV series Dr. Kimbell was played against the obsessive policeman Girard, in the Hollywood version they end up both pursuing a criminal drug manufacturer who was responsible for the killing of Kimbell's wife. Both men are highly professional, motivated by a concern for justice, and present positive male role models. It is indeed amazing how moralistic the basically amoral business machine of Hollywood can be at times, and how saturated with political messages the seemingly apolitical Hollywood entertainment often is. Indeed, one of the successful liberal epics of its day, *Schindler's List* (1993), also fits into this paradigm, showing the transformation of a basically amoral, opportunistic German businessman into a Mensch concerned with justice and the saving of Jewish lives.

Thus, the sustained reaction against Reaganite masculinization that Jeffords analyzes is no doubt visible in both Hollywood film and U.S. society during the late 1980s and 1990s. I think Jeffords is mistaken, however, when she relates this to the shift from the Reagan to Bush administrations. She cites Bush's inaugural rhetoric of "a kinder, gentler nation" and "a thousand points of light" as Bush's attempt to differentiate himself from Reagan and to redefine American political and moral values. Yet in retrospect, Bush is most notable for pursuing the military adventures of the Panama invasion and the war against Iraq. Moreover, Bush showed no more concern for justice or sensitivity toward suffering or problems of ordinary Americans than Reagan—which is one of the reasons that Bill Clinton was elected president.

Hence, one can agree with Jeffords that in the culture at large there was indeed a shift against Reaganist ultramasculism, a shift that resulted in the defeat of George Bush by Bill Clinton in 1992. Identifying Bush as part of the shift is a mistake, however, despite his slogan promising "a kinder, gentler nation," coined by speechwriter Peggy Noonan but hardly expressive of George Bush's policies as president. Rather, I would interpret the redefinitions of masculinity during Bush's reign as the resurgence of Hollywood liberalism, a force never vanquished even during the Reagan years, and as symptomatic of the fierce battles around gender that have challenged prevailing definitions of masculinity and femininity since the 1960s. U.S. society is not only a contested terrain around more narrowly defined political ideologies such as liberalism and conservativism, but also a place where gender itself is contested with competing models of masculinity in play. Hollywood films articulate the competing political discourses and the struggles over masculinity and the definitions of men and women. Thus, the conflicting Hollywood versions of masculinity articulate competing models currently in conflict in many domains of social and political life.

Masculinity, like femininity, is a social construct that is periodically contested, put into question, and shifts, and that is subject to negotiation, revision, and development. Yet some dominant models, such as the more sensitive male of the later 1960s and early 1970s, emerged both in media culture and as the ideal of the women's and men's movements. Also appearing during the late 1960s and 1970s, in media culture and everyday life, was the confused male, uncertain of his gender role, which was followed by images of the assertive conservative male hero and supermale of the later 1970s and 1980s, the subjects of Jeffords's analyses. During this entire period, and currently, however, more liberal models continue to contest the hyperconservative model, just as conservative models are themselves constantly revising their own figures, as in Clint Eastwood's *Unforgiven* (1992).

Indeed, Jeffords's "hard-body," highly macho male was visible throughout the 1970s, and though the figure became dominant during the 1980s, it was contested even then. Jeffords fails to note the intense contestation of all of Reagan's social agenda and ideologies throughout the 1980s, especially over gender politics. She fails to note the trend in '80s films for independents to enter the mainstream and to offer a greater range of representations of gender than in previous epochs of Hollywood film. Yet she does illuminate the dominant trends of the era that shifted from moves to represent more sensitive and empathic males in the 1960s and '70s to the superhero hard bodies of the Reagan era. And though Jeffords fails to articulate the conflicting ideals of the Reagan period, she does nicely capture the move away from the Reaganite ideal in post-Reagan politics and culture.

In fact, the present is marked by persistent fierce cultural wars between conservatives and their liberal and more radical antagonists that continue to be played out in Hollywood films and other forms of media culture. Masculinity, as noted, is a cultural construct that is always up for grabs. Competing social groups and movements have conflicting ideals of masculinity and femininity, which in turn get articulated in Hollywood films and other arenas of media culture. The contest of representations played out in film, television, and other forms of media culture are thus deeply political and subject to the vicissitudes of contemporary politics.

In a way, Jeffords registers this continuing struggle, concluding her book with a study of how *Unforgiven* shows that the Reaganite hard body has not vanished, but she argues that the film suggests that a strong masculinity must be tempered by concerns for justice, thus infusing liberal concerns into the conservative masculinist scenario. But in fact the conservative and masculinist hard-body hero never disappeared and has been deployed in numerous films during the 1990s, transcoding conservative discourses in the continuing intense culture wars of the period. At times, opposing liberal models became hegemonic, and perhaps the popularity of more sensitive and humane male heroes points to shifts in public opinion or at least the presence of more progressive ideals of masculinity in U.S. culture. But at the same time that more liberal male figures appeared in popular films, a virulent backlash against women also appeared, and Jeffords fails to register the extent of this continuing backlash against feminism in U.S. culture and society.

Backlash: Hollywood's War Against Women

Susan Faludi's *Backlash* (1991) demonstrates systematically the ways that the media, culture, and fashion industries and the economic and political establishment reacted against feminism during the 1980s. For Faludi, *Fatal Attraction* (1987) is *the* backlash movie of the 1980s, demonstrating that the condition of independence and professional career success, celebrated by some versions of feminism, produce neurosis and desperation that can border on psychosis. The film's villainess, Alex (played by Glenn Close), seduces a married male, Dan Gallagher (played by Michael Douglas), and then proceeds to pursue him obsessively, seeking to destroy his marriage and to possess him for herself.

Faludi points out how the film was initially intended to be a sympathetic portrayal of the dilemmas of a single independent woman, and the original version makes her a tragic victim of her situation, showing her committing suicide alone in a bathtub. But the final version of film revises that ending, having the wife shoot the single woman, whom *Fatal Attraction* positions the audience to hate by portraying her as an evil threat to the happy family. One key scene shows Alex voyeuristically watching a happy family scene in which Dan gives his daughter a rabbit, while his wife looks on with affection. The scene dramatizes precisely what this single career woman is missing, and she vomits as she realizes all that she lacks.

The other side of *Fatal Attraction* is that it provides a morality tale for men, warning that if they stray from matrimonial monogamy—even once—it could wreak disaster and destroy what the film presents as most important in life. *The Hand That Rocks the Cradle* (1992) contains similar problematics in favor of the traditional family and traditional women's roles at the expense of single women. In its melodramatic plot, a happily married woman, Claire Bartel (played by Annabella Sciorra), reports that her gynecologist sexually molested her; other women report the same, and he commits suicide, causing his wife, Peyton (played by Rebecca De Mornay), to miscarry. In a revenge plot, Peyton enters the Bartel home as a nannie to their two children and proceeds to attempt to destroy the wife, getting revenge for her husband's death.

In one scene, a black handyman catches Peyton breastfeeding the Bartels's newly born baby, and she gets him fired with false accusations that he sexually molested the young daughter. The image of the single woman with child represents a norm for women that is denied to Peyton, who is driven to psychotic extremes to try to fulfill this role. And in both films it is the wife who, fighting for her family, kills the evil threat to their familial happiness.

Fatal Attraction and *Hand That Rocks the Cradle* contrast bad and good women, with traditional women represented as good, while the sort of independent professional woman celebrated by certain versions of feminism, or single women per se, are depicted as lacking and are driven to vile and destructive behavior. *Basic Instinct*, by contrast, simply vilifies women per se in its story of a successful woman writer (played by Sharon Stone) whose family, lovers, and enemies are shown as mysteriously murdered. The striking thing about this film is the extent to which it vilifies *all* of its women characters. Its convoluted plot makes it ambiguous as to whether the woman writer, or a woman police psychologist obsessed with the writer, are really guilty of the crimes. Two other major women characters, the writer's lesbian lover and an older woman, are also revealed to be mass murderers who killed their families, thus representing women per se as evil and vicious—traditional sexist stereotypes.

Basic Instinct also vilifies lesbians as "perverted" and predatory, and portrays women as wanting to assume male phallic power and control. Indeed, the film can be read as an alarmist allegory concerning what women would do if they were to assume phallic power. Both the writer in *Basic Instinct* and the character Alex of *Fatal Attraction* can indeed be read as derisive vehicles of phallic power run amok with knives and ice picks, crude Freudian symbols of the violent and murderous phallus, used as murder weapons of choice.

Jeffords thus plays down the prevalent contemporary Hollywood theme of the vilification of women, especially strong, independent women who do not fill the traditional gender role as subservient and domestic wife and mother. These films and others, such as *Single White Female, Body of Evidence, The Temp, The Crush,* and *Death Becomes Her,* vilify single women, objectifying them as vicious predators and witches, in sharp contrast to "good" traditional women. Likewise, horror films continue to vilify women, while comedies, dramas, and other films continue to objectify women as objects of the male gaze.

Thus, to properly analyze the sexual politics of the present age, one must depict the media culture constructions of both masculinity and femininity and the ways that relations between men and women, sexuality, and other relations (women-women, men-men, etc.) are portrayed. Failing to analyze the system of gender relations leads Jeffords to stress the liberalization of representations of men during the post-Reagan era, which are often at the expense of more negative representations of women. Though it is admirable for cultural theorists to focus on representations of men, and while Jeffords's analysis of masculinization provides a much-needed antidote to feminist theory that focuses solely on representations of women, a truer picture would focus on the system of gender relations, analyzing the system of representations of men, women, and their modes of relation to each other in various types of media culture.

Gender relations are part of a differential system of power and domination, with unequal power relations producing domination and subordination. The representations of media culture can either contest such representations, attacking domination and/or depicting gender relations of equality, or can produce representations that legitimate and naturalize relations of gender inequality; or they can, of course, be ambivalent and rent with contradictions. Some films combine negative and positive representations of women, or provide more liberalized representations of men at the expense of negative images of women (e.g., *City Slickers* depicts the liberalization of men at the expense of negative stereotypes of Jewish women, and *Kramer versus Kramer, Ordinary People,* and *Author! Author!* present positive images of nurturing men at the expense of negative images of women—see the analysis in Kellner and Ryan 1988).

Jeffords's excellent analyses of the Hollywood constructions of masculinity thus provide a useful supplement to the analyses of constructions of femininity and representations of women that have dominated much feminist cultural theory, but both sides of the equation and the system of gender relations as a whole now need to be analyzed, deconstructed, and reconstructed as part of a social project of the radical reconstruction of gender and social relations—a key part of the project of radical democracy.

Concluding Remarks

For the most part, Jeffords's *Hard Bodies* brilliantly documents the fascinating conjunction between media culture and politics in contemporary Hollywood film, and I do not have the space here to discuss the full range of her provocative readings of Hollywood film in the age of Reagan and Bush. Yet she occasionally stretches in her correlations of politics and culture, as when she interprets the *Back to the Future* films in terms of Reagan's rewriting of history (73). Her correlations of the Doc character and Reagan (77) is a stretch, as is her correlation of Bush as Batman (96). Her reading of *Robocop* (106) misses the satire, as does her reading of the *Back to the Future* films. The contradictory moments of many Hollywood films are assimilated too quickly to specific political discourses, and she doesn't indicate how the conservative or liberal films sometimes undercut their own ideological problematics, or how audiences can read these films against the grain. She also does not systematically engage the problematics and interplay of gender, race, and class in her analyses and make clear how films that are liberal on gender can be reactionary on race and class—though occasionally she brings race and class into her readings of gender, as in her discussions of *Unforgiven* and the *Lethal Weapon* films.

Yet Jeffords convincingly demonstrates how political Hollywood film is, how attuned it is to the factional struggles of the day, and thus demonstrates the need for political critique to grasp the messages and effects of the Hollywood ideology machine. But Jeffords does not really offer an adequate explanation of *why* such an often uncanny correspondence exists between dominant political discourse and the ideological discourses of Hollywood film. She mentions that the movie business, in which the product is a multimillion-dollar investment, has confidence that the films will tap into and speak to people's experiences and feelings. But this is only part of the story. Films also transcode political discourses, transforming the figures, discourses, and representations of the 1960s counterculture, for example, into cinematic forms in '60s films such as *Easy Rider* or *Woodstock*. Other films of the era transcoded conservative discourses into antisixties backlash texts (e.g., *The Green Berets, Dirty Harry*, etc).

Likewise, Hollywood films over the last decades have transcoded the competing liberal, conservative, and radical discourses into social texts, drawing on the themes, concerns, and discourses of the day to attract popular audiences to their products. Furthermore, some Hollywood creators *are* political and use their cinematic artifacts as vehicles for their own ideologies. This is clearly the case for Stallone, Chuck Norris, Globus-Golem, and the Hollywood Right, but also the case for the Hollywood Left, including Jane

Fonda, Robert Redford, and Oliver Stone. These folks have amassed significant cultural power and can use it to advance their own politics.

Jeffords's views of dominant models of masculinity tend to be too monolithic, underplaying the contestation of dominant models and constant struggle over gender politics of competing groups. She follows Robin Wood (1986) in seeing the 1970s' Hollywood film as primarily articulating disintegration, and she follows Cagin and Dray (1984) in stressing the socially critical nature of seventies Hollywood "political cinema." The alternative—the correct one, as Michael Ryan and I argued in *Camera Politica* (1988)—is to see the decade as one of intense political contestation between liberals and conservatives, with more radical voices, who attained some visibility, especially from 1967 to 1971, pushed into the margins.

Yet many of Jeffords's readings of individual films are brilliant and provoke reflection on the politics of culture and the way that the contest of representations produces subject positions that articulate the conflicting political discourses of the day. Her focus on representations of masculinity supplements feminist theory that focuses on representations of women and suggests to contemporary cultural theory the need to analyze representations of both masculinity and femininity, the differential system of gender relations, and the ways that the representations of media culture intersect with the political discourses and struggles of the day.

References

Cagin, Seth, and Philip Dray (1984). *Hollywood Films of the Seventies*. New York: Harper and Row.

Faludi, Susan (1991). *Backlash*. New York: Crown.

Jeffords, Susan (1989). *The Remasculinization of America*. Bloomington: Indiana University Press.

———— (1994). *Hard Bodies. Hollywood Masculinity in the Reagan Era*. New Brunswick, NJ: Rutgers University Press.

Kellner, Douglas, and Michael Ryan (1988). *Camera Politica: The Politics and Ideology of Contemporary Hollywood Film*. Bloomington: Indiana University Press.

Wood, Robin (1986). *Hollywood from Vietnam to Reagan*. New York: Columbia University Press.

7

Toward a Polymorphous Perverse Curriculum[1]

Deborah P. Britzman

Eve Sedgwick (1990) inaugurates her study *Epistemology of the Closet* with a grand narrative gesture she calls "risking the obvious" (22). The phrasing is deceptive in its simplicity, because when it comes to the language of sex (and the closet, after all, is about that curious referentiality, that "open secret" of sex) what is obvious for some becomes for others something to disavow. When speaking about sex, there is that queer contradiction between the ambiguity of language itself and the dominant insistence upon the stability of meaning in sex practices. As Cindy Patton (1991, 374) wryly observes, "The language of sex is so imprecise, so polyvalent that it is 'hard' to know when we are talking about sex and when we are talking about business or politics or other weighty matters [like education]." We are left with the questions of what is imagined when sex is imagined and what is imagined when what is euphemistically called "sex education" is imagined. To return to Sedgwick's formulation, what can "risking the obvious" and placing the obvious at risk *mean* when the labile subject of sex is so conspicuously contested, masked, rated, counted, disavowed, and made synonymous with one's identity?

Our topic becomes even more complicated when one tries to plot the imaginative geography of sex,[2] or when one tries to read sexuality through a favorite theory, instruction manual, or even the views of what can only be called an army of professionals. To muck up matters even more, when inserted into the school curriculum or the university classroom—when, say, education, sociology, or anthropology gets its hands on sexuality—the language of sex becomes explication-like and then, well, desexed. Even more, when the topic of sex becomes like a curriculum and stuck to the underaged (and here, I mean the legal categories of children and youth), one can barely separate its objectives and fantasies from the historical bundles of anxieties, dangers, and predatory discourses that seem to render some sex intelligible as other sex is relegated to the unthinkable and the morally reprehensible. And one might acknowledge the dreariness of even the "thinkable" version that makes sex into a danger and a duty to perform. There, sex becomes something that disturbs innocence and the everyday. It becomes indistinguishable from that strange economy of affects that Jonathan Silin (1995), Eve Sedgwick, and Shoshana Felman (1987) all term "our passion for ignorance."

With all of these lacuna in mind, Sedgwick persists in her willingness to place at risk the obviousness of sex. Structured as axioms, her first one states: "People are different from each other" (23). She plays with all sorts of differences while still managing to admit the impossibility of exhausting the possibilities and hence of finally accounting for all the differences between, within, and among individuals. And a certain geometric quality is allowed because she begins not with cultural universals but with a certain curiosity about polymorphous actions or capacity for humans to be exponential in their strategies of meaning. Here are a few examples:

- Even identical genital acts mean very different things to different people.
- To some people, the nimbus of "the sexual" seems scarcely to extend beyond the boundaries of discrete genital acts; to others, it enfolds them loosely or floats virtually free of them.
- For some people, it is important that sex be embedded in contexts resonant with meaning, narrative, and connectedness with other aspects of their life; for other people, it is important that they not be; to others it doesn't occur that they might be.
- Some people's sexual orientation is intensely marked by autoerotic pleasures and histories—sometimes more so than by any aspect of alloerotic object choice. For others the autoerotic possibility seems secondary or fragile, if it exists at all. (25–26)

Sedgwick is interested in a sort of difference that "retains the unaccounted-for potential to disrupt many forms of the available thinking about sexuality" (25). It is a project akin to what George Bataille (1986) calls "erotism," a certain subjective practice that allows for a question, for the self to be called into question. Something similar guides this present essay, where I move back and forth between the issues raised in the edited volume *Sexual Cultures and the Construction of Adolescent Identities* and the contest of discourses that endeavor to link sex with education. Throughout this essay, three versions of sex education are discussed: the normative, the critical, and the one not yet tolerated. I call the last form "the polymorphously perverse." At times, distinguishing the normative from the critical version becomes difficult because of the latter's reliance on engaging the terms of the former. And yet, in order to consider questions of implication, one must be willing to make an exploration of what it means to link together these two dynamics: sex and education. In this essay, I also engage some of the theories of Freud and Foucault as a lens through which the Irvine text might be read, for the Irvine text provides an important occasion for thinking the unthought-of sex education. And, in thinking about what might constitute such an odd couple, that is, sex and education, we may as well raise difficult questions like: Can sex be educated, and can education be sexed? What might sex education be like if it could become indistinguishable from what Foucault (1988), in one of his last works, called "the care of the self" as a practice of freedom?

Could such an exploration be what Freud (1968, 194) had in mind when, in his inaugural study of sexuality, he termed children "little sex researchers"? The idea that a relation might exist between sexuality and curiosity allows us to question both the limits of sexuality, in what is euphemistically termed "sex education," and its beyond: the transgressions, pleasures, and inexhaustible sensualities, or, in Foucault's often-cited phrasing, the capacity to "produce pleasure with very odd things, very strange parts of our bodies, in very unusual situations" (cited in Halperin 1995, 88).

If sex is such a labile subject in its aims, knowledges, pleasures, and practices, then what exactly can be said of sex? Are its labile qualities the thing that has allowed educators to remain so keen on arguing for and against sex, on linking the construct of appropriate sex to the construct of age appropriateness, and on worrying over which knowledge holds in which bodies and in what circumstances? These worries are not new, and their history seems caught in strange repetitions. As early as 1895, debates over whether sexuality should be placed in the school curriculum occurred in the United States (Hale 1995)—even as, one might say, sex was already there. To continue our little chronology of despair, we can go back to what might now be read as one of the first journals (dated around 1863) written by one student teacher, the hermaphrodite Alexina Herculine Barbin. In this *Bildungsroman*, just at the moment when the question, "Do we truly need a true sex?" was answered with an emphatic "Yes!" (Barbin 1980, vii), our student teacher sadly ponders a melancholy chronology that demands life be separated into a "before sex and after sex." Barbin laments what has been lost when what is lost is the freedom of being without a definitive sex, or, in Foucault's phrase, "the happy limbo of a non-identity" (xiii).

Forty years later, Freud notes in his first essay on sexuality, published in 1905, that what characterizes the literature of psychological development is the contradiction between the paucity of materials on the sexuality of children and the proliferation of interdictions on their bodies. Freud then argues that sexuality begins at the beginning of life and therefore is indistinguishable from any other bodily experience because the body is all. Further, he insists that sexuality is originally polymorphously perverse and hence not organized by object choice, true sex, and so on.[3] And in answering the question of why so many interdictions are stuck to the child's body, Freud attributes the adult's intolerance of children's sexuality to the adult's forgetting of its own infantile sexuality. The dynamic is termed "infantile amnesia," a curious category that suggests that infantile memories of eroticism are buried and therefore preserved in repression. Education, organized as it is by adults, offers tribute to this burial, this forgetting, or, again, this making of the "passion for ignorance." For remember, in Freud's view, there is nothing innocent about forgetting, slips of the tongue, jokes, indeed, all forms of parapraxes—those bungled actions that can be observed daily in and out of classroom life. But in thinking about this first form of forgetting, where children's sexuality slips between the fault lines of adult recall, Freud locates a second structure of forgetting: education. This allows for the psychoanalytic idea that the very grounds of education require the restriction of sexual pleasure. But there is more. By imagining that sexuality is akin to normal development and by forgetting that perversity is the grounds of possibility for sexuality itself, the apparatuses of education, law, and medicine must normalize sexuality to the confines of object choice. Sex, in the normative developmental model of education, then becomes a problem of specifying the proper object and conforming to the interdictions of morality and the state.

Anna Freud (1979) would continue the psychoanalytic critique of education. Her lectures to teachers suggest three ways psychoanalysis could be useful to education: as offering criticism to educational methods, as extending teachers' knowledge of human development, and, in Anna Freud's words, as "endeavor[ing] to repair the injuries which are inflicted upon the child during the processes of education" (106). Anna Freud is even more specific: "It should be said that psychoanalysis, whenever it has come into contact with pedagogy, has always expressed the wish to limit education" (96). We are left with another queer contradiction: if education demands the renunciation of instinct, how is sex education even possible? Or what can be the aim of sex education if the object of education is in the renunciation of sex?

Michel Foucault teaches us how tricky are the actions of renunciation. And in specifying its tricks, Foucault (1990) offers another way to think about sex, one that emphasizes its invention, or what is commonly termed "construction," as opposed to supposed "true nature." Foucault terms the wish for sex to have a true nature "the repressive hypothesis," or the historical fantasy that there was a time before sexual repression and now is the time for discovering the secret of sex. While the proliferation of talk shows work this fantasy with great glee (providing, by the way, a stage for our army of professionals to extend the confessional into the living room and the studio audience), Foucault argues that sex is not the liberation of repression. Rather, as myth, desire, and representation, sex has a historicity. His interest is in how the surfaces of bodies have been inscribed by, and therefore have come to take on, new forms of intelligibility through the contradictory workings of modern knowledge.

For Foucault, the historicity of sex can be more accurately spoken of as a burgeoning nineteenth-century discourse. Knowledge of sexuality targets and produces a series of imagined problem populations: "the masturbating child,"[4] "the hysterical woman," "the pervert," and "the malthusian couple" (105). Such a strange cast of characters, made from the stuff of unspecified actions, becomes translated into knowable identities, examples of the value and the strategies of various eugenics movements. One could say that such characters become the poster people for eugenics campaigns. More specifically, such identities become the anchorage points and props for various forms of racism.

But at the same time that bodies became the site of problems as the targets of these new forms of knowledge, Foucault emphasizes yet another dynamic. And here is where the repressive hypothesis fails. With the making of these new and knowable historical identities came the demands of those so identified, demands that structure such present social movements as feminism, gay and lesbian civil rights, children's rights, and antiracist education. Essentially, this proliferating geometric design is what Foucault means by power, or "manifold relations of force" (94). What made such identity categories hold good, then as now, were the burgeoning social hygiene movements variously termed as pedagogy, criminal justice, psychology, anthropology, medicine, and sociology, *and* the burgeoning movements that demand civil rights. The apparatuses that give sex meaning allow modern knowledge to take hold of the body and, of course, for the body to resist modern knowledge.

Thus Foucault offers us another way to think about sexuality, not as development but as historicity:

> Sexuality must not be thought of as a kind of natural given which power tries to hold in check, or as an obscure domain which knowledge tries gradually to uncover. It is the name that can be given to a historical construct: not a furtive reality that is difficult to grasp, but a great surface network in which the stimulations of bodies, the intensification of pleasures, the incitement to discourse, the formation of special knowledges, the strengthening of controls and resistances, are linked to one another, in accordance with a few major strategies of knowledge and power. (105–106)

To conceptualize sex as that "great surface network" allows one to ponder the specific relations made intelligible when sex becomes coupled with education. We might think how sex becomes subjected to larger questions that organize pedagogical efforts and that span relations between children and adults, between home and school, and between identity and its representation.[5] We might also consider the possibility that knowledge itself is insufficient in our time of the pandemic known as AIDS.

Janice Irvine's edited collection might be read as wavering between the theories of Freud and Foucault.[6] Parts of the collection address the "silences" and "repressions" that structure most sex education, while other chapters engage the social effects (in terms of what must be excluded and rendered as deviant) of a sex education that can imagine sex as having a true nature only if it is white, middle class, and heterosexual. The critique of sex education and the sorts of remedies the text offers will be returned to a bit later. What brings this collection together, however, is an attention to the question of how various strategies of knowledge seem to transform sex into education and into the identities of adolescents. The volume is further focused by an emphasis on a prevention model of sex education: prevention of bodily harm (where sex education becomes a protective knowledge of various sexually transmitted infections and early pregnancy avoidance); protection against homophobia, racism, and sexism (where sex education critiques practices of subordination); and prevention of stereotypes of femininity, disabilities, and school textbooks (where sex education critiques representations of the body). Within these forms of protection, one also finds the advocacy of imagining sex education as an opportunity for curiosity, bodily pleasures, and the development of strategies for social negotiation that are central to the care of the self. All of the authors work within the framework of social science; many practice in the field of preventive health.

The book's opening premise is ethical: "We want more than for some adolescents merely to survive an epidemic. We aspire to a world in which they all can develop rich and satisfying sexualities" (ix). The problem, then, for the text and for the reader is to imagine which knowledges will allow for new practices of the self when the dominant knowledges of sexuality are so caught up in discourses of moral panic, protection of innocent children, and the dangers of explicit representations of sexualities. More pointedly, when sex gets into the hands of mainstream politicians, social policymakers, religious fundamentalists of every ilk, and those whose project is the centering of what queer theorist Michael Warner (1993, xxi) terms as "heteronormativity in social theory," what's a curriculum to do? If everything causes sexuality, or more interestingly, if anything can make sexual pleasure and therefore make sexuality perverse, then what should be the subject of sex education?

But alas, the subject is dual. And this is signaled in the title of the text, "sexual cultures" and "adolescent identities." Writing within what might loosely be called poststructuralist theory, most authors maintain the necessity of considering both adolescents and culture as social constructions. They try to maintain that difficult and slippery argument that constructions or representations, though imaginary and historical, take hold so well precisely because they are animated by their social effectivity. But in positing a phenomenon as a construction as opposed to an always-already-there thing, what is at stake? The arguments against social construction have been with us for a while. For those who refuse discourse theory, the debate tends to stall between the contradictory assertions that either there are adolescents or there are no adolescents. Either there is culture or there is no culture. A different way of thinking about constructions or inventions might begin with another look at Foucault's deconstruction of the repressive hypothesis, for the repressive hypothesis is a sort of conceptual fortress that preserves the ground for such distinctions as those between innocence and guilt, normality and deviance, and nature and culture.

The repressive hypothesis would say of adolescents that there once was an unencumbered or true adolescence that became subject to all sorts of worries. First adolescents were carefree; now they are careless. The productive hypothesis would say that such worries produce what we call "the adolescent" or, as Irvine writes, that "recently invented life stage shaped by economic and political influences" (7). In the productive hypothesis, what seems to be at stake is how the body is read (and not whether there is a body) when the body is assumed to stand in for adolescents. In the case of culture, the repressive hypothesis would posit culture as a transhistorical and unitary set of behaviors, customs, modes of address, and so on, passed down through generations. The seamless picture becomes distorted only when a culture becomes interfered with by an outside. In this hypothesis, culture is the sacred object and becomes the sacred ruin through no fault of its own. Moreover, to return to one's culture becomes a journey back to *a priori* origins. The productive hypothesis reads suspiciously, positing culture as far more contentious and as requiring the processes—as a condition of making and recognizing its members—of regulation and exclusion. And, even these processes of distinction would produce new cultural forms and new sorts of demands.

From these sorts of assertions one can then question the fault lines of discourses on sex that advocate cultural appropriateness and age appropriateness. For if both of these terms are constructed terms, then along with the construction comes a target for appropriateness. This, after all, is the limit of appropriateness and where critical models of sex education may become indistinguishable from normative models. Should sex education even be coupled with appropriateness of any kind? What is appropriate for who if culture has that teleological talent for excluding its members on the basis of cultural appropriateness? Can a notion of appropriateness ever become uncoupled from developmental theory?[7] Or to exceed our present limit and perhaps begin with the perverse: what if sex education became a lifetime study of the vicissitudes of knowledge, power, and pleasure?

Irvine signals some of the above tensions when she states the text's problematic:

> Although effective research and education on adolescent sexuality can only proceed from a standpoint of strong cultural analysis, there is some complexity to this task. . . . In sexuality research . . . one must negotiate the tension between simplistic overgeneralization about culture and [in the words of Carol Vance] "the anarchy of sexual idiosyncrasy." (9)

With Vance's phrasing, we are back to Sedgwick's axioms and the difficulty of pinning down our unruly subjects or even provisionally risking any form of essentialism.

These are significant tensions because they point to the necessity of calling into question three dynamics: research, education, and culture. Each dynamic has become significantly troubled in our time of AIDS. But in allowing for such tensions, this volume also centers the question of responsibility and what responsibility might mean when one faces the conditions that youth and adults confront as they fashion their lives. Every author advocates for a recognition of the complexities of youth in all their varied sizes, shapes, orientations, and interests. Many of the chapters are quite clear on the need for a sex curriculum that is unapologetic in the issues it raises, in the subjects it spans, and in the critique of the double-edgedness of such sex binaries as the public and private, the cultural and the individual, the masculine and the feminine, the normal and the pathological. Most if not all of the chapters consider the insights of antiracist education and anti-homophobic inquiry, and pay close attention, particularly in those chapters that draw their discussions from ethnographic research, to the very specific kinds of negotiatory strategies different genders and cultural groups will have to invent if safer sex is to be possible and pleasurable. This is the strong sense of culturally appropriate sex education, where curriculum would be an incitement for students to make culture and to refuse their own cultural superstitious categories that require, as a condition of their intelligibility, dynamics such as gender inequalities, hatred of homosexuality, and inter-dictions that silence public talk about sex.

On the other hand, this text exhibits a weaker sense of culturally appro-priate curriculum, where certain knowledge becomes affixed only to cer-tain populations and therefore where education—as a provision of information on cultural attributes—takes precedence over sex. The prob-lems indicated above become secondary for, more often than not, the information models assume the sort of stability that is irrelevant to con-duct, sex, and sociality and that information will be no problem to the informed. This is not to say that youth should not consider cultural rela-tions or that youth should not have access to accessible information. It is to insist, however, that cultural relations and information of any kind be taken as symptomatic rather than curative and final, and as subject to the work of those who engage its myriad meanings. Moreover, in safer sex edu-cation, matching knowledge to identities cannot admit the crucial under-standing that one's sexual conduct is conduct, not identity. What seems to be at stake here is how one engages dynamics of cultural relations, specific information, and the discourses of sex.

It may be more useful to consider Jonathan Silin's (1995) notion of a socially relevant sex education, that is, curricular endeavors unafraid to con-sider children and youth as "little sex researchers" interested in the vicissi-tudes of life and death. Pedagogical efforts could become unsatisfied with the pinning of knowledge to specific identities and more restless—or better, polymorphous in its perversity—in what can be imagined when sex is imag-ined and in what can be acknowledged when the erotics of pedagogy and knowledge are acknowledged. For if we take seriously social theories about the historicity and contentiousness of constructions, then pedagogy might begin with the assumptions that identities are made and not received and that the work of the curriculum is to incite identifications, not close them down.

Those authors in the Irvine volume who write about ethnic groups and questions of sexuality insist that educational intervention programs and curriculum must be culturally specific and appropriate to that culture's way of life. Behind this demand are important critiques of sex education as being Eurocentric in its reliance on developmental theories (and its central tasks of individuation, separation, and autonomy as a universal quest); homophobic in the narrowing of sex to the mechanics of reproduction and in its advocacy of heterosexual romance and marriage; masculinist in its focus on males as either predators or people capable of being calmed and in its refusal to consider female desire; racist in its depiction of whiteness as the universal measure for beauty, power, and status; and suicidal in its refusal to address safer sexual practices. These sorts of critiques point more to the need for sex education to be antiracist, antihomophobic, and feminist than for it to protect culture per se.

Given these sorts of critiques, two kinds of interventions are advocated. One is a disassembling of racism and Anglocentric visions of the body and of the other body. In concrete terms, many of the chapters argue for the centering of Asian, Latino, and African American bodies in sex education. Moreover, in decentering the persistent racism of sex education, a kaleidoscopic vision of such categories as nation, immigration, generation, language, geography, home, family, literacy, and so on, are required because such categories are central to the fashioning of sexuality. The other intervention concerns the argument for a culturally appropriate curriculum. Here is where the strong and the weak versions of appropriateness coexist in tension. Readers of this text might well engage the problem of how sex can be culturally appropriate, and, if it can be, what of perversity?

For a pedagogy to be made from this text, perhaps the central problem concerns what educators do with the kinds of information and advocacy this text offers. This collection should not be taken as "sensitivity training." Nor should it be taken as an anthropological tour through the lives of the Other, perhaps another version of sensitivity training. I do think this text allows for important questions. What values, orientations, ethics, and singularities should a socially relevant sex education appeal to if a culture is not a tidy safe house or if culture produces its own set of inequalities along the lines of gender, socioeconomic status, sexual practices, age, and concepts of beauty, power, and the body? If adolescents are a social construction as well and hence have no universality except for the fact that, in North American contexts, this contruct takes the form of an extralegal status of citizenship and is thus subject to the control of parents and schools and if certain other constructions, such as HIV, STDs, unplanned pregnancies, and various sexualized forms of violence, place adolescent bodies at risk, then how are educators and students to engage ethically within a sex education viewed as indistinguishable from a practice of freedom and as a care of selves? For these questions to remain important, educators must not simply debate them, make a decision, and then serve them up as an easy-bake sex education curriculum. Shall we admit that nothing about sex education is easy and that if the concern is to make a curriculum that does not incite curiosity, sex education will continue to signify "our passion for ignorance"?

Given such heteroglossic contexts—and this text does well in suggesting the complexity of forces that engage sexuality—perhaps part of what is needed are curricular endeavors that begin with antiracist, antisexist, and antihomophobic suppositions. But such suppositions may well go against notions of cultural appropriateness and age appropriateness. What is being advocated here is a curriculum that refuses the grounds of eugenics and social hygiene and that can come to its own social relevancy because it is fashioned by those participating and is capable of pushing the limits of critique and pleasure. But in making such a curriculum, can sex education exceed sociological categories and be more than a semester where bodies are subject to the humanistic constructs of self-esteem and role models and to the endless activities of voting on knowledge and the finding of stereotypes? More to the point, can sex be thought of as a practice of the self rather than a hypothetical rehearsal, as in preparation for the future? And if such questions can be thought about seriously, one might just as well consider *not* how sex can fit into the curriculum but rather how sex might allow the entire disciplinary enterprise of education to be reimagined for education to incite ethical projects of caring for the self.

Such projects are occurring. But more often than not, they exist outside of public education, beyond the confines of disciplined knowledge and the defensiveness of official school talk. The projects may be known for their contention, for their refusal to fit into tidy categories, for the debates they allow, for the practices that become possible. And these are precisely the dynamics that education disavows. But one can still think of the poetry of Essex Hemphill and Marilyn Hacker, the dances of Bill T. Jones, the essays of Pat Califia and Joan Nestle, the films of Derek Jarmen, Maria Luisa Bemberg, and John Greyson, the novels of Toni Morrison, Samuel Delany, David Feinberg, and Henry Roth, the collection of short essays and stories published by Plume called the *High Risk* series. And just as Sedgwick's list of axioms should invite the reader to produce one's own, so, too, with this present list. For the thing in common to both lists is the invitation to think, the invitation to imagine as Foucault imagines, the capacity to "produce pleasure with very odd things, very strange parts of our bodies, in very unusual situations."

For such conversations to even become thinkable in relation to education, educators will be required to get curious about their own conceptualizations of sex and, in so doing, become advocates for the explorations and curiosities of others. For when one becomes a "little sex researcher," one is interested in the study of pleasures and in the detours taken. When one can study the histories sex provokes, the perversities it might imagine and perform, then one is likely to engage as well in the study of where knowledge breaks down, becomes anxious, is built again. The curriculum moves toward the polymorphously perverse and onto Bataille's notion of "erotism" when the problem becomes the making of questions that can unsettle the finitude that education has become. And if the question can tolerate its own perverse journey, then maybe a certain curiosity can be made. But it will have to begin, as the first few lines of Essex Hemphill's poem "Now We Think" begins, with a practice of care for the self:

> Now we think
> as we fuck

Notes

1. The issues raised in this essay are elaborated and revised in Deborah P. Britzman, *Lost Subjects Contested Objects: Toward a Psychoanalytic Inquiry of Learning.* (Albany: SUNY Press, forthcoming).

2. In a taken-for-granted way, the geography of sex suggests the geographical sites where sex occurs. Cindy Patton, however, disccusses a stronger sense of this term in chapter 2 of *Last Served.* "The Gendered Geopolitics of Space" is an overview of the epidemiology of global AIDS in terms of migration patterns and global population displacements. Patton also makes the significant point that travelers perform sexuality differently than when at home, and thus the term "geography of sex" signals something about the traveler, not the site. Patton uses the term "sexual landscape" and advises the following, which I hope readers will keep in mind throughout my essay: "Truly comprehensive approaches to safer sex will view all sexuality as the mingling of potentially different sexual cultures, requiring each of us to be educated and to educate others about the variety of possibilities for creating sexual indentities and sexual practices which can stop the [AIDS] epidemic" (48).

3. In its common usages, the term "perversion" connotes a moralistic judgment on transgressing social convention, nature, and what is accepted as "normal." This essay works with the term "perversity" in the psychoanalytic sense. There, perversity invokes any sexual activity that deviates from coitus with a person of the opposite sex for the purpose of reproduction. Essentially and regardless of object choice, perversity refers to every other practice of pleasure that has no reason other than pleasure. Laplanche and Pontalis (1988, 307–308) offer the following observation:

> So-called normal sexuality cannot be seen as an *a priori* aspect of human nature [and citing Freud]: ". . . the exclusive sexual interest felt by men for women is also a problem that needs elucidating and is not a self-evident fact." . . . One could . . . define

human sexuality itself as essentially "perverse" inasmuch as it never fully detaches itself from its [infantile] origins, where satisfaction was sought not in a specific activity but in the "pleasure gain" associated with functions or activities depending on other instincts. Even in the performance of the genital act itself, it suffices that the subject should develop an excessive attachment to forepleasure for him [or her] to slip toward perversion.

Throughout this essay, my use of perversion is meant to signify actions without utility rather than the unfortunate moralistic usage that structures homophobic discourse.

4. The "masturbating child" is an interesting case and a crucial trope in the early discussions in the United States over the aims and goals of sex education. It can be said that the ghost of the masturbating child haunted the "resignation" of Surgeon General Joycelyn Elders and, earlier in this century, the development of Kellogg Corn Flakes, originally promoted for its capacity to curb boys from masturbating. For a long discussion of the relation between social hygiene movements and sex education, see Nathan Hale Jr., *Freud and the Americans: The Beginnings of Psychoanalysis in the United States. 1876–1917* (New York: Oxford University Press, 1971).

5. Simon Watney makes similar points in his essay "School's Out." He offers not "the usual question of what children supposedly want or need from education," but "what it is that adults want or need of children in the name of 'education' " (398).

6. My use of Freud and Foucault throughout this essay is not meant to set up an opposition between their theories, specifically because both theorists center the question of the body, and its history. When it comes to sexuality, the question of surface or interiority cannot be distinguished, for with both theorists, sexuality is a relation. Thus this essay considers what these theorists have in common: a study of limits and of the intolerable, and a concern for diminishing the pain of suffering.

7. For the best discussions of how the construct of age appropriateness and its discourses of development deny the sexuality of children and produce the exclusion of gay and lesbian bodies, see Jonathan Silin's (1995) stunning critique of developmental psychology in chapter 4 of *Sex, Death and the Education of Children* (1995), "Developmentalism and the Aims of Education," and see Simon Watney's essay "School's Out."

References

Barbin, H. (1980). *Herculine Barbin: Being the Recently Discovered Memoirs of a Nineteenth-Century French Hermaphrodite*. Introduced by Michel Foucault. New York: Pantheon Books.

Bataille, G. (1986). *Erotism: Death and Sensuality*. San Francisco: City Lights Press.

Felman, S. (1987). *Jacques Lacan and the Adventure of Insight: Psychoanalysis in Contemporary Culture*. Cambridge: Harvard University Press.

Foucault, M. (1988). *The Care of the Self,* Vol. 3 of *The History of Sexuality*. New York: Vintage.

——— (1990). *The History of Sexuality: An Introduction, Volume 1*. New York: Vintage.

Freud, A. (1979). *Psycho-Analysis for Teachers and Parents*. New York: Norton.

Freud, S. (1968). *The Standard Edition of the Complete Psychological Works of Sigmund Freud, Volume 7 1901–1905*. London: Hogarth.

Hale, N. (1995). *Freud and the Americans: The Beginnings of Psychoanalysis in the United States, 1876–1917*. New York: Oxford University Press.

Halperin, D. (1995). *Saint Foucault: Towards a Gay Hagiography*. New York: Oxford University Press.

Hemphill, E. (1992). *Ceremonies: Prose and Poetry*. New York: Plume.

Irvine, J., ed. (1994). *Sexual Cultures and the Construction of Adolescent Identities*. Philadelphia: Temple University Press.

Laplanche, J., and Pontalis, J.B. (1988). *The Language of Psychoanalysis*. London: Karnac Books and the Institute of Psycho-Analysis.

Patton, C. (1991). Visualizing Safe Sex: When Pedagogy and Pornography Collide. In ed. *inside\out: Lesbian theories, gay theories*, D. Fuss, 373–86. New York: Routledge.

———— (1994). *Last Served? Gendering the HIV Pandemic*. London: Taylor and Francis.

Sedgwick, E. (1990). *Epistemology of the Closet*. Berkeley: University of California Press.

Silin, J. (1995). *Sex, Death and the Education of Children: Our Passion for Ignorance in the Age of AIDS*. New York: Teachers College Press.

Warner, M., ed. (1993). *Fear of a Queer Planet: Queer Politics and Social Theory*. Minneapolis: University of Minnesota Press.

Watney, S. (1991). School's Out. In *inside/out: Lesbian theories, gay theories*, ed. D. Fuss, 387–404. New York: Routledge.

8

And I Want to Thank You, Barbie

Barbie As a Site for Cultural Interrogation

Claudia Mitchell and Jacqueline Reid-Walsh

Barbie is a problem for many—a deep problem.

 Barbie is an American icon: the product of an adult's fantasy of a girl-child's toy. Or is Barbie the adult's toy and the child's fantasy? What happens when the adult's fantasy collides with the child's fantasy? Sparks fly. You would have no "Angry Women" issue of RE/SEARCH without Barbie. This book is the answer to millions of prayers. At last revealed—all that misplaced Barbie angst, all that childhood conditioning, torture and repression. A home for brave Barbie survivors who can finally step forward. "My name is . . . and I had a Barbie." (xvi)

So runs the introduction to *Mondo Barbie: An Anthology of Fiction and Poetry* edited by Richard Peabody and Lucinda Ebersole. In their introduction they situate for feminist scholars who have already begun to interrogate and revision popular culture texts associated with women the most problematic cultural icon of girlhood—Barbie. Linda Hutcheon in *The Politics of Postmodernism* observes, "The postmodern is seemingly not so much a concept as a problematic: 'a complex of heterogeneous but interrelated questions which will not be silenced by any spuriously unitary answer' (Burgin 1986, 1989, 163–64)" (1989, 15). The "spuriously unitary answer" that has almost universally accompanied Barbie since her birth 35 years ago, from adults, particularly women, and almost assuredly from feminists has been a flat rejection of Barbie and everything she appears to stand for: beauty, the male gaze, body, fashion, femininity, materialism, big business, and mass marketing. In this paper, we enter into this discourse and argue that Barbie exists as a perfect cultural site for interrogating the margins, borders, and contradictions of our lives as girls and women.[1]

In this paper, we attempt to illuminate the dilemmas and contradictions in the lives of women by understanding the dilemmas and contradictions that surround Barbie-as-text in the lives of girls. Our interest in exploring these contradictions in the lives of women by interrogating the culture of girls is not without precedent. In one sense, the work of Luce Irigaray (1991) in writing that "men's culture is regularly valorized and women's culture devalorized" (38) situates for us a concern for the devaluing of the culture of girls and women. Indeed, we would argue that the spuriously universal "no" to Barbie parallels the spuriously universal "no" to romance reading that Janice Radway (1984) takes on in *Reading the Romance*.[2]

In interrogating Barbie as a cultural site, we acknowledge—as do Lorraine Gammon and Margaret Marchmont in *The Female Gaze: Women as Viewers of Popular Culture*—that:

> Popular culture is a site of struggle. . . . It is not enough to dismiss popular culture as merely serving the complementary systems of capitalism and patriarchy, peddling "false consciousness" to the duped masses. It can also be seen as a site where meanings are contested and where dominant ideologies can be disturbed. (1989, 1)

Such meanings and ideologies have already been "disturbed" by feminist scholars in interrogating the popular culture of adolescent girls and women: ranging from addressing the devaluing of romance reading (Janice Radway 1984; Linda Christian-Smith 1990), romance writing (Jayne Ann Krentz 1992; Gemma Moss 1989), fiction reading (Claudia Mitchell 1982, 1994), soap operas (Christine Geraghty 1991), diary and journal writing (Cinthia Gannett 1992). Like Gammon and Marchmont, these scholars have chosen not "to dismiss the popular by always positioning ourselves outside it" (2), and in so doing have acknowledged that it is "from popular culture . . . that women (and men) are offered the culture's dominant definitions of themselves" (2).

Lyn Mikel Brown and Carol Gilligan in *Meeting at the Crossroads: Women's Psychology and Girls' Development* contend that by focusing on the critical points in girls' lives, we can understand more fully our lives as women. In essence, these writers argue that we need to go back to the time before adolescence if we are to understand women's psychology, and to include in research girls who are in their earlier stages of development. In focusing their most recent scholarship on the lives of girls who are in the second and third grade, Brown and Gilligan situate for us the girls who are developmentally still in their Barbie-playing stage. We draw further support for this investigation from Carol Gilligan in her essay "Women's Psychological Development: Implications for Psychotherapy," where she describes a type of revision and "covering over" that seems to accompany girls as they pass out of childhood into early adolescence wherein they begin to revision their relational world as girls as " 'false' or 'illogical' or 'stupid' " (Brown and Gilligan 1992, 7).

> This act of revision washes away the grounds of girls' feelings and thoughts and undermines the transformatory potential which lies in women's development by leaving girls-turning-into-women with the sense that their feelings are groundless, their thoughts are about nothing real, what they experienced never happened, or at the time they could not understand it. (7)

The fiction and poetry offered in *Mondo Barbie*, the recent flurry of popular interrogations of Barbie on talk shows such as *The Shirley Show*, and the plethora of articles in the newspapers surrounding the "Math class is tough" episode[3] all suggest to us that, at least within a white, middle-class, heterosexist framework, many women would like to deny that Barbie ever happened.[4] Such a position is confirmed in our own informal explorations on the meaning of Barbie with young university women and one group of female academics. It is also supported by the work of Emily Hancock, who in *The Girl Within: A Groundbreaking New Approach to Female Identity* looks at the need to uncover the layers within the experiences of women in order to understand their development. Though accounting for the spuriously unitary "no" that accompanies Barbie beyond the scope of this paper, we do see this paper as a first step in acknowledging that Barbie is a cultural site "in her own right." In so doing, we consider that unless we can understand the roots of our own positioning (i.e., our lives as girls, or how we see girls' lives), we remain in the position occupied by the teachers in Brown and Gilligan's study *Meeting at the Crossroads*, who, while intending to offer a supportive and encouraging environment to adolescent girls in their school, are described by the girls as contributing to their loss of voice. They appeared to the girls to be offering contradictory messages about being autonomous and being nice.

In the remainder of this paper we attempt to situate contradiction in the lives of girls and women through an interrogation of the cumulative cultural text of Barbie. In our analysis we employ the term *text* as used by cultural theorist John Fiske to include the primary texts (Barbie and her accompanying paraphernalia), related texts that include the texts of critical reception, and the texts of the readers (players of Barbie) themselves. Though we focus only on the primary text in this paper, our attention is less on Barbie, the 11 ½-inch doll that has been around since 1959, and more on a text of Barbie that includes print and play paraphernalia. It is not our intention to "cover over" the physical features of the 11 ½-inch fashion doll other than to say that Barbie is only one (and is "the" one) of many fashion dolls that have womanly bodies and fashionable clothing. It is also not our intention to "cover over" the consumer world that Barbie represents. As Ellen Seiter (1993) takes up in *Sold Separately* in her social and economic analysis of "buying happiness, buying success," the mass marketing of toys and educational products from the 1940s and '50s onward already signals children as part of consumer capital. Mattel's Barbie is just another part of the Fisher Price–Lego world.

Barbie as Text

Sidney Ladensohn Stern and Ted Schoenhaus observe in their book *Toyland: The High-Stakes Games of the Toy Industry* that the 1987 slogan "We Girls Can Be Anything" encapsulates Barbie's long-lasting appeal. As they describe it, Ruth Handler, the originator of the doll, first had the idea for it when she noticed that her daughter Barbara and her friends preferred to play with paper dolls that were adult or teenage rather than with baby or child dolls. As she observed the girls at play, she was apparently struck by the hours that they would devote to creating new situations: "If we were only in the doll business, she would think, we could three-dimensionalize that play pattern and we would really have something" (60).

Over the years Barbie has been positioned as a bride, a friend, a date (mostly with Ken, but as Stern and Schoenhaus point out, she did apparently two-time Ken for Derek in her days as a rock star in 1986), a fun-loving vacationer in Hawaii, and a backyard weekender with barbecues, pool parties, and tennis games. Most recently she has taken to rollerblading. She has also had a multitude of careers, occupying over the years and altering with the times occupations such as an astronaut, marine biologist, fashion designer, fashion model, teacher, nurse, doctor, flight attendant, ballet dancer, and rock star. She has even presented papers at conferences.[5] In all of these positions and occupations she has remained an 11 ½-inch doll; although her hair and skin have changed color, her makeup coloring has changed with the times—from bright red lips to pastels and back again— and her measurements have altered slightly. What does change continually are the artifacts and paraphernalia that surround the 11 ½-inch doll (friends, clothing, appropriate scene markers). In a sense, the 11 ½-inch doll is the equivalent of the Lego starter set.

What follows are our close readings of four related Barbie texts: the Barbie collector cards; *Barbie* and *Barbie Fashion* comic books; *Barbie, The Magazine for Girls*; and the Barbie game "We Girls Can Do Anything." In interrogating the ideology of these relatively recent phenomenon we ask the question: What do these artifacts mean in the development of the nineties girls who will become young women at the turn of the century?

Barbie Collector Cards

The hockey and baseball trading card industry has been around for a long time, catering primarily, although not exclusively, to young and not-so-young males as buyers, sellers, and traders. Such cards have a photograph of a well-known or not-so-well-known player on one side, and on the reverse side relevant sports trivia (e.g., number of home runs, batting average, history of the player, career events such as being voted in the Hall of Fame). Barbie collector cards,[6] which exist in at least two languages, French and English, follow a similar format, having a picture on one side along with a collector number and a year (from 1959 to 1993). These pictures of Barbie alone and with her friends or of friends alone, such as Skipper or Ken, frequently exist as tableaux where the characters are situated historically (e.g., in appropriate 1959, 1960 dress) as well as in narrative form in that the picture suggests a script or story. These tableaux resemble the tableaux that girls create as part of playing Barbies. Note, too, that these tableaux are essentially what Mattel sells in the Barbie Picnic, Barbie Music Class, or the dozens of other Barbie paraphernalia. The reverse side of the card is inscribed with two types of text: a short narrative text of the scene on the picture side—always with a title such as "Daydreaming among the ruins," "A jump ahead of the rest," or "Ride 'em Ken"—and a feminist history question, "Famous Women." For example, on the picture side of #171 we are introduced to Korean Barbie, and on the back the narrative "What's in the attic" provides for a fuller description of Korean culture:

> Korean Barbie is visiting her friend in Seoul, the capital of South Korea. After lunch, Barbie explores her friend's house. "I wonder what surprises are in the attic?" Barbie says. She opens the attic door, looks around, and finds an old trunk hidden in the corner. Inside the trunk Barbie discovers a toy yong. Its serpent body is covered with scales. It has long claws, wings, and is said to breathe fire. What is a yong? A dragon.

This narrative is followed by a "Famous Women" question:

> Q. An English novelist and literary critic, my husband and I founded a publishing house that published many of my own writings. Attacks of mental illness led to my suicide. Who am I?
> A. Virginia Woolf (1881–1941)

In #159, one of the 1982 cards, Barbie is depicted in a fashionable parka, sitting on a sleigh being pulled by huskies. In the narrative on the back, we are introduced to a "North to Alaska" scenario:

> It's early winter in Alaska for Eskimo Barbie. To keep warm Barbie bundles up in a thick, warm coat. Today she is driving a dogsled to join Ken and his friends. They are fishing through holes in the ice. "Did you bring along an extra pair of mukluks?" yells Ken as he sees Barbie arrive. "My feet are wet and dry boots will keep me warm." Do you know what mukluks are? Mukluks are boots.

Following this narrative is the "Famous Woman" question:

> Q. I first began my career under the direction of Ma Rainey. I was most successful in the years from 1923 to 1930 during which time I recorded "St. Louis Blues" with Louis Armstrong. Who am I?
> A. Bessie Smith (1894–1937)

On #146 of the French language cards the following question appears:

> Q. Romanciere acadienne, mes romans evoquent l'histoire et la vie du peuple acadien. Qui suis-je?
> A. Antoinine Maillet (1929–)

Questions span the lives of Barbara Ann Scott, Roberta Bondar, Beatrix Potter, Anne Frank, Catherine Parr, Anne of Cleves, Grandma Moses, Indira Gandhi, Elizabeth Taylor, and Iseult, to name only a few. Leading feminists such as Marie Therese Forget Casgrain appear, as well as political refugees such as Carmen Gloria Quintana, who, having been persecuted by General Pinochet of Chile, survived and was "healed in Montreal and later returned to Chile in 1987" (#145). We would see these cards as an example of allowing girls to recover feminist history, or of offering girls the opportunity to become through history feminist historians. At the same time, we see the cards signaling contradiction and interrogation.

Barbie and *Barbie Fashion* Comic Books

Barbie and *Barbie Fashion* comic books come out monthly through Marvel Comics. Each issue is made up of at least three "full-length" episodes, advertising, and a letter to the editor section. The comic book episodes deal with Barbie and her friends. The title of our paper is taken from one of these episodes, where Barbie is presented as a student teacher. In this episode, "The Art of Teaching" (*Barbie* 1, no. 23), we see Barbie arriving at a high school, briefcase in hand, wearing a short but not immodest pleated skirt, coordinating jacket, and hair tied neatly back. "Today is the first day of school! Even though I've studied art appreciation for many years, I'm still a little nervous about 'student teaching,' " the caption says.

As Barbie makes her way through the halls of the high school, which has as its motto "Knowledge through learning," she worries to herself, "I hope I'll be a good teacher. . . . And that the students learn a lot from me." They do, as Jessica tells her at the end, when Barbie gets her out of the censure of the Pink Sweater girls and into an after-school art club. The students in Barbie's classes, too, are likely to learn a lot. We see Barbie delivering a well-organized and well-executed lesson on different historical periods in art history. Through the use of a slide projector and slides, Barbie's students and the young readers are introduced to Rembrandt, Monet, Picasso, and Warhol. She talks about particular movements in art as well, naming realism, impressionism, cubism, and pop art. Barbie has the full attention of her students, the slide projector works well, the students remain orderly. The most that a university supervisor would offer as criticism is that in the teaching episode she does not involve the students greatly in discussion. However, through Jessica we gain some idea of the impact of the lesson.

In another comic book episode, "The Volunteers" (*Barbie Fashion* 1, no. 26), Skipper, Barbie's little sister, spends the Thanksgiving holiday volunteering at a shelter for the homeless. She misses Barbie and her friends but at the same time is thankful for meeting all sorts of people, including Julie and her two children, Jennifer and Deborah, and doing something useful. Meanwhile, Barbie, who misses Skipper observes: "We missed Skipper at dinner today, but I'm so proud that she's helping other people" (10). Ultimately, however, Barbie and friends (Ken, Theresa, and Midge) bring a special dessert over to the shelter, joining Skipper after all. In the final scene, we see Skipper bringing Barbie et al. and her new friends at the shelter together:

SKIPPER: Julie, I want you to meet Theresa. She runs a day care center. Maybe she has room for Jennifer and Deborah.

THERESA: Well, Skipper, thanks to Barbie* we've built an extension and now I can take in more children.

We also see Barbie taking on other important personal and social issues, such as eating disorders, which are addressed in "Barbie as role model" (*Barbie Fashion*, 1, no. 27). In this episode, Jennifer, Skipper's friend, is reprimanded by the teacher for not paying attention and afterward reveals to Skipper that she is on a diet: "I want to be like your sister Barbie! Her picture is in all the magazines." She goes on: "Everybody likes her because she is so pretty. I want everybody to like me, too!" Skipper tells Barbie of her concern about Jennifer's eating and Barbie suggests that Jennifer spend the day with her. Jennifer arrives at Barbie's house just as she is about to eat breakfast, much to Jennifer's astonishment:

JENNIFER: You're eating cereal and whole wheat toast! But isn't bread fattening?

BARBIE: Bread is less fattening if I spread it with margarine, Jennifer, and the carbohydrates* in cereal and bread give me the energy I need to get through the day. Carbohydrates help me to concentrate too.

JENNIFER (thinking to herself): Gee . . . maybe that's why I've been having trouble concentrating in school. Maybe that's why I feel so tired.

They then dash through the day, meeting stylists and a photographer, and eating lunch (a nutritious one). Each scene offers versions of the same message:

RACHEL(Fashion stylist): A scarf should look good with this number. . . . And they (these fashions) look best on healthy figures! They don't look good at all on skinny models.

BARBIE (at lunch, and in response to Jennifer ordering the small salad only): I'll have your lunch special.

JENNIFER: A baked potato? Aren't potatoes fattening?

BARBIE: Potatoes, especially the skins are very nutritious, Jennifer. . . . And remember they're only fattening if they've been deep fried or if you add butter or sour cream . . .

RICARDO (Photographer): Hi, Barbie—ready to start modelling?

BARBIE: Yes I am. This is Jennifer. She'd like to be a model too.

RICARDO: Well, Jennifer, this fall I'll be taking pictures of teenagers for an ad campaign. . . . But the teenagers in my pictures have to look healthy! Here's my card. If you can gain about five pounds by fall, call me!

*This apparently refers to an episode in no. 20.

The contradiction that Barbie raises in this episode mirrors perfectly the contradiction offered in magazines for adolescent and adult women such as *Cosmopolitan* or *Seventeen*, and even the earlier version of *Ms.* magazine: the message of eating right, and the image of the models who can never be too thin.

Some issues of race do come up, both in terms of representation as in "The Volunteers," where several of the other volunteers are black, and where Julie, who runs her own day care, is black. In "Barbie in the Fix-up Mix-up" (*Barbie Fashion* 1, no. 23), Barbie's friend Christie, who is black, apparently has no date for the Harvest Ball because her boyfriend, also black, Brad, must go to visit his sick aunt. Ken, it just so happens, is entertaining his out-of-town friend from childhood, Jay, also black, for a few days, and Jay can take Christie to the dance. Aunt Thelma makes a remarkable recovery, however, and Brad becomes available for the dance—leaving Christie with two dates. Fortunately, Christie's friend Noel comes along on the evening of the dance looking for a good book to read because she wasn't invited to the ball. A light bulb goes on in Christie's head, and everyone has a date for the dance. Arguably race is not addressed explicitly, and no interracial dating takes place. At the same time, however, in one of the letters to the editor, we do encounter race:

> Dear Barbie:
> I am a big fan of yours. I get Barbie comics! I like your comics. I am from Whiteriver, Arizona. I'm an Apache Indian. But it doesn't matter what we are, right? I collect lots of Barbie dolls.
>
> Eds.
> You're absolutely right, Davina! The world is a very colorful and interesting place because there are many different kinds of people in it! For all our differences, we're still very much the same. (*Barbie Fashion* 1, no. 23)

That there have been generations of Barbiephiles is addressed in the letters, adding to our sense of Barbie as a cumulative cultural text both in terms of the range of her paraphernalia and in terms of her longevity. For example:

> Hi, my name is Michelle. I like your comic a lot. My grandmother had some Barbies. When my great-grandma moved, the movers threw them out . . .
>
> Eds.
> Many of our readers write to tell us that their mothers or grandmothers used to play with Barbies when they were young. We think this is part of what makes Barbie so special!

That Barbie now exists as an historical phenomenon linked to contemporary girlhood offers a strong "interrogative possibility" for girls and women across generations. The texts of the comics exist, too, as an historical phenomenon linked to the recent range of didactic "issue books" published for young children on topics such as family violence, divorce, AIDS, and gay families.

Barbie, the Magazine for Girls

Barbie, the Magazine for Girls is published five times a year. It is a glossy format magazine that includes a short editorial in each issue—"Love from Barbie,"—letters to the editor (Barbie, of course), book reviews, crossword puzzles, interviews (with child media stars such as the boys who play the three brothers on *Home Improvement* [Winter 1993]), arts and crafts, and a "send in your drawings" feature. The Winter 1993 issue includes articles on how to have a successful pajama party, recipes for tacos, a biography and pictures on a real-life hairstylist, a travelogue on New York City, a "When I grow up . . ." column featuring wildlife rehabilitator Joan Seward, and a scientific and creative piece on snow. Also included are ads for Barbie paraphernalia, both to play with and to wear, as well as public service ads sponsored by the Environmental Defense Fund and the Women's Sports Foundation. A section called "We're with Barbie!" features pictures and testimonials regarding Barbie collections. Again, the generational factor appears. As one young collector/reader writes: "I am really 'Into Barbie!' My mother and I not only collect new Barbie dolls, but we also look all over the country for old dolls from 1959–1966. Our collection grows everyday!"

In scanning the pages of this magazine, the Barbie paraphernalia and the prominence of the color pink take our attention in one direction. At the same time, the interviews and informational articles take our attention in another direction. This division is itself sufficient for the magazine to "disturb." For example, nothing in the interview with the wildlife rehabilitator suggests that she played with or endorses Barbie. Moreover, the ad "Career Moves" on the opposite page sponsored by the Women's Sports Foundation is directed toward parents: "To find out how sports and physical activities can help your daughter, write to . . ." (38).

On other pages, the images of Barbie paraphernalia for sale are difficult to separate from articles about Barbie-as-body. These pages match the intertextuality of the Saturday morning cartoons and the commercials, as identified by Marsha Kinder in her book *Playing With Power.*

"We Girls Can Do Anything" Game

The game "We Girls Can Do Anything" that Mattel (1991) has produced is not quite so liberating that Barbie can be or do anything she wants, but she does have a number of options, including "a glamorous actress, a graceful ballerina, an out-of-this world pilot," a doctor, musician, or fashion designer. As the creators describe it, the players can "travel the path that leads to the career of your dreams." The game is one of chance; two to four players, ages five and up, each pick what they want to be from the six options. Through a series of turns where they spin the needle, they head for the center of the board. The player who gets to the center first very simply gets to do what she has chosen to do. Though a few career setbacks are possible, the game is quite straightforward and "aboveboard." Only one player can win, but the rules are very explicit, and anyone can win.

This game contrasts with the game "Beauty and the Beast" marketed by Disney for players five and up. On the surface this game seems less competitive, and players are invited to "help Belle break the spell." Either Belle or Gaston climbs a stairway, depending upon the moves of the players. If Belle gets to the top first, the Beast is transformed into the prince. The goal then is to have Belle get to the top first. The game appears less competitive because a player doesn't really win or lose but, rather, has the chance to assist either Belle or Gaston. If the game is fully "deconstructed," however, one finds that Gaston has fewer chances to gain access to the top of the stairway. In a sense, the game is "rigged" and raises a number of questions about collaboration and winning.

Discussion

We would see these Barbie texts as offering a challenge both to feminists and to their daughters in terms of interpretation. As Stern and Schoenhaus observe, Barbie has always been controversial, with her most vehement critics in the early years being men who opposed her predatory behavior.[7] Now, her most ardent critics are women.

The emphasis on beauty and consumerism are obvious targets, as is the "Math class is tough" incident or "The Case of the Talking Barbie Doll," which raised important issues about Barbie as a role model.

Indeed, Mattel was sharply criticized by many groups of educators as well as feminist groups, including the American Association of University Women. The recent attention to "body as curriculum" (Lesko 1985) brings into question issues of weight obsession, eating disorders, and low self-esteem. Where Barbie was once positioned as at least having a career, in

1993 she is almost totally defined by her leisure possessions. As Stern and Schoenhaus conclude: "Barbie has come a long way. In the 1960s she was considered a perfect bitch. Today she is regarded as a complete bimbo" (63). These criticisms may be taken as signals of the contradictions that present themselves: Barbie as a doll to be played with by little girls *and* occupying a "sexuated" space (Irigaray 1992); Barbie as manifesting an impossible standard of beauty; Barbie as having it all—an impossible standard of beauty, occupying a sexuated space, and maintaining a full-time glamorous career; and finally, Barbie in a world of heightened consciousness regarding the environment, social justice, and social action, and yet occupying the space of heightened consumer and glamor.

Each successive version of Barbie brings with it new contradictions. If Barbie has always occupied this position of contradiction, we would argue that in her most recent manifestations she comes "dangerously close" to being positioned as Barbie-as-interrogator. What does it mean that Barbie exists as feminist historian through collector cards that allow girls and their mothers to "recover" women's history? What does it mean that Barbie addresses eating disorders, or makes it possible for a day-care center to be enlarged? How do little girls connect these texts? Are these just "politically correct" trappings that sell a Barbie who continues to epitomize conventional femininity in all its manifestations, or do these texts in their very handling of feminist history, social responsibility, and "career choice" heighten yet another contradiction: Barbie is beautiful *and* serves the poor and hungry, or Barbie is beautiful *and* cares about feminist history.

Critical reflection, skepticism, and resistance are all attributes of what Kathleen Weiler describes as an "interrogating" ideologies stance: "where consciousness is interrogated, where meanings are questioned, and means of analysis and criticism of the social world as well as of a text or assignment are encouraged" (1988, 114).

Many feminist researchers who explore the culture of girlhood and early adolescence—such as Gemma Moss, Linda Christian-Smith, Valerie Walkerdine, Pam Gilbert, and Carol Gilligan—all identify some form of resistance and interrogation as central to the development of the contemporary young woman. We are not arguing in this paper that eight-year-old girls ought to take up critical interrogation. Rather, by extending the text of Barbie to include not only the Barbie doll and her clothing but also the full range of artifacts that define Barbie as a cumulative cultural text, we move Barbie into a broader discourse about popular culture as a site of interrogation. We include both an interrogation of the possible contradictions contained within the texts and the interrogation of the texts of critical reception that almost ensure that the play and pleasure of an eight year old must eventually be "covered over." Clearly we need to gather more data on how women view, remember, and position Barbie in their own history, and we also need to focus more closely on the contemporary players themselves and what they do with Barbie in their play. To return to Linda Hutcheon and the problematics of the postmodern, we see the postmodern of Barbie as being one that follows the code of interrogation. For this we want to thank you, Barbie!

Notes

1. In using the term "interrogate," we mean a questioning of basic premises that underpin generally held assumptions about girls and women. For us, "interrogating" is the process of laying bare culturally held assumptions about women that have been given the authority of logical absolutes. In using the term this way, we apply the ideas of feminist theorists Mary Eagleton, Catherine Belsey, and Alice Jardine.

2. Elsewhere we argue that there is nothing in the popular culture of boys and men (including G.I. Joe, Nerf Bow and Arrow, Legos, televised football games, or Zany Grey) that rivals the devaluing of Barbie or romance reading. The paper "Sweet Valley High, Seventeen," presented at the CRIAW conference in Edmonton, 1991, contains a more detailed account of the gendering of toys. As is argued in the paper, clearly many people buy toys for their own children, and almost all of the mainstream "popular culture" toys have their own ideological baggage, ranging from the territoriality and acquisitiveness of Legos, to the war-games of G. I. Joe or Nerf Bow and Arrow to the codes of beauty and romance contained with Starlight Sparkles and Barbie dolls.

3. Here we refer the reader to a series of newspaper accounts about the talking Barbie who in one of her manifestations says, "Math class is tough" ("All this fuss over Barbie's math sentence doesn't add up," *Montreal Gazette*, 19 October 1992; "Why All the Barbs for Barbie?" Kathleen McDonnell, Facts and Arguments, *Toronto Globe and Mail*, 4 November 1992).

4. Here we acknowledge the participation of the women who attended the "We Girls Can Do Anything, Can't We?" session as part of the Noon-hour Seminar Series of the McGill Centre for Research and Teaching on Women, 24 March 1993. We also acknowledge the students of the Women's Studies Interdisciplinary Seminar, McGill University, Fall 1992.

5. Here we are grateful to Theresa Moretti, who shared her extensive "popular culture" sleuthing on Barbie at the Annual Popular Culture Conference, Louisville, Kentucky, 16–19 March 1992.

6. Here we are grateful to Krista Walsh and Dorian Mitchell, who allowed us to interrogate their collections of Barbie cards.

7. As Stern and Schoenhaus note:

> Even the *Nation* worried about Barbie (on the same page as an essay on Khrushchev). "Teen-focused play-fantasies are rearranging the souls of girls between the ages of 6 and 15," it revealed. "Barbie threatens to make a generation of vipers that will cause men to plead for the return of momism." The ideal woman was a happy homemaker, and Barbie was just too independent. Besides, Ken was obviously just a sex object, a face-man to accompany Barbie wherever she wanted to go. (1990, 62).

References

Brown, L. M., and C. Gilligan (1992). *Meeting at the Crossroads: Women's Psychology and Girls' Development*. Cambridge: Harvard University Press.

Burgin, V., ed. (1986). *The End of Art Theory: Criticism and Postmodernity*. Atlantic Highlands, NJ: Humanities Press.

Christian-Smith, L. (1990). *Becoming a Woman Through Romance*. New York: Routledge.

Fiske, J. (1989). *Understanding Popular Culture*. Boston: Unwin.

Gammon, L., and M. Marchmont, eds. (1989). *The Female Gaze: Women as Viewers of Popular Culture*. Seattle: Real Comet Press.

Gannett, C. (1992). *Gender and the Journal: Diaries and Academic Discourse*. Albany: State University of New York Press.

Geraghty, C. (1991). *Women and Soap Opera: A Study of Prime Time Soaps*. Oxford: Polity.

Gilligan, C. (1991). *Women, Girls and Psychotherapy: Reframing Resistance*. New York: Haworth Press.

Hancock, E. (1989). *The Girl Within: A Groundbreaking New Approach to Female Identity*. New York: Fawcett Columbine.

Hutcheon, L. (1989). *The Politics of Postmodernism*. New York: Routledge.

Irigaray, L. (1992). *Je. tu. vous: A Culture of Difference*. London: Basil Blackwell.

Kinder, M. (1991). *Playing with Power in Movies, Television and Video Games*. Berkeley: University of California Press.

Krentz, J. A., ed. (1992). *Dangerous Men and Adventurous Women: Romance Writers on the Appeal of the Romance*. Philadelphia: University of Pennsylvania Press.

Lesko, N. (1985). The Curriculum of the Body in a Girls' Parochial School. Paper presented at the annual meeting of the American Education Research Association, Chicago, Illinois.

Mitchell, C. (1982). Exploring the aesthetic response: "I just read novels and that sort of thing." *English Quarterly* 15: 67–77.

——— (November 1991). *Seventeen*, soap operas and Sweet Valley High: Isolating Girls in Their Reading of Popular Culture. A paper presented at the CRIAW conference, Edmonton, Alberta. November

——— (1994). Reading in Popular Culture. *Textual Studies of Canada: Canadian Journal of Cultural Literacy* 4: 69–80.

Moss, G. (1989). *Un/popular Fictions*. London: University of London Press.

Peabody, R. and L. Ebersole (1993). *Mondo Barbie: An Anthology of Fiction and Poetry*. New York: St. Martin.

Radway, J., (1984). *Reading the Romance*. Chapel Hill: University of North Carolina Press.

Seiter, E. (1993). *Sold Separately: Children and Parents in Consumer Culture*. New Brunswick, NJ: Rutgers University Press.

Stern, S. L., and Schoenhaus, T. (1990). *Toyland: the High-Stakes Games of the Toy Industry*. Chicago: Contemporary Books.

Weiler, K. (1988). *Women Teaching for Change: Gender, Class and Power*. New York: Bergin and Garvey.

Race Matters

9

The Problem with Origins

Race and the Contrapuntal Nature of the Education Experience

Cameron McCarthy

> Epic discourse is a discourse handed down by tradition. By its very nature the epic of the absolute past is inaccessible to personal experience and does not permit an individual, personal point of view or evaluation. One cannot glimpse it, grope for it, touch it; one cannot look at it from just any point of view; it is impossible to experience it, analyze it, take it apart, penetrate into its core. It is given solely as tradition, sacred and sacrosanct, evaluated in the same way by all and demanding a pious attitude to itself.
>
> — M.M. Bakhtin, *The Dialogic Imagination*

The publication in the late eighties and early nineties of such culturally narrow-minded texts as Allan Bloom's *The Closing of the American Mind* (1987) and Dinesh D'Souza's *Illiberal Education* (1991) and the neonationalist response of Afrocentric writers such as Molefi Asante ushered in a phase of eruptive particularism in discourses within education on culture and race. This new phase in education and in social life is marked by a revivified investment in ethnic symbolism and an almost epic revalorization of the ethnic histories and origins of some embattled dominant and subordinant groups. We are living in a time which racial hysteria and racial anxiety ride the undersides of the public discourse on schooling and society as rapid demographic changes alter the racial and ethnic configuration of America. These developments have spawned what I wish to call the new essentialisms that have infected popular and academic theories of race. An increasingly rigid and constricted language has overtaken the discussion of racial inequality and racial antagonism in education. This is powerfully reflected in contemporary discourses of cultural exceptionalism, the declaration of privileged epistemologies, and the balkanizing identity politics that now inform ethnic prioritization and race-based agenda-setting practices of embattled social groups in education.

In this essay, I offer a critique of essentialist theories of race. I suggest that such theories have limited explanatory and predictive capacity with respect to the operation of race in education and in daily life. Further, I argue that one cannot understand race by looking at race alone. One must look at the dynamics of class, ethnicity, and gender. These dynamic variables operate in contradictory and discontinuous ways in the institutional setting. Dynamics of gender and class often cut at right angles to race. For example, working-class black women and men have radically different experiences of race relations than their middle-class counterparts because of the ever-widening economic divide that separates different groups of black people in the United States. In addition to critiquing contemporary theories of race, I will look at a number of ethnographic examples of contradiction in the experience of racial inequality that underscore the heterogeneity associated with the operation of racial dynamics in schooling. Finally, I will draw some conclusions about curriculum and educational reform that take the complexity and the heterogeneity of race into account.

The Problem of Race, The Problem of Origins

In a recent *New York Times Book Review* article, Henry Louis Gates (1991) relates a story that has made its rounds in the jazz world. The story takes the form of an answer to what Gates calls "the perennial question: Can you really tell?" The question is about racial authenticity, racial origins, and their predictive capacity with respect to cultural behavior and meaning of style. Can you really tell who is the black one, who is the white one? According to Gates:

> The great black jazz trumpeter Roy Elridge once made a wager with the critic Leonard Feather that he could distinguish white musicians from black ones—blindfolded. Mr. Feather duly dropped the needle onto a variety of record albums whose titles and soloists were concealed from the trumpeter. More than half the time, Elridge guessed wrong. (Gates 1991, 1)

What Gates fails to mention is the fact that the blindfold test has been an institution of the *Down Beat* jazz magazine for well over a quarter century now and that white jazz musicians presented with the blindfold test regularly confuse black musicians with white ones and vice versa. The problem of racial origins and racial authenticity is a problem all around. The elusiveness of racial identity not only affects blacks, it also affects whites. Racial identities can never be gathered up in one place as a final cultural property. And, as we approach the end of the twentieth century, what seemed like stable white ethnicities and heritages in an earlier era is now entering a zone of recoding and redefinition. Michael Omi and Howard Winant (1991) put the problematic of waning white ethnicity in this post–civil rights era in the following terms:

> Most whites do not experience their ethnicity as a definitive aspect of their social identity. They perceive it dimly and irregularly, picking and choosing among its varied strands to exercise, as Mary Waters (1990) suggests, an "ethnic option." The specifically ethnic components of white identity are fast receding with each generation's additional remove from the old country. Unable to speak the language of their immigrant forbears uncommitted to ethnic endogamy, and unaware of their ancestor's traditions (if in fact they can still identify their ancestors as, say, Polish or Scots, rather than a combination of four or five European—and non-European!—groups) whites undergo a racializing panethnicity as "Euro-Americans." (17)

Nowhere is this sense of the "twilight of white ethnicity" felt more deeply than on American college campuses. In these deeply racially balkanized and polarized sites of the American education system, we are entering the Brave New World of the post–civil rights era—a new world registered in the popular culture by such films as *Falling Down* (1993), *White Palace* (1990), and *Dances with Wolves* (1990)—a world in which the proliferation of ethnic diversity has led to a heightened state of race consciousness on the part of minorities and whites. The post–civil rights era is the era of the displaced and decentered white subject. And white students on college campuses find themselves positioned as the antagonists in an unpredictable racial drama in which middle-class subjects speak in the voice of the new oppressed—a progeny spawned in an era of the discourse of racial resentment and reverse discrimination. For instance, white students interviewed in a recent study on racial diversity (Institute for the Study of Social Change 1990) conducted at Berkeley emphasized a sense of racial encirclement, ethnic instability, and the new conflictual nature of identity. A few examples of comments made by white students and recorded in the report underscore these new dilemmas over racial/ethnic identity:

> Student Comment I: Many whites don't feel like they have an ethnic identity at all and I pretty much feel that way too. It's not something that bothers me tremendously but I think that maybe I could be missing something that other people have, that I am not experiencing. (37)

> Student Comment II: Being white means that you're less likely to get financial aid. . . . It means that there are all sorts of tutoring groups and special programs that you can't get into, because you're not a minority. (37)

Student Comment III: If you want to go with the stereotypes, Asians are the smart people, the Blacks are great athletes, what is white? We're just here. We're the oppressors of the nation. (37)

These stories of racial/ethnic instability come at a critical juncture in debates on racial inequality, racial identity, and curriculum reform in the field of education in the United States. They also point to the crisis in the theorization of race and racial logics in education. But this is also, paradoxically, a time that is seeing the emergence of a peculiar language of racial and ethnic certainty, of panethnic camps drawn tightly around specular origins. The world is a vast Lacanian mirror in which theorists of racial purity and racial essence see themselves standing in front of their ancestors. It is the perfect image, the snapshot of history collected in the nuclear family photo album. It is the story of the singular origin, the singular essence, the one, true primary cause. The old Marxist and neo-Marxist orthodoxies of class and economic primacy in education debates are rapidly being replaced by the new panethnic cultural assertions of racial origins. The proponents of western civilization and Eurocentrism and their critics, the proponents of Afrocentrism, now argue for the heart and soul of the educational enterprise (this is not of course to suggest an equal deployment of material and political resources here, for in some ways, the playing out of this conflict involves a certain encirclement of black intellectual thinking). Conservative educators such as Diane Ravitch join conservative ideologues such as George Will in insisting, for instance, that "our country [the United States] is a branch of European civilization. . . . 'Eurocentricity' is right, in American curricula and consciousness, because it accords with the facts of our history, and we and Europe are fortunate for that" (Will 1989, 3). Europe, through this legerdemain, is collapsed into the United States without any difficulty. History and tradition in this country are seen as interchangeable with those of Europe.

On the other hand, Afrocentric theorists such as Molefi Asante (1987) argue for the panethnic unity of all black people of the diaspora, pointing to the origins of African people in the "spatial reality of Africa." We are in the historical moment of what Stanley Aronowitz and Henry Giroux (1991) call the "politics of clarity." Of course, it is important to emphasize here that Afrocentrism is a liberatory discourse. When one reads the work of Asante, Jawanza Kunjufu, and others, one recognizes immediately a sustained effort to connect to an intellectual and political history of struggle waged by racially subordinated groups in the United States. But Afrocentrism also contains within its discourse a language that masks issues of contradiction and discontinuity within the diaspora, between the diaspora and Africa, between different economically and socially situated African Americans and other minority groups, and between differently situated men and women.

Beyond these concerns is the issue of the intellectual and cultural worker and his or her problematic relationship to anything that begins to sound like a singular cultural heritage or cultural stream. A necessary condition of dynamic intellectual and cultural work is that the intellectual worker have the flexibility to draw on the wellspring of history, to draw on the variety of cultural resources that fan out across the myriad groups that make up this society and the world. "Culture," writers such as Coco Fusco, Cornel West, and Stuart Hall suggest, is a hybrid. For that matter, race is a hybridizing process as well: it is the product of encounters between and among differently located human groups. By hybridity here, I am not referring to a Joseph-coat trope of difference—the proverbial social quilt that happily embraces a cornucopia of differences, laying down these agreeable differences, one after the other, side by side. Instead, I am drawing attention to the contradictory nature of identity formation and the fact that, to use the language of Hall, "dominant ethnicities are always underpinned by a particular figured masculinity, a particular class identity," and so forth (1993, 31). Any group or individual always has competing identities, competing interests, needs, and desires wrestling to the surface. In saying this, I am not denying that certain stabilities are associated with race. I am not here denying the persistence of what Hall (1989) calls "continuities" between, say, the peoples of Africa and the peoples of the Afro–New World diaspora. Nor am I trying to contest the fact that brutal realities are associated with patterns of racial exclusion in the United States. What I am saying is that racial difference is the product of human interests, needs, desires, strategy, capacities, forms of organization, and forms of mobilization; and that these dynamic variables, which articulate themselves in the form of grounded social constructs such as identity, inequality, and so forth, are subject to change, contradiction, variability, and revision within historically specific and determinate contexts. "Race" is a deeply unstable and decentered complex of social meanings constantly being transformed by cultural and political conflict (Omi and Winant 1991). Racial identities are therefore profoundly social, historical, and variable categories.

Against the grain of this historical and social variability, Afrocentrics and Eurocentrics now argue for school reform based on the narrow limits of ethnic affiliation. For the Afrocentric, the intolerable level of minority failure in school is a result of the fact that minority, particularly African American, cultural heritage is suppressed in the curriculum. Black students fail because schools assault their identities and destabilize their sense of self and agency (a good example of this thesis is to be found in *Countering the Conspiracy to Destroy Black Boys* by Jawanza Kunjufu [1990]). For the proponents of western civilization, western cultural emphasis in the curriculum is color-blind. Black students fail because of the cultural deprivation that exists in their homes and in their communities. Literacy in western civilization would be the best antidote for failure among the black poor. As E. D. Hirsch (1987) suggests, broad cultural literacy would help disadvantaged black youth enter the mainstream.

This essay is written in response to this moment of race/ethnic-based diagnosis of inequality in education and prescription for change. This is a diagnosis that is driven by a peculiarly recalcitrant concept of race that is discursively based in nineteenth-century biology and naturalization of human distinctions. A nineteenth-century concept of race now inhabits much mainstream and radical thinking about inequality in education. Race theory is particularly unreflexive about the category of "race" itself. Educational theories of racial inequality are at bottom still informed by notions of "essences," notions of near-indelible characteristics in culture, linguistic style, cognitive capacity, family structures, and the like. I set myself up against these essentialist approaches to the theorization of racial inequality and racial identity in education. By "essentialist," I am referring to the tendency in current mainstream and radical writing on race to treat social groups as stable or homogeneous entities. Racial groups such as "Asians" or "Latinos" or "blacks" are therefore discussed as though members of these groups possessed some innate and invariant set of characteristics that set them apart from each other and from "whites." Feminist theorists such as Michele Wallace (1990) and Teresa de Lauretis (1984) have critiqued dominant tendencies in mainstream research to define differences in terms of transcendental essences. Wallace, for example, maintains that differences in the political and cultural behavior of minority women and men are determined by social and historical contingencies and not some essentialist checklist of innate, biological, or cultural characteristics.

Following Wallace, I argue that current tendencies toward essentialism in the analysis of race relations significantly inhibit a dynamic understanding of race relations and race-based politics in education and society. I argue further that essentialist thinking about race contributes to the increasing balkanization of cultural and public spaces in education and society. Common to these approaches to race and education as well as some of the more recent formulations around multiculturalism is a tendency to undertheorize race (Ogbu 1992; Tiedt and Tiedt 1986). Within these paradigms of education theory and social theory, racial antagonism is conceptualized as a kind of deposit or disease that is triggered off into existence by some deeper flaw of character or society. I inflect the discussion of race away from the language of deprivation and cultural and economic essentialism that now dominates the research literature on racial inequality. The fact is that racial differences are produced. These differences, as Edward Said (1985) points out, are "the product of human work." Racial relations of domination and subordination are arranged and organized in cultural forms and in the ideological practices of identity formation and representation inside and outside social institutions such as schools—what Louis Althusser (1971) calls the "mise-en-scène of interpellation." I am therefore interested in the ways in which moral leadership and social power are exercised "in the concrete" and the ways in which regimes of racial domination and subordination are constructed and resisted in education.

The theoretical and methodological issues concerning race are complex and therefore require a comparative and relational approach to analysis and intervention in unequal relations in schools. Such analysis and intervention must pay special attention to contradiction, discontinuity, and nuance within and between embattled social groups, what I have called elsewhere the process of "nonsynchrony" (McCarthy 1990). Rather than treating minority groups as homogeneous entities, I point to the contradictory interests, needs, and desires that inform minority behavior in education, culture, and politics and define minority encounters with majority whites in education and in society. By invoking the concepts of contradiction and nonsynchrony, I wish to advance the position that individuals or groups, in their relation to economic, political, and cultural institutions such as schools, do not share identical consciousness and express the same interests, needs, or desires at the same point in time (Hicks 1981, 221). These discontinuities in the needs and interests of minority and majority groups are, for example, expressed in the long history of tension and hostility between the black and white working class in this country. Also of crucial importance within this framework are the issues of the "contradictory location" (Wright 1978) of the "new" black middle class within the racial problematic and the role of neoconservative black and white intellectuals in redefining the terrain of contemporary discourse on racial inequality toward the ideal of a "color-blind" society (McCarthy 1990). Just as important for a relational and nonessentialist approach to race and curriculum is the fact that minority women and girls have experiences of racial inequality that are radically different from those of their male counterparts because of the gender difference (Wallace, in her book *Invisibility Blues* [1990], calls these dynamics "negative variations"). A relational and nonessentialist approach to the discussion of racial identities allows for a more complex understanding of the educational and political behavior of minority and majority groups. I argue for such an understanding of racial inequality, one that focuses on the contradictory and highly nonsynchronous formulation of racial subjectivity and identity and the dynamic intersection of race with class, gender, and nation. I believe that any strategy for educational reform in the area of race relations must take this complexity into account.

Contradictions in the Experience of Racial Inequality

As Michael Burawoy (1981) and Mokubong Nkomo (1984) make clear with respect to South Africa, economic divides that exist between the black under-class from the Bantustan and their more middle-class counterparts who work for the South African state (the police, nurses, Bantustan bureaucrats, etc.) often undermine black unity in the struggle against racial oppression. Similar examples exist in the United States, where some middle-class minority intel-lectuals such as Shelby Steele and Thomas Sowell have spoken out against affirmative action and minority scholarship programs in higher education, suggesting that such ameliorative policies discriminate against white males. And indeed, a 1990 ruling by Michael Williams, who then was the U.S. Department of Education's assistant secretary for civil rights, maintained that it was illegal for a college or university to offer a scholarship only to minority students (Jaschik 1990). The irony of such a ruling coming from an assistant secretary for civil rights is surpassed by the irony of the fact that Williams is a black man. Without these scholarships, a number of very talented members of minorities would not be able to pursue higher education. Here again, the "point man" on a reactionary Republican policy that effectively undermined the material interests of African Americans and other minority groups was a neoconservative member of the emergent minority middle class.

One should not, however, draw the conclusion that contradictions asso-ciated with race and specific social policies such as affirmative action affect only blacks. These dynamics are also reflected in the politics of identity for-mation among Asian Americans. Let us look at two examples of the contra-dictory effects of inclusionary and exlusionary ethnic practices among Asian Americans and Pacific Islanders. In order to consolidate and extend their political clout and benefits from land trust arrangements, native Hawaiians voted four-to-one in January 1990 for a highly inclusionary definition of their ethnic identity—one that expanded the definition of their people to anyone with a drop of Hawaiian "blood." "Previously," Omi and Winant write, "only those with at least 50 percent Hawaiian 'blood' were eligible for certain benefits" (1991, 9). They also point to the exclusionary effects of intraethnic contradictions in the politics of Asian American identity forma-tion and affirmative action policy:

> By contrast, in June 1991 in San Francisco, Chinese American architects and engineers protested the inclusion of Asian Indians under the city's minority

business enterprise law. Citing a Supreme Court ruling which requires cities to narrowly define which groups had suffered discrimination to justify specific affirmative action programs, Chinese Americans contended that Asian Indians should not be considered "Asian." At stake were obvious economic benefits accruing to designated "minority" businesses. (Omi and Winant 1991, 9)

The contradictory phenomenon of racial identity formation in this post–civil rights era also manifests itself inside schools. Linda Grant (1984) calls attention to these discontinuities in terms of the operation of gender at the classroom level. Based on the findings from a study of "face-to-face interactions" in six desegregated elementary school classrooms in a midwestern industrial city, Linda Grant concludes that "black females' experiences in desegregated schools ... differ from those of other race-gender groups and cannot be fully understood by extrapolating from the research on females or research on blacks." Among other things, the teachers (all women, three blacks and three whites) she observed did not relate to their black students and white students in any consistent or monolithic way. Grant places particular emphasis on the way in which black girls were positioned in the language of the classroom and in the informal exchanges between teachers and students. She notes the following:

> Although generally compliant with teachers' rules, black females were less tied to teachers than white girls were and approached them only when they had a specific need to do so. White girls spent more time with teachers, prolonging questions into chats about personal issues. Black girls' contacts were briefer, more task related, and often on behalf of a peer rather than self. (Grant 1984, 107)

Although these teachers tended to avoid contact with black male students, they were still inclined to identify at least one black male student in their individual classroom as a "superstar." In none of the six desegregated classrooms was a black girl identified as a high academic achiever. Instead, Grant said, black girls were typified as "average achievers" and assigned to average or below-average track placements and ability groups. Gender differences powerfully influenced and modified the racially inflected ways in which teachers evaluated, diagnosed, labeled, and tracked their students. Grant therefore points to a hidden cost of desegregation for black girls:

> Although they are usually the top students in all-black classes, they lose this stature to white children in desegregated rooms. Their development seems

to become less balanced, with emphasis on social skills. . . . Black girls'
everyday schooling experiences seem more likely to nudge them toward
stereotypical roles of black women than toward [academic] alternatives.
These include serving others and maintaining peaceable ties among diverse
persons rather than developing one's own skills. (1984, 109)

While black girls have a differential experience of schooling, one in
which their talents are marginalized and delegitimated, black boys often
experience a profound alienation from an academic core curriculum.
Teachers in the urban setting, even black middle-class teachers, tend to distance themselves from black boys, as Grant (1985) points out. The following excerpt taken from my ethnographic work in an inner-city high school
in a large western city is yet another illustration of what I call nonsynchrony.
This research was conducted in the summer of 1990 and involved an evaluation of Teacher For America's Summer Institute. (Teach For America is
the much-talked-about volunteer youth organization that has sought to
make a difference in the educational experiences of disadvantaged
American youth. The organization, patterned on the can-do humanism of
the Peace Corps, recruits graduates from elite universities and colleges
around the country to serve a two-year stint in needy inner-city and rural
public school districts. At its annual Summer Institute held at the University
of Southern California, corps members or teacher recruits undergo an
eight-week crash course in teaching methods and classroom management.
They spend four of these weeks as interns in Los Angeles inner-city schools.)
In what follows, I will give an extended account of the operation of nonsynchrony in a classroom that I observed as part of my research study of Teach
For America's Summer Institute. This extended account is drawn from my
fieldnotes. It is intended to get at some of the dynamism of racial identity
formation in the inner-city classroom in which, often, the conflictual loyal-
ties, needs, desires, and interests of black adolescent males collide with the
needs and desires of teachers and other adult staff. The school under study
is St. Paul's High School.

Identities in Formation: Notes from an Inner-City Classroom
I report on a class that was taught by a Teach For America intern,
Christopher Morrison. Christopher, who is white, was about twenty-two
years old at the time of the study. He hails from the South and has some mil-
itary training. His assignment to do a four-week teaching stint in Golden
Arches High School was his first exposure to an inner-city school.
Christopher's cooperating teacher was Ms. Marshall, a black woman in her

early sixties, close to retirement. She exuded an air of having seen it all. The students in Christopher's classroom were predominantly African American. This classroom that I am about to describe was taken over by accounts of police violence. Christopher had introduced the topic of police harassment based on some queries made by one of his students the previous day. But in the torrent of accounts offered by the students, Christopher lost control of the class. So did Ms. Marshall.

What was fascinating about this development was the sharp, unpredictable collision of interests, needs, and desires that fragmented the classroom as a learning community. Even more important within this framework were the lines of division that cut through racial affiliation, pure and simple. The black cooperating teacher, Ms. Marshall, seemed (because of dynamics of age, class, and gender) remarkably alienating to her students, even though she clearly empathized with their stories about harassment and humiliation. Black male students did affect a difficult but clearly emergent bonding with Christopher. This relationship was not unproblematic, however, as we will see in moment.

Before the class started, Christopher had indicated that his lesson would deal with "Imperialism in South Africa and India." This was to be part of a unit on "The Building of Empires." There were seventeen students in the class: one Hispanic and six African Americans, nine males and eight females. Students trickled into the class, one by one and sometimes in twos. It was 10:27 A.M. Seven minutes after the period was supposed to begin, the lesson started. Students hurriedly wrote down the assignment that was on the chalkboard for the period. Christopher had written up this assignment in bold letters. Here, he was emulating his cooperating teacher, Ms. Marshall, who was inclined to write an enormous amount of work on the board. The objective seemed to be to keep the students occupied. Nevertheless, Christopher wrote the assignment in this manner on one of the three large chalkboards in the classroom:

Period 2, 31 July 1990   Ms. Marshall
                 WORLD HISTORY
I. READ CH. 28, 518–538
II. SECTION REVIEWS I—4, IV—13
II-1, 3, 4, V—ALL
III-3, 4, VI—ALL

As Christopher was about to address the class, a black student came sauntering in dressed in blue overalls. He wore a red, gold, and green belt around his waist—the colors of black solidarity associated with the Rastafarians of

Jamaica and radical black groups like the Nation of Islam. Morgan, one of the students whom Christopher had identified to me as a gang member, shouted: "Hey Morrison, don't you notice the beautiful colors that our brother is wearing. That's powerful! That's powerful!" "Yes," said Christopher, "they are beautiful." Christopher then shifted the topic adroitly. "Before we begin the lesson today, I just wanted to let you know that I did some research on the question that Ramon asked yesterday. Tell them the question you asked, Ramon!" Ramon obliged: "Can the police arrest you for what he thought?" The temperature in the classroom instantly changed—some students were already itching to jump in and say their piece. Christopher responded, "Well, I talked to a police officer of the L.A. Unified System, and he said that chances are, if the police picked you up, it may be because somebody called in."

Morgan, who had established himself as a spokesperson for his peers inside and outside the school, was quick to note, "They have to have probable reason." As would become clear later, Morgan had a history of run-ins with the police. "For instance, one day I was cruising up the road to Marsha, one of my friends, who tell me she was having some trouble with this dude. He was pushing her around. And I, I had my Wankar and my 45 in my pocket. And they [the cops] stop me, man. They stop me. Now they had no probable reason, no probable reason. And they knew it, man. They knew it." Christopher asked politely, "And what did you do?" Morgan was incredulous at the question: "What do you mean? I told them they had no probable reason." "Probable cause," Christopher corrected. "If you had a gun on you, then you gave them probable cause." Morgan shouted, "What do you mean by that, Mr. Morrison. I did not do anything. I was only carrying my Wankar [students laughed]."

By now the floodgates were open. Elvis, another black student, asked the cooperating teacher, "And how do you feel about the police, Ms. Marshall?" Ms. Marshall, a little upset with the defiant language of her students, told them that their defiance endangers them in their encounters with the police:

> I say if you walk like a duck and you hang out with ducks, then you are a duck. I believe that some of the things they (police) do are not right. But you guys sometimes walk around without any books like the rest of the guys on the street. If you do that, they [the police] will pull you over. [Here, Ms. Marshall appeared to be speaking out of a sense of concern, even a sense of fear, about her students' confrontation with the police. Maybe, as a black woman, she felt specially responsible for telling these students how to survive]. . . . One day I saw them [some police officers]. They had this guy spread eagle against this car. And they were really harassing him. You

should not hang out with those guys [here, guys seemed to be an euphemism for "gang bangers"] . . . don't hang out with the Bloods, or the Cribs, or the Tigers.

This got Rasheed really upset: "What do you have against the Tigers? The Tigers don't do anybody anything." Again, Christopher tried to subtly change the topic to diffuse the tension in the room. "Let me tell you a story about myself," he said, "maybe this will help. Once I had some friends. They were hanging out on the college campus. But they did not look like college students. They were white, but they had long hair."

A number of students interjected, "You mean like a hippie." "Like a hippie," Christopher said. Then he continued with his story, "They arrested these guys. You have to understand that the police go on images. They rely on images. They need categories to put people in so that they can do their work. And sometimes these categories are right. And if you, Morgan, had a gun, then you gave them probable cause. You fitted into one of their categories." Morgan seemed dismayed. But he was emphatic: "It wasn't the gun. They were just riding through the hood. If I had given them any trouble they would have sweated me." Christopher disagreed with this assessment of danger: "I don't think they would do that to you. You can complain if you feel that your rights have been abused. Look, people are being blown away at a faster rate than ever in this country. Just don't give them cause. If you got something [a gun] on you, then that is giving them cause."

Ms. Marshall supported Christopher: "When a group of you guys are hanging out together, that gives them cause for concern. You don't even carry books. You need to be nonthreatening." Rasheed was indignant: "You mean to say that if I am going around with my friends at night I need to haul along a big old bunch of books over my shoulder." Misha, a black female, joined in: "There are cops who walk around killing people at random. I have friends of mine whose houses have been bust into. That is why if any of them [police] comes to my house, I will take out a knife and go [motion indicating stabbing a fictional police officer], 'Oops, sorry, I didn't know you was a cop.'"

Elvis contended: "I will kill a cop." An uncomfortable silence fell in the room: "If you kill a cop, you will be dead!" said Ms. Marshall. "Well," said Morgan, "cops is a gang. They been going around with colors. They got cars that say that they are from the L.A. Police Department." By now, it was already thirty minutes into the period. Christopher said, "I want to wrap this up because I have got to move on. Now, has anybody here ever been frisked? The way to stop yourself from being harassed by the police is to be as nonthreatening as possible. If you say, 'Yes, sir' and 'No, sir,' it will help.

You can't turn this into a thing about power. The minute they start to feel threatened, they are going to search you."

I was amazed at how the actors in this classroom drama kept searching for some kind of understanding of the others and yet kept missing each other like ships in the night. First, Christopher, trying to understand these inner-city kids but ultimately constrained by being so white and middle class in his values and understandings. Second, Ms. Marshall, who grew up in an age when children—particularly black children—were less assertive with adults and who, fearing the worst, wants to save her students from danger. And then the students, black teenagers in search of identity and self-assertion. Being black and from the inner city made them—especially the males— particularly vulnerable to police harassment. They were trying to understand these two adults who were telling them to be "nonthreatening" in the face of harassment from the police. They were particularly dismayed by Ms. Marshall, who was preaching compromise. But Ms. Marshall persisted:

> You guys [referring to her male students] start this stuff at school. You get angry at the teacher because that person is an adult. . . . If you do that with the police you will get into trouble. . . . You need to keep your mouth shut. You must remember that he [the police officer] has the advantage. He has a billy club, he has a gun.

Morgan interrupted: "And what about free speech! . . . You talk funny. You're funny that way. The last time I talked with you, you said, 'Go with the flow.'" "The question is not one of right and wrong. It is a question of who has the power," Ms. Marshall replied. "I don't understand you," Morgan said. "Your position is lame, lame, lame." Another male student, Raymond, seemed to side with Ms. Marshall: "If you don't give them [the police] no head, they won't beat you." The sharpest exchanges were those among Morgan, Raymond, and Ms. Marshall. Christopher felt that the students were being disrespectful to Ms. Marshall. "Morgan and Raymond, show some courtesy here!" he said.

Raymond was struggling with what was being proposed about their relationship to the police: what is the right thing to do? There was no answer to this question. Clearly, Ms. Marshall and Christopher wanted to wrap up the discussion about police harassment and get back to the formal curriculum. Ms. Marshall attempted to bring about closure: "I would just like to say to those of you who had these experiences [encounters with the police] that I wish to thank you for sharing them with us because all of us haven't had those experiences." But Morgan would not let her get away with this: "So what is the conclusion? What is the conclusion?"

Christopher tried to be direct and honest: "There is no conclusion. What I am saying is this; I once had a billy club on my neck too, but I am here. I have a degree, and I am teaching. And this is because I was not hostile back to the police. . . . And isn't that the goal? Isn't the goal to be left alone? If you don't give them reason to be hostile to you, maybe they won't beat you [Christopher's voice trembled a little when he said this, as though he was experiencing an internal conflict. He seemed to be losing faith in what he was telling the students]. Anyway, you need to get to your test."

In this way, Christopher made an awkward transition to the review exercises that the students had to complete in the period. Somewhat ironically, these review exercises were on "The Building of Empires" unit in Welbak's *History and Life* textbook. Student participation in the proceedings in the classroom changed from the vigorous but inconclusive discussion about what to do about police harassment to overt and covert forms of resistance to the routinized curriculum assignment. A notable feature of the latter part of this eventful double period was the fact that many of the girls, for the most part silent throughout the informal discussion of police harassment, came into their own and dominated the formal curriculum—the question-and-answer session associated with the review exercises.

This example of the classroom culture of an inner-city school in Los Angeles foregrounds in quite a striking manner the specificity of inner-city black male youth experiences of schooling—a context in which the repressive arm of the state seems ever near (for instance, the Los Angeles school system has its own police force). In such a context, academic experiences are deeply informed by social deprivation and inequality. The intensity of this deprivation and inequality and social violence contributed to these students' alienation from the formal school curriculum. Their teachers were at a loss as to how to bridge this huge gulf between lived experience outside the school and the formal requirement of participation and achievement in the classroom. They opted instead for a form of defensive teaching and a routinized curriculum as a sort of holding strategy—one that was constantly subverted by nonsynchronous dynamics of race, gender, class, and age. Though reports of police harassment were not everyday classroom events, the students clearly were under stress, overdetermined by dynamics of class, gender, race, and age that intensified misunderstandings between themselves and the two teachers. Christopher Morrison and Ms. Marshall positioned themselves differently in relation to the issue of police harassment versus adolescent rights and self-assertion. Christopher, white, hip, but with a military background and a conservative upbringing in the South, tried to cross the enormous racial gulf and to reach out and touch his black students. But his basis of affiliation drew on the raw material of a relatively privileged background. As a middle-class white person, he felt "the system" worked. All one had to do was to obey the law and "complain" when the policing institutions of the state treated you unfairly. On the other hand, Ms. Marshall tried to empathize. She reached back across the years of her life and drew on encounters in which the system worked against black people. The police were gratuitously violent toward black men. In her opinion, black youth were vulnerable to an inequality that reflected itself in the unregulated power of the police. Since power was unequal, Ms. Marshall suggested to her students that they avoid confrontations with the police, even in cases when the students were "in the right." Both teachers in their different ways suppressed the students' questions about representation and identity—difficult questions about self-assertion before the law. Again, the issues of racial solidarity or racial response to inequality and racism seemed to be subverted, marginalized, or just simply displaced by dynamics of ethnicity, class, gender, and age.

Conclusion

The point that I want to make here is that you cannot read off the educational, cultural, or political behavior of minority and majority youth or adults based on assumptions about race pure and simple. Different gender and class interests and experiences within minority and majority groups often cut at right angles to efforts at racial coordination and affiliation. In each of the examples of nonsynchrony discussed earlier—the case of black middle-class bureaucrats versus Bantustan peasants and workers, and the struggle against racial domination in South Africa, or black girls' differential academic experiences in a desegregated classroom, or inner-city black male youth, police harassment, and the difficulties of affiliation for their black and white teachers, or in the cases of intraethnic conflict and instability among Asian Americans and among white youth—dynamic variables of gender, class, and race/ethnicity, seem to confound one another. These realities were reflected in highly complex and deeply unstable sets of racial effects that imperiled race-based predictions, solutions, or modifications, pure and simple. To predicate race relations reform in education on the basis of static definitions of what white people are like and what minorities are like can lead to costly miscalculations that can undermine the goal of race relations reform in education itself.

My principal theoretical and methodological concern is therefore to stress the importance of social context, nuance, and language in understanding the dynamics of race relations. I also want to emphasize the need to pay attention to the differential patterns of historical and contemporary incorporation of minority and majority groups into the social and cultural relations that exist in the school setting. Of course, in affirming the positive moment in history and culture, we should not fall back on the idea of race as some essentialist or primordial expression of language and cultural solidarity. Neither should we rush headlong into the politics of cultural exceptionalism or the celebration of cultural diversity for its own sake. For as Abdul JanMohamed and David Lloyd (1987) argue, "Such pluralism tolerates the existence of salsa, it even enjoys Mexican restaurants, but it bans Spanish as a medium of instruction in American schools" (10). Rather than taking the easy path to exceptionalism, I maintain that critical and subaltern educational activists must begin to see racial difference as *one*, not the *only*, starting point for the drawing out of the various solidarities among subordinated minority youth and adults and working-class women and men over our separate but related forms of oppression. Indeed, the failure of progressive groups to see the limitations of a calcified position around racial identity contributed to the paralysis around the nomination of the ultra-conservative black judge Clarence Thomas to the U.S. Supreme Court. One cannot read off racial interests or diagnose racial politics by looking at racial experience alone—even if this experience places you in Pin Point, Georgia, the ominous location of Thomas's origins. Such intensely complex problematics help to underline the fact, as Toni Morrison has forcefully put it, "that the time for undiscriminating racial unity has past. . . . [We are] in a new arena, and the contestants defy the mold" (1992, xxx).

The challenge before us is to move beyond tendencies to treat race as a stable, measurable desposit or category. Racial difference is therefore to be understood as a subject position that can be defined only in what Homi Bhabha (1992) calls "performative terms"—that is, in terms of the effects of political struggles over social and economic exploitation, political disenfranchisement, and cultural and ideological repression. In this respect, discourses on racial inequality in education cannot be meaningfully separated from issues such as police brutality in African American and Latino neighborhoods or the sexual and mental harassment of minority women on the shop floor. Nor can oppression and inequality be meaningfully confronted by simply adding more "sensitive" curriculum materials or "new voices" to the school syllabus (Carby 1990, 1992). We come to recognize that examining race relations is critical, not simply for an understanding of social life as it is expressed in the margins of American society, but also ultimately for an understanding of life as it is expressed in its very dynamic center. For as Stuart Hall (1981) reminds us:

> If you try to stop the story about racial politics, racial divisions, racist ideologies short of confronting some of these difficult issues; if you present an

> idealized picture of a "multicultural" or "ethnically varied" society which
> doesn't look at the way racism has acted back inside the working class itself,
> the way in which racism has combined with, for example, sexism working
> back within the black population itself; if you try to tell the story as if some-
> where around the corner some whole constituted class is waiting for a green
> light to advance and displace the racist enemy . . . you will have done
> absolutely nothing whatsoever for the political understanding of your
> students. (68)

The complex dynamics of the operation of race identified by Hall caution
against dogmatism and totalizing solutions to the problem of racial inequality and racial antagonism in education and society. But these same contradictions behoove us to guard against quietism and cynicism. As a further
corollary to this, we should by now be disabused of the idea that the contradictory politics and practices associated with racial and identity formation
address only the experiences of minority individuals and groups. In this
essay, I have sought to draw attention to the fact that these discontinuities
and contradictions also apply to whites. Much work needs to be done to
understand and intervene in the ways in which whites are positioned as
"white," in the language, symbolic, and material structures that dominate
culture in the West and the United States. We need to move beyond static
definitions of whites and blacks as they currently pervade existing research
in education (Fusco 1988; Roman in press). This means, for example, that
we should not continue to position all whites as the Other of multicultural
curriculum reform and other transformative projects in education. It means
that in every local setting, particularly in the urban setting, we must find the
moral, ethical, material, and political resources for generalized affective
investment in schools. Such an investment must be grounded in a critical
reading of the differential needs of embattled urban communities and
the particular needs of inner-city school youth. Such a "differential
consciousness" (Sandoval 1991) must constantly challenge individual constituencies to think within but at the same time to think beyond the particularity of their experiences and interests. Schools cannot continue to
function as armies of occupation in the inner-city setting but must become
arenas in which diversifying urban communities can participate in building
new solidarities for educational access, mobility, and affirmation for minority youth. Ultimately, then, a vigorous attempt to read the dynamism and
complexity of schools as social institutions that are deeply infiltrated by
society and stratified by difference, unstable alliances, needs, desires, and
interests is a vital first requirement in thinking through the parameters of
race relations reform in education.

References

Althusser, A. (1971). Ideology and ideological state apparatuses (Notes towards an investigation). In L. Althusser, *Lenin and Philosophy and Other Essays* (121–73). New York: Monthly Review.

Aronowitz, S., and Giroux, H. (1991). The politics of clarity. *Afterimage* 19 (3): 5, 17.

Asante, M. (1987). *The Afrocentric Idea.* Philadelphia: Temple University Press.

Bakhtin, M. M. (1981). *The Dialogic Imagination,* Ed. M. Holquist, trans. C. Emerson and M. Holquist. Austin: University of Texas Press.

Bhabha, H. (1992). Postcolonial authority and post modern guilt. In L. Grossberg, C. Nelson, and P. Treichler, eds., *Cultural Studies* (56–68). New York: Routledge.

Bloom, A. (1987). *The Closing of the American Mind.* New York: Simon and Schuster.

Burawoy, M. (1981). The capitalist state in South Africa: Marxist and sociological perspectives on race and class. In M. Zeitlin, Ed., *Political Power and Social Theory,* vol. 2; 279–335. Greenwich, CT: JAI Press.

Carby, H. (1990). The politics of difference. *Ms.,* September/October, 84–85.

——— (1992): The multicultural wars. *Radical History Review* 54 (Fall): 7–20.

De Lauretis, T. (1984). *Alice Doesn't: Feminism, Semiotics, and Cinema.* Bloomington: Indiana University Press.

D'Souza, D. (1991). *Illiberal Education: The Politics of Race and Sex on Campus.* New York: Free Press.

Fusco, C. (1988). Fantasies of oppositionality. *Screen* 29 (4): 80–95.

Gates, H. (1991). "Authenticity," or the lesson of little tree.– *New York Times Book Review,* 24 November 1991, 1.

Giroux, H. (1992). *Border Crossings: Cultural Workers and the Politics of Education.* New York: Routledge.

Grant, L. (1984). Black females' "place" in desegregated classrooms. *Sociology of Education* 57: 98–111.

——— (1985). *Uneasy Alliances: Black Males, Teachers, and Peers in Desegregated Classrooms.* Unpublished manuscript. Southern Illinois University of Carbondale Department of Sociology.

Hall, S. (1981). Teaching race. In A. James and R. Jeffcoate, eds., *The School in the Multicultural Society* (58–69). London: Harper & Row.

——— (1986). Gramsci's relevance to the analysis of race. *Communication Inquiry* 10: 5–27.

——— (1989). Cultural identity and cinematic representation. *Framework* 36: 66–81.

——— (1993). What is this "black" in black popular culture. In G. Dent, ed., *Black Popular Culture* (21–33). Seattle: Bay Press.

Hicks, E. (1981). Cultural Marxism: Nonsynchrony and feminist practice. In L. Sargeant, ed., *Women and Revolution* (219–38). Boston: South End Press.

Hirsch, E. D. (1987). *Cultural Literacy.* Boston: Houghton Mifflin.

Institute for the Study of Social Change (1990). *The Diversity Project: Final Report to the Chancellor*. Berkeley: University of California Press.

JanMohamed, A., and Lloyd, D. (1987). Introduction: Minority discourse—What is to be done? *Cultural Critique* 7: 5–17.

Jaschik, S. (1990). Scholarships set up for minority students are called illegal. *Chronicle of Higher Education* 37 (15): A1.

Kunjufu, J. (1990). *Countering the Conspiracy to Destroy Black Boys*. Chicago: African American Images.

McCarthy, C. (1990). *Race and Curriculum*. London: Falmer.

Morrison, T. (1992). Introduction: Friday on the Potomac. In T. Morrison, ed., *Racing Justice, Engendering Power: Essays on Anita Hill, Clarence Thomas and the Construction of Social Reality* (vii–xxx). New York: Pantheon.

Nkomo, M. (1984). *Student Culture and Activism in Black South African Universities*. Westport, CT: Greenwood.

Ogbu, J. (1992). Understanding cultural diversity and learning. *Educational Researcher* 21 (8): 5–14.

Omi, M., and Winant, H. (1991). Contesting the meaning of race in the post–civil rights period. Paper presented at the annual meeting of the American Sociological Association, August 23–27.

Roman, L. (in press). White is a color! White defensiveness, postmodernism, and anti-racist pedagogy. In C. McCarthy and W. Crichlow, eds., *Race, Identity and Representation*. New York: Routledge.

Said, E. (1985). Orientalism reconsidered. *Race and Class* 26 (1): 1–15.

———(1992). Identity, authority, and freedom: The Potentate and the traveler. *Transition* 54: 4–18.

Sandoval, C. (1991) U.S. third world feminism: The theory and method of oppositional consciousness in the postmodern world. In *Genders* 10: 1–24.

Tiedt, I., and Tiedt, P. (1986). *Multicultural Teaching: A Handbook of Activities, Information, and Resources*. Boston: Allyn & Bacon.

Wallace (1990). *Invisibility Blues*. New York: Verso.

Waters, M. (1990). *Ethnic Options: Choosing Identities in America*. Berkeley: University of California Press.

Will, G. (1989). Eurocentricity and the school curriculum. *Baton Rouge Morning Advocate*, December 18, 3.

Wright, E. O. (1978). *Class, Crisis and the State*. London: New Left Review.

10

Trading Races

Majorities, Modernities; A Critique

Mike Hill

> The only endangered species is the White Anglo-Saxon Male.
> —Congresswoman Helen Chenowith, R-Idaho

If you read your glossy magazines after the bombing of the Oklahoma City Federal Building in April '95, you will remember seeing on the cover of *Time* a photo of the alleged perpetrator—blond-haired, blue-eyed white guy Timothy McVeigh. You would have also noticed the caption emblazoned in the lower left-hand corner of the photo, which read in block letters: "THE FACE OF TERROR." Inside the magazine, you would have read how "a sense of guilty introspection swept the country when the FBI released the sketches of the suspects, distinctly Caucasian John Does one and two."[1] The "terror" at issue in *Time* and on its cover is twofold, I think: most obviously, there is the "terror" of the bombing itself. People died. The news displayed the carnage in sometimes graphic detail. Other people felt terrified. But there is a secondary terror at work here as well, a terror that draws a bead on whiteness itself and its apparent coconspirator, masculinity, in a more revealing way. WASP masculinity is here tagged by the magazine with a "distinction" the news typically locates elsewhere. For an "introspective" white majority (conceived as the "nation"), *Time* places an assumedly benign and banal-looking white male face into terrifying proximity with everything WASPishness is purportedly not: noticeable, peculiar, divisive. In marking McVeigh's indifferent white face with its newly discovered "terror," a "nation" of readers experienced, I suspect, a kind of chiasmatic reflective gaze, looking both at themselves and at somebody different.

Things are similar in theory. Following numerous appeals within the last five years or so (mostly) by well-known black feminists,[2] a spate of monograghs, edited volumes, special journal issues, feature articles, conference panels, and popular magazines continue to hold forth on the question of whiteness.[3] If with less "terror" than in the real world, recent debates over race in and about academe have blown the lid off white racial indifference. Whiteness no longer very easily maintains its remarkable historical capacity to remain, as it were, unremarkable. The boilerplate story of whiteness today is that its fragility has gone too long unsaid. Whiteness is a *faux* neutrality, a liberal ruse that has worked since the Enlightenment to keep race matters distinct and at a comfortable distance from the dominant and, heretofore anyway, silent majority.[4]

As the dust begins to settle on what I'll sheepishly call a "first wave" of work on whiteness (as if whiteness hasn't been the unacknowledged topic of modern knowledge and its very substance all along), it seems right to pause a moment and think critically about what is starting almost to look like a white Renaissance. In this sometimes heady age of multicultural curriculum revision,[5] and with the emergence of identity politics as a distinct institutional force (there are currently more than 800 ethnic studies programs in U.S. universities[6]), the recent turn to whiteness is indeed a curious thing. How sorry it would be if the epistemological challenge to whiteness produced its sneaky ontological comeback, if the puissant banality of whiteness and its imminent critique eventuated somehow in the benevolent takeover of what were once its margins.

So perhaps there is a *third* white terror besides the ones captured and fostered by *Time* magazine after the Oklahoma bombing—a terror manifest when the study of whiteness ends up running interference for difference-sensitive white academics to finally get a bit of the Other. The charge is tempting to make. As it becomes possible to speak in quantitative as well as qualitative terms about "the new whiteness studies," the likely effect of margin poaching is something those of us working on what thirty-odd years ago *Ebony* magazine called America's "white problem" ought to take in earnest.[7] Addressing whiteness critically provides an inherent positional awkwardness if you happen beyond even your best intentions to be identifiably white, and this awkwardness is far from politically irrelevant. Indeed, rather than seeing the irony apparent in work on whiteness as unintended (and therefore politically nettlesome) critical fallout, why not begin from that place and see if the difficulties regarding such a slippery topic as whiteness might be, in fact, difficulties that are at least in some limited way politically constitutive?

Participants in (and performers of) "the new whiteness studies" take for granted now that white hegemony depends largely on the clever stratagems by which whiteness and white folks keep silent the powerful fiction of race. We take for granted, in other words, that "the white Anglo-Saxon male" *is* and ought to be—as Congresswoman Chenowith says with a categorically different agenda—"endangered." If this is happening with as-yet-unaccountable awkwardness and some irony, it is happening with relatively little regret. But ought we (can we) sweep the irony evidently immanent to the formation of "the new whiteness studies" under the rug of political good conscience?

Irony is typically defined as a force that splits and multiplies the formerly coherent (coherent, like whiteness, because it is both overspoken and unspoken); and irony is defined, too, as something that happens not necessarily with the ironist's complete consent (desire here being dislodged as well). I would obviously not be the first to speak of irony as a political force, but I think its implications are essential for evaluating white critique. Whiteness thought through the irony of its lasting claim on our attention becomes both an identity problem (which white critics appear only too glad to address) and a knowledge problem (which, at some level anyway, returns less happily to tag the white critic with the charge, perhaps, of a sneaky "ethnic" takeover). In short, it is unlikely that the political force of "the new whiteness studies" can be reliably cordoned off from the political symptoms it bears. White writing arrives ultimately, and like it or not, at the conditional ambivalence of itself, and it does so, one hopes, to perform in some necessarily strange combination both its power and fragility so that postwhite associational possibilities might be arranged.

Below I want to discuss three recent and important books on whiteness and, in particular, how each eventually comes up against the performative condition of white ambivalence I am trying to describe. The ironic condition of the subject made multiple—that is, of whiteness *both* "massified" and disintegrated by differences usually contained outside its purported neutrality—is precisely where a "second wave" of work on the topic might begin.[8] I want to suggest, in other words (and perhaps you see this coming now), that the material stakes of whiteness are also the theoretical stakes of modernity.

Debunking Whiteness, Rebunking Modernity?

> Whiteness is a very modern thing.
>
> —W.E.B. Du Bois

Ruth Frankenberg's *White Women, Race Matters* is an agenda-setting book.[9] This is so less perhaps because of what it says about whiteness (though this is by no means trivial) than how it goes about saying it. The book is based on a series of conversations. Frankenberg talks about whiteness with thirty white California Bay Area women in the two years between 1984 and '86. Each of the book's core chapters focuses on a different category of white women, their different stories, and different issues about race that come up in the course of the exchange. Chapter 3, for example, addresses growing up white; chapters 4 and 5, interracial sexuality. Each chapter contains a series of what Frankenberg calls "narratives." Each narrative is discussed (one could as easily say read, interpreted, or retold), and then provisional conclusions are drawn. Each conclusion establishes, more or less, how white women are "marked by the interlocking effects of geographical origin, generation, ethnicity, political orientation, gender . . . and how each are [sic] inscribed . . . into a shared history of race in the United States and beyond" (18).

It cannot be said today in the wake of so much work on whiteness (though it could have been ten years ago, when the narratives were told and heard) that this book contains many substantive surprises about the shibboleth of white neutrality. To deny "the apparent emptiness of whiteness" as the "location of the unmarked and unnamed" (2, 16–17) is, thanks in part to Frankenberg's success, standard fare these days in discussions of race. The book reads convincingly if not originally that whiteness and white folk are hegemonic on the grounds of "universality," "purity," and "the setting and marking of boundaries" that keep whiteness itself a nonracialized (i.e., unmarked) category (99). It is no doubt important to point out specific cases and individual narratives that help make whiteness available for critique. However, I would argue that what makes *White Women* an agendasetting book is, first, the singular distance it goes in attaching (or inviting us to attach) the problem of white neutrality to its theoretical motor, the "liberal humanist" stance of "universality" (147); and, second, for going the further and more nettlesome distance of holding itself accountable to the implications of that critique.

A local and specific critical ethnography and one without apology, *White Women* rightly attaches to representations of whiteness a politics that worries representativity itself. The epistemological problem of internal neutrality, what Frankenberg a propos Gayatri Spivak calls the "epistemic violence" of "rationalized colonial domination" (16), is central to the ontological problem of whiteness. Put simply, *White Women* realizes that naming what whiteness *is* (and what it refuses to become) necessitates talking about what knowledge *does*. What knowledge does in this case is withhold from whiteness (white authorship included) the slick veneer of racial empiricism, and of white representivity as such. This book is thus a critique of white majoritarian thinking that targets equally the principles of modernity upon which

writing itself works. It posits in the first instance that majority discourse—
the privilege of white neutrality that say "We are all of us the same"—is
unremittingly intertwined with the modernist project of representative
knowledge. To the extent that white subjectivity sustains its normative value
by remaining somehow outside the differences it wants to name (in
Lacanian or Althusserian terms, a "subject/object adequation"), the very
grounds from which the white critic speaks to interrogate whiteness
becomes simultaneously her target.

Thus, the agenda-setting premise of *White Women*, and equally the
premise of feminism since the late seventies, might then be summed up as
follows: "We act from within the social relations and subject positions we
seek to change" (5). Frankenberg writes, "I viewed myself as much as the
women I interviewed as situated within the relations of racism" (30); "my
examples illustrate the ways my own 'caughtness' in the relations of racism
limited my speech" (39); and "I can see myself working from within the discourse I am seeking to challenge" (40–41). Like no other "scholarly" book on
the topic known to me, *White Women* is clear and careful not to re-establish
the ontological ruse of white unaccountability through the epistemological
back door. By refusing to evoke the kind of "power evasiveness" identified in
the least progressive white storytellers the book examines, it also refuses the
habitually modernist take on writing and thinking as "objective" enterprises
(we are, after all, only talking about thirty Bay Area women, hardly a "representative" sample). By opting for a cross between James Clifford's interested
ethnography and a kind of feminist-inspired Barthesian narratological ethics,
White Women insists that the awkwardness of knowing and the impossibility
of being are, for whiteness, one and the same, two problems designated by
the fragility of "representation" itself. The challenge put forth in this book,
then, is to debunk the (ontological) neutrality of whiteness without rebunk-
ing precisely that condition in the (epistemological) form of modernity. This,
as I'll make clearer below, is a tall order.

Ceci n'est pas une White Guy

> Ceci n'est pas une pipe.
>
> —René Magritte

I suggested above that *White Women* invites us to consider that the primary
effect of white critique is to make whiteness something else again, that is, to
bear a new distinction thought through the classificatory rearrangements of
race, gender, and/or class. If thinking differently about whiteness necessarily
implicates white authorship in some, let's say "terrifying," proximity with

what it doesn't want to be (in Frankenberg's case, implicated by the racism she wants to challenge), and if it is a false sense of modernist "object adequation" that keeps the white critic so distanced, then I think the so-called postmodern idea of the multiple subject might deliver the political goods over which materialist critics have been stomping their feet for a long time.[10] "This is not a pipe," according to Magritte. It's a painting, or a word (or an epigram), and with a certain amount of critical attention, it is something else again. The "white problem" as we approach a second wave of work upon it is, I think, analogous: on the one hand, we desire to critique and displace white neutrality, to mark and make it something other than simply given, something other, that is, than just white; but as work on whiteness mounts, there emerges discomfort (redressed by Frankenberg as self-implication) that we still attend to whiteness at all. How, then, to account for—and I put this as awkwardly as it is in practice—the desire (for white desire) to desire something else? In the midst of a disintegration of white neutrality, and given the ambivalences come lately by its amassing critique, can it be said about those who might resist the power that usually names them, that "this is not a white guy"?

In *How the Irish Became White*, Noel Ignatiev gives a provocative historical argument toward thinking through the invention and, from there, the contemporary disintegration of whiteness.[11] Whiteness is less the unspoken identity of privilege into which one is, or is not, "naturally" born than it is a set of historical relations through which Irish immigrants played out a host of competing economic and national interests. To this end, chapter 1 discusses the abolitionist and 1840's home rule activist Daniel O'Connell. In the figure of O'Connell, certain Enlightenment terms such as "inalienable rights" are seen to be characteristically wrought with contradiction. In both O'Connell and the soon-to-be whitened Irish of his day are seen two impossibly antagonistic elements: on the one hand, the "rights"-based Enlightenment ideology of individuality and "liberty," which dictated an abolitionist stance; on the other hand, however, that same abolitionism perceived by the U.S. government as pro-British, which Irish Republicans would have seen as anathema. What we get in O'Connell, then, is a political split over which the U.S. Irish had eventually to choose. To oppose slavery and ignore the emergent color line would have meant, in effect, British loyalty. Thus, caught between national independence and racial equality—and, paradoxically, according to the Enlightenment principles that produced the rhetoric for both—the Irish are tragically maneuvered by their U.S. allegiances into choosing antiabolitionism. They chose, simultaneously, to become white.

The split in political identity that leads by default to a version of whiteness that our historical moment falsely assumes to be neutral begins with the figure of O'Connell. But it is a condition replayed throughout *How the Irish*

Became White. In chapter 2, for example, Thomas Brannagan has a "divided soul" (57) over the question of racial "sameness." Brannagan exalts Africa at first, producing (as is not historically uncommon) the well-intended idea of Africa as feminized regeneration, a thing of beauty and fertility in the white imaginary and, thereby, a fleeting version of what (white) humanity might have been. After an uprising against whites in Haiti, however, Brannagan's benevolent Christian humanism turns without missing a step to a program of colonialist containment (55). Chapter 3 introduces John Binns, a similarly conflicted Jacobin agitator and devout Jacksonian. Binns achieves the status of white working-class hero, fighting indefatigably for radical labor rights and gaining success within the white labor movement, but proportionate only to his proslavery stance.

Consistent among these and other similarly divided white Irish characters in *How the Irish Became White* is the practice of resolving political conflicts by choosing coherence in that falsely configured, depoliticized zone of white racial neutrality. Similar to *White Women* in effect, this book marks whiteness as historically frail and internally conflicted. Its frailty is never more dramatically nor convincingly displayed than at the historical moment when the Irish were caught within the contradictions of Enlightenment vagaries—that is, caught for a fleeting moment in the mid-nineteenth century between the ideological emergence of "white" assimilation and the unconstructed ontological options the Irish might otherwise have had. Terms such as "universality," "liberty," "individuality," and so on, which seemed to promise economic autonomy and republican independence, in point of historical fact functioned on behalf of whiteness to close down politics and end African/Irish relational (not individual) rights. Indeed, the implicit and most powerful lesson of this book (and this speaks directly to the new labor history associated with Herbert Gutman) is that the materialist struggle over class inequity is, by historical necessity, a struggle that also involves the classificatory habits under which identities may and may not cohere. Insofar as working-class radicalism has subscribed to a rights-based politics of individualism—wherein "liberty," "freedom," "universality," and "humanity" are somehow meaningful outside the need for categorical counter-maneuvers attendant to race—then working-class struggle is historically doomed to reinvent the very inequities it means to take down. For the Irish, the Enlightenment meant a "freer," emergent, white-Irish middle class. "Freedom" here depends on how the "free" exclude and exploit. Those "of color" with whom nineteenth-century white labor competed were marked differently from those who, in the name of "liberty" and other historical fictions, proceeded to become economically stable and white.

The ruse of white neutrality duly noted, the common work of universalism and racism described, *How the Irish Became White* has weaknesses that are in the end as far reaching as the book's unimpeachable strengths. Indeed, the very problem of collective neutrality that founded the white race and positioned the Irish within it (O'Connell's pitch for "liberty," Binns's Jacobinism) is inexplicably and circuitously reintroduced as exactly the kind of world the book imagines before and after whiteness. For a book that rightly breeds political suspicion about internal neutrality, *How the Irish Became White* begins with the confusingly pat theoretical statement, "The only race is the human race" (1). Recall, one of the things that the book details remarkably well is that, when the (Enlightenment) terms of inclusiveness are at work historically ("liberty," "liberty for all," the "people," "citizens," etc.), that the malignant social relation we call whiteness is also most effectively at work.[12] While whiteness appears representative, it is in fact divisive. But how one arrives at an alternate state of "representivity" (here put as "humanity") is a crucial question, and one even more crucially omitted.

It is, after all, part of the historical scoop that whiteness as a collectivity that naturally coheres is a fiction we need to abolish immediately (this is the charge of the "new abolitionism" espoused in Ignatiev's provocative journal *Race Traitor*, the subtitle of which is "Treason to Whiteness Is Loyalty to Humanity"). Yet there is no explanation whatsoever of how the "humanity" in question in the book's introduction (and at several points throughout), and for that matter, other ideas—the "natural sympathies" (96) that the Irish allegedly had for their fellow man when they were just "Green" (3), and the "general knowledge of humanity" (130) we're asked to draw upon for understanding the Irish; I could go on—function in any less problematic or mystifying ways than they did when O'Connell et al. tried to repair their internal dividedness through the ontological fiction of whiteness. *How the Irish Became White* in other words provides no explicit basis for thinking about which collectivities might be conceivable other than the ones the book so rightly critiques. Indeed, this book seems at points to reinscribe the historical ruse of transparent and neutral collectivities—alas, the defining problem of the white race—and repeat precisely the false reparations its troubled Irish subjects perform in choosing whiteness in the nineteenth century. O'Connell's dilemma as a split political subject returns in the book's elementary appeal for a kind of "humanity" magically rid of the most objectionable features of whiteness, itself constructed as an apolitical totality.

O'Connell and his whitening Irish compatriots chose whiteness to repair a sense of internal division. This is a lesson that *How the Irish Became White* both offers and abandons. Even if with a certain nostalgia for probably nonexistent better days, one must begin the critique of whiteness with the now common feminist admission that (recalling Frankenberg) we're a part of the very power relations we want most to change. Irish identity is in the past multiply interested and incommensurably construed, and the fear and loathing of this strange multiplicity is a problem implicit to the histories of whiteness we may or may not write today. In the critical rediscovery of whiteness and in the critique of majority discourse at our own historical moment, why not suspect that O'Connell's ontological ambivalence persists?

After White Guys: Toward a Mass/Minority Discourse?

> I'm going to push the envelope this time. I think the heartbeat of this country is the white majority, and I'm speaking for them.
> —David Duke, as candidate for U.S. Senate

If Fred Pfeil is right in *White Guys*, white ambivalence most certainly does persist. It persists in the mind-boggling populism witnessed as I write this chapter (Pat Buchanan's presidential campaign being both white inspired and allegedly anticorporate), and it persists in any number of less odious mass cultural locations where white masculinity as we know (or knew) it is beginning to finally unravel. Like *White Women* and *How the Irish Became White*, *White Guys* insists that whiteness is not an internally neutral state of being. It contains multitudes, if only these were recognizable. Whiteness and white guys contain "modalities . . . riven by contradictions and fissures, . . . subject to flux" and, therefore, one hopes, "not imperiously closed to change" (x). Whereas in *How the Irish Became White* the historical contradictions of white Irishness are detailed as political failures and then inexplicably recouped with an ahistorical and inexplicably whitelike totality (i.e., "humanity"), *White Guys* takes an important page from feminism and is, therefore, a more politically astute if similarly conflicted book. The white guy in mass culture at his best is neither a historical mutation (a split subject outside "humanity"), nor is he politically unsalvageable for thinking anew about race, gender, and, ultimately, class. Ambivalences here are shrewdly cast as the inevitable political limits of (white) mass culture and, furthermore, as the condition of categorical change.

Of particular importance in *White Guys* is the fact that its pop-culture icons struggle not just with but, in finer moments, against their own variously constructed, defended, surrendered, and otherwise worn-out white masculinities. Indeed, white-guy angst itself has important political uses. It reveals the increasingly ruthless working conditions of the current labor market, a distinctly hostile time to maintain postwar notions of white-skin privilege. Something not unlike Ignatiev's O'Connell, Pfeil's Rambo is a

white "subaltern subject" on the edge of revolutionary political concious-
ness (6), "dreaming together" his leftward anti-establishment leanings
(for O'Connell et al., read Irish republicanism/radical labor), with a debilitating rightward hostility toward the nonwhite Other (for O'Connell,
antiabolitionism/the black wage worker). Though Rambo is by no means
brought on board Pfeil's "left" (a left in regard to which Pfeil himself feels a
familiar white-guy angst), Rambo and his male rampage counterparts bear
within them features of an emergent post-white-political imaginary (33).
For all of its problematic macho *ressentiment*, the *Die Hard* series brings big
business and corporate well-fare down at the behest of a class warrior waiting to be named (Pfeil doesn't miss the populism connection either). In the
male rampage film and elsewhere, *White Guys* identifies episodes of
"left-populist eat-the-rich joy" (23).

However, the book wants us sometimes to resist these "joys," and, even if
one agrees to ward off those pleasures that politics cannot defend, the precise
distinction between offensive and political "joys" is not altogether clear. On
one hand, this book offers nuanced theoretical readings of mass culture as
exhibiting the "symptomatic irresolutions" of (maybe) an emergent post-
white-guy radicalism. On the other hand, the dismissals that exist in the
politically safer chapters of the book make for (as is said of the very "white
guys" in the book) problems that are similarly "symptomatic" of white
ambivalence *qua* resistance. In short, *White Guys* itself performs the ambivalence it locates within mass culture, where the correct political legislation of
white-guy pleasure is notoriously confounded and most difficult to describe,
as long as you happen to be white. In other words, this book seeks to formulate political potential from mass culture, but when it tries to divide white
guys too neatly into good guys and bad guys, the firmer critical ground of
cultural representivity shifts, and that almost progressive white-guy ambivalence located out there comes ruthlessly home. The "antagonistic linkages"
that put the male rampagers politically up for grabs, for example, are denied
rock 'n' roll in chapter 3. Rock (and not just corporate rock as the title
indicates) is, it seems, flattened out as "ready access to the resources of femininity and blackness yet with no obligation to either women or blacks"
(79). That Bruce "The Boss" Springsteen becomes an obscurantist rip-off
artist and puppet of white-right Reaganomics, "like the visible bosses owning and running the plant" (86), seems a curious assertion given the serious
attention paid that other Bruce (Willis) in chapter 1. Indeed, this book
exhibits what is arguably the most important and, as yet, unresolved problem with Birmingham Cultural Studies and its U.S. incarnation—that is, the
unwieldy combination between a persistent left-Leavisite suspicion of the
masses on the one hand, and, on the other, a political pragmatism that wants

to take and make work the flickers of radical consciousness more or less where they are found. In the sense that this confronts the cultural studies practitioner with the impossibility of avoiding an up-close critical engagement with the cultural processes s/he wishes to distinguish, such a quandary is well suited for the study of whiteness, particularly by white folk.

So why not consider the ambivalence of *White Guys* (the book) in the same way it invites us to read the ambivalence of the "white guys" pinched between its covers? Consider the white guy *in* mass culture: he experiences real economic troubles, which he works out, for better or often for worse, on the grounds of gender and race. He feels, more or less, ambiguous about his politics because he realizes as a "post-Fordist subaltern" that the things he wants to oppose, namely big business and the government (recall *Times* "terror"), are the very things that before global economic restructuring had so securely sustained him. Marxists would rightly identify this ambivalence as an ideological problem. The (white male) subject who is interpellated by ideology recognizes somehow (by either good art or, sometimes, even in mass culture) that the desires that are not his own and that trouble how he thinks of himself are necessary for imagining the good life, precisely because they are radically other than his own. Call this a white racial unconscious. The feminist update of this is that we are, we white folk in particular, positioned within and are in no small measure an effect of the very relations of power we now want most to change. We are, in part anyway, the object of a critique we are also performing, and the effects of that performance by logical extension cannot be self-assuredly known by white folk before they actually exist. Simply put, the political effects of "the new whiteness studies" are best evaluated from positions that are other than white.

White-guy ambiguity in mass culture is thus thought of as a necessary stage in the development of a politics they (and we) haven't learned yet to own. This, on a sympathetic reading of, say, the *Die Hard* films or of *Falling Down*, seems permissible. Indeed, because nothing is in place conceptually to entertain both a simultaneous withering away of white masculinity *and* the commitment to collectivities within which whiteness might be effectively dispersed, abolished, and dismissed, white ambivalence might well be read as a step toward a radical remaking of ourselves. The emergent leftward lean traceable in mass culture presumes for white guys a giving up of white masculine identity and a simultaneous giving over to identities white guys can't both own and remain monolithically male, heterosexual, and white. The complicated task of locating in mass culture what I would call a "mass minority discourse" is summed up in more conventional terms in *White Guys* by referring to the "consumerist individualism" versus "the collective will" (200) debate and by calling alternatively for "a new masculinity"

(228) based on a more "public and collective politics" (229, 238, 258). Rather like the ironic split that has unintentionally conditioned "the new whiteness studies" on the whole, white-guy desire and identity is itself being displaced if not rewritten by way of mass culture, and we who choose to account for this are given here the opportunity to step between a displaced, heretofore silent majority, and the likes of David Duke.

So with this proposition in mind about white-guy ambivalence *in* mass culture, consider again the white guy *on* mass culture. He is detailed with great care and at some length in Pfeil's quasi-autobiographic introduction (he appears too in the description of, and sheepishly skeptical participation in, the "men's movement," chapter 5). The introduction to *White Guys* begins with a "socially significant" fear about whiteness (i)—that is, with explicit ambivalence over whether or not a white guy has any political business at all fighting against "the idea that white straight masculinity is unified" (viii). The introduction quotes at length Stephen Heath's well-known opening salvo in *Men in Feminism*, marking how Heath is in fact a split subject wanting, he hopes not in bad faith, to give up the very masculinity from which, in both senses, he speaks "out of." Heath wonders whether his "desire to be a subject there too in feminism—to be a feminist—is then only also the last feint in the long history of their colonialization" (xi). Pfeil begins *White Guys* with this quote in a way that takes us directly to the emergent irony of white critique. His ambivalence is expressed thus: "It is not clear that there is much room within progressive culture for any version of white straight masculinity to take its place in the ensemble of other racial, sexual, and gender identities" (ix); and similarly, he reveals the fear that "I will be assailed by those men and women [on the left] with whom I have worked . . . accused of being merely another crypto-macho Bruce Willis fan under feminist sheepskin" (x). Accordingly, and in anything other than in typical white-guy fashion, he continues: "I push my fears back and take the hands down from my face" (xi).

The anxiety held forth here by the subject who names *White Guys* (I mean, by its author) is concomitant with the anxiety that the book tries, sometimes more and sometimes less successfully, to identify someplace else. *White Guys* is thus emblematic of certain complex forms of reversal implicit in "the new whiteness studies." Here, for better or worse, is a critical practice that, unlike Black, Asian, or Latino studies, works in the context of a desire to disintegrate the very object of its thought. Such work may well provide cause for a good round of political "assailing" from the various lefts that progressive "white guys" evidently both fancy and fear. That particular arrangement of white negation known as the blame game may be one way to speak politically; but I think there are others as well.

Does "whiteness," in some now specifiable sense, inadvertently comply with the skin privilege it used to take for granted? Most definitely, but on the order of feminist thought, one hopes not absolutely. Will the current burst of attention to "whiteness," some may say its most "terrifying" appearance, occasion a certain amount of discord on behalf of identity politics as they were before, that is, before "whiteness studies" unleashed the apparent portability of difference? Most likely. But one affirms these questions precisely to the extent that they reveal the undeniable peculiarity that white people continue to exist at all.

Notes

1. Elizabeth Gleick, "Who Are They?" *Time* (May 1995): 46.

2. Among black feminist calls for the critical examination of whiteness, see: Hazel Carby, "The Politics of Difference," *Ms.* (September 1990), 84–85; bell hooks, "Representing Whiteness," *Yearning: Race, Gender, and Cultural Politics* (Boston: South End Press, 1990); and Toni Morrison, *Playing in the Dark: Whiteness and the Literary Imagination* (New York: Vintage, 1992). Black writers have called for a full-scale critique of whiteness at least since Du Bois.

3. Scholarly journals that have done (or are doing) special issues on whiteness include *Socialist Review*; *Lusatania*; *the minnesota review*; *Transition*; and *American Quarterly*. Also see Noel Ignatiev's *Race Traitor: Treason to Whiteness is Loyalty to Humanity*. For a good write-up on the new whiteness studies, see Liz MacMillan, "Lifting the Veil of Whiteness: Growing Body of Scholarship Challenges Racial 'Norm'," *Chronicle of Higher Education* (8 September 1995), sec. A, 23. Among recent collections on whiteness, see Annalee Newitz and Matthew Wray, eds., *White Trash: Race and Class in America* (New York: Routledge, 1996); and my edited volume, *Whiteness: A Critical Reader* (New York: NYU Press, 1997). For a review of white critique after 1990, see Shelly Fisher Fishkin, "Interrogating 'Whiteness,' Complicating 'Blackness': Remapping American Culture," *American Quarterly* 47.3 (September 1995): 428–66.

4. A *locus classicus* of the critique of whiteness as unmarked is Richard Dyer's essay "White," *Screen* 29.4 (1988): 45–64.

5. Among the many "multiculturalisms" running around these days, the most politically troubling is what Peter McLaren calls "liberal multiculturalism." According to McLaren, "liberal multiculturalism" essentializes ethnic difference or treats race as a lifestyle issue. It opts for a "diversity" of fixed identities instead of the political transformation of identities joined together by critique. See McLaren's "Multiculturalism and Postmodern Critique," in Henry A. Giroux and Peter McLaren, eds., *Between Borders: Pedagogy and the Politics of Cultural Studies* (New York: Routledge, 1994).

6. See Gretchen M. Bataille, et al., *Ethnic Studies in the United States* (Garland: Hamden, 1996).

7. See the edited volume subsequent to the *Ebony* special issue, *The White Problem* (Chicago: Johnson Publishing, 1966). For a transcription of a recent lively debate on the proliferation of work on whiteness, see Mike Hill (moderator), "A Marxist Literary Group Symposium on Whiteness," *minnesota review* 47 (Spring 1997).

8. Elsewhere I describe this process in more detail as "mass minority discourse." See my "Vipers in *Shangri-la*: Whiteness, Writing, and Other Ordinary Terrors," in Mike Hill, *Whiteness*; I explore gender and race as problems of categorical interrelation in, "White Was

(the White Race)?: Memories, Change," *Postmodern Culture* 7.2 (January 1997) : [electronic publication]. www site is www.iath.virginia.edu/pmc.

9. Ruth Frankenberg, *White Women, Race Matters: The Social Construction of Whiteness* (Minneapolis: University of Minnesota Press, 1993).

10. "Postmodernism" is probably not a useful term outside very specific contexts that range across the political spectrum. My ideas about the "massification" of white neutrality is more directly in line with the tradition of historical materialism, in particular work on the "masses" as historical agents. See, in particular, Etienne Balibar, *Masses, Classes, Ideas: Studies on Politics and Philosophy Before and After Marx* (New York: Routledge, 1994).

11. In this respect, the book resembles in intent the seminal work of Ted Allen and David Roediger. See Allen, *The Invention of the White Race*, vol. 1 (London: Verso, 1994), and Roediger, *The Wages of Whiteness* (London: Verso, 1991).

12. The ideology of rights is most effectively taken to task by work known today as "Critical Race Theory." See Derrick Bell Jr., "Racial Realism," in Kimberlé Crenshaw et al., eds., *Critical Race Theory* (New York: New Press, 1995), 302–14.

11

Race, Schooling, and Double Consciousness

The Politics of Pedagogy in Toni Morrison's Fiction

Susan Searls

> The history of the American Negro is the history of this strife,—this longing to attain self-conscious manhood, to merge his double self into a better and truer self. In this merging he wishes neither of the older selves to be lost. He would not Africanize America, for America has too much to teach the world and Africa. He would not bleach his Negro soul in a flood of white Americanism, for he knows that Negro blood has a message for the world.
>
> —W.E.B. Du Bois, *The Souls of Black Folk*

The artistic and cultural work of Toni Morrison attests to the truth of W.E.B. Du Bois's 1903 prophecy that the problem of the twentieth century would be the problem of the color line. Among the most important public intellectuals of the century, Morrison, like Du Bois, has emphasized the primacy of the pedagogical in her literary and critical writings, drawing attention to the ways in which knowledge, power, and identities are produced under specific conditions of learning within the academy and outside of it. Central to the pedagogy of both Du Bois and Morrison are the cultural traditions of African Americans and their accessibility to future generations of black intellectuals. In 1946 Du Bois wrote:

> The experience through which our ancestors have gone for four hundred years is part of our bone and sinew whether we know it or not. The methods which we evolved for opposing slavery and fighting prejudice are not to be forgotten, but learned for our own and others' instruction. . . . The problem of our children is distinctive: when shall a colored child learn the color line? At home, at school or suddenly in the street? What shall we do in art and literature? Shall we seek to ignore our background and graft on a culture which does not wholly admit us, or build anew on that marvellous African . . . heritage. (1973, 144).

Situated in the distinctive African American cultural traditions to which
Du Bois once alluded, Morrison's literary work valorizes the "discredited
knowledges" of the folk: traditional African cosmology and the lore of
African Americans, the centrality of community, and the importance of the
African ancestors—values and value systems that challenge the hegemonic
paradigms privileged by the academy (James 1995).

Du Bois theorized about the education of black people under the shadow
of Jim Crow; race was *the* defining principle of one's social existence. For
Morrison, the category of "race" is under erasure. "For three hundred years
black Americans insisted that 'race' was no usefully distinguishing factor in
human relationships," Morrison asserts. "When blacks discovered they had
shaped or become a culturally formed race, and that it had specific and
revered difference, suddenly they were told that there is no such thing as
'race,' biological or cultural, matters and that genuine intellectual exchange
cannot accommodate it" (1989, 3). Whereas Du Bois challenged the
assumption that the cultural difference of African Americans was a marker
of inferiority, Morrison attempts to rescue the politics of difference from
the jaws of racial indifference.

Of course, the assertion of black inferiority and the retreat into
color blindness both function to preserve white cultural hegemony.
Accommodating a different strategy for perpetuating racial exclusion,
Morrison's project extends beyond the Du Boisian preoccupation with the
real contributions of black Americans to their country by engaging the degree
to which the construction of "white Americanism" is dependent upon a silent
and abiding Africanist presence. In a collection of lectures on the history of
American civilization given at Harvard, *Playing in the Dark*, Morrison writes:

> For some time now I have been thinking about the validity or vulnerability of
> a certain set of assumptions conventionally accepted among literary histori-
> ans and critics and circulated as "knowledge." This knowledge holds that
> traditional, canonical American literature is free of, uniformed, and unshaped
> by the four-hundred-year-old presence of, first, Africans and then African-
> Americans in the United States. It assumes that this presence—which shaped
> the body politic, the Constitution, and the entire history of the culture—has
> had no significant place or consequence in the origin and development of that
> culture's literature. Moreover, such knowledge assumes that the characteris-
> tics of our national literature emanate from a particular "Americanness" that
> is separate from and unaccountable to this presence. (1992, 4–5)

The literary imagination is of primary importance to Morrison because it
reveals not only the invention of literary "blackness" but also its role in the

construction and elevation of literary "whiteness." Foregrounding the absence of critical discussions of race in the academy, Morrison exposes how agendas in literary criticism have historically disguised themselves and thus diminished the study of literature itself:

> When matters of race are located and called attention to in American literature, critical response has tended to be on the order of a humanistic nostrum—or a dismissal mandated by the label "political." Excising the political from the life of the mind is a sacrifice that has proven costly. . . . A criticism that needs to insist that literature is not only "universal" but also "race-free" risks lobotomizing that literature, and diminishing both the art and the artist. (1992, 12)

Though *Playing in the Dark* constitutes her most explicit challenge to the politics of knowledge and authority in the academy, it is in Morrison's fiction writing, which explores the dynamics of institutionalized racism, education, and identity formation, that one finds specific elements of her pedagogy at work.

In what follows, I want to take up some of the critical responses of a largely white establishment to Toni Morrison, whose cultural work invokes the political and pedagogical—as opposed to the aesthetic and humanistic—as part of a broader attempt to revive the imperative of racial justice that, as John Brenkman forcefully argues, has been absent from public discourse since the civil rights movement of the 1960s (see Brenkman 1995). Despite Morrison's radically antiracist and antisexist politics, critics have accused her of being appropriated by the dominant order. Of those critics, Denise Heinze is particularly worth attention. Though Heinze's *The Dilemma of "Double-Consciousness"* is to be credited for attempting to take up black literature within the context of black culture, it exemplifies a form of criticism that misrepresents and undermines the historical traditions and experiences that inform black cultural criticism and literature. I want to connect Heinze's use of Du Boisian double consciousness as a way of theorizing Morrison's alleged appropriation by the dominant white culture with the recent attacks on black public intellectuals charged with "selling out" in the interests of gaining the fame and popularity that white-liberal and left-liberal audiences can confer. Second, I want to focus on the ways in which Du Boisian double consciousness can be used in theorizing the relationship between institutionalized racism and the construction of black American identities in Morrison's fiction. By focusing on three novels by Morrison—*The Bluest Eye* (1970), *Tar Baby* (1982), and *Beloved* (1987)—I hope to demonstrate how double consciousness and double vision foster the potential for a pedagogy of creative

resistance to racial domination as well as resourceful self-definition and ethnic formation in different black communities in Morrison's novels.

Double Consciousness and the Dilemma of Appropriation

That the March 1995 cover of the *Atlantic Monthly* bore a raised black fist
with the caption "The New Intellectuals," while *The New Republic* of the
same month grimly announced "The Decline of the Black Public Intellectual," attests to the fact that the powerful ambivalence that white America
has harbored historically toward black scholars, critics, and artists has not
diminished. Reminiscent of the conservative backlash that followed the
Harlem Renaissance of the 1920s when Ralph Ellison noted, "We are no
longer in vogue," so too it appears that in the era of Newt Gingrich and the
New Republicanism, progressive black intellectuals such as Toni Morrison,
Cornel West, Michael Dyson, and bell hooks, among others, will be met
with a mixture of bewilderment, paternalism, and rage. Though Robert
Boynton's "The New Intellectuals" had none of the venom of the attack on
Cornel West in *The New Republic*, Boynton provides a scurrilous comparison between the new black intellectuals and the mostly Jewish intellectuals
who gathered around the *Partisan Review* in the 1940s and 1950s.

For Boynton, the marginality of the New York intellectuals attests to
their authenticity as cultural radicals who could not be seduced by the so-
called American mainstream. Boynton nods significantly to the media
attention lavished on several noteworthy black scholars and murmurs
"sellout." According to Boynton and many other critics, the public sphere
forged by black artists and intellectuals has not only gone mainstream; it is
also encumbered by their insular academicism and professional jargon.
Rather than acknowledge the legitimacy of the contributions of black
Americans in deepening and extending the possibilities of democratic
public life, Boynton becomes, despite himself, one of the many "besieged"
cultural conservatives brought to crisis over the pluralization of literacies
and their attendant forms of authority.

Boynton suggests that for those black intellectuals found worthy of
assuming the "particular burden of the American intellectual," there
emerges a real quandary. He argues:

> Having distinguished themselves by their analysis of racial subjects, they
> must now widen their scope and address broader political questions; having
> received accolades as academic specialists, they must now address a general
> audience. Secure in their place at the center of mainstream intellectual
> culture, they must now endure the criticisms of those who accuse them of
> having shed their "authentic" minority identification and of selling out. (56)

Given the announcement that black intellectuals are in decline at the same time that Boynton critiques their rising influence, one can rightly question the security of black intellectuals' place in the "mainstream." Not only is Boynton seemingly unaware that the new black intellectuals, like generations of black intellectuals before them, have always addressed "broader" social issues such as democracy, freedom, capitalism, gender roles, and education, but he also suggests that to speak to such concerns in large public forums is to forfeit one's "authentic minority identification."

Similar charges of appropriation have dogged artist/intellectual Toni Morrison both in the media and in the academy. Such criticisms need to be taken seriously not only in the interests of defending notions of equity and racial justice that certain concessions to the status quo jeopardize, but also for the ways in which such accusations can be used to dismiss significant critical interventions in public life. Morrison has received much national and international recognition, including a Pulitzer Prize for her novel *Beloved* and the Nobel Prize for Literature in 1993. In addition to receiving several other awards and honors, her fiction and criticism have regularly appeared on the *New York Times* best-sellers list and among Book of the Month Club selections. Widely acknowledged in the academy, Morrison's fiction has prompted several book-length critical studies and dissertations in addition to hundreds of essays in diverse scholarly journals.

Denise Heinze establishes the cultural and political context for Toni Morrison's rise to literary fame in her introduction to *The Dilemma of "Double-Consciousness": Toni Morrison's Novels.* Du Boisian double consciousness provides the theoretical means by which Heinze explicates Morrison's novels as well as its acceptance by the so-called American mainstream. For Heinze, double consciousness is simply "a state of affairs in which an individual is both representative of and immersed in two distinct ways of life" (5). Morrison's popularity, she argues, is a result of "a rare accommodation of two often competing literary selves" (5). Moreover, Morrison's successful career "appears to have transcended the 'permanent condition' of double-consciousness that afflicts her fictional characters" (10). I hope to demonstrate that Heinze's use of double consciousness to explain what she describes as Morrison's "irresolute" responses to white society does little justice to Du Bois's conception of black American identity.

In order to demonstrate that Morrison's responses to white society is "irresolute" rather than "oppositional," Heinze draws on cultural reproduction theory. According to this perspective, when a social group is not in control of its literary production, it must become aware of how the group that is in control is using the literature. Aware of the ways in which literary texts get appropriated by institutions to the degree that they reflect and legitimate dominant social values and practices, Heinze sees the success of an artist who is frequently read as "oppositional" as somewhat of an anomaly. Reviewing Toni Morrison's recent successes, the critic finds grounds to raise the critical question of whose interests her novels serve. Heinze wonders if Morrison's novels "function in the same way that the ghost of Beloved does—to haunt and torment a guilty conscience in need of absolution and redemption, for in each of her works Morrison launders one American ideal after another, while a huge contingency of Americans—male and female, black and white, rich and poor—wildly cheer her on" (3).

In this scenario, the critic reads the tension generated by Morrison's work as a result of her desire to voice a rage intent on demystifying American cultural hegemony on the one hand, and provide a kind of cathartic absolution for the guilty on the other. Invoking what appear to be contrary aims in Morrison's fiction, Heinze builds a case to argue that the author "both subverts and maintains, is exploited by and exploits the literary establishment" (10).

Morrison's acceptance by dominant white society, then, is the product of "a rare accommodation" achieved through Morrison's use of the conventions of traditional (read: white) literature as well as black cultural forms and meanings. Ironically, Heinze lauds Morrison's alleged accommodation in the "humanistic nostrum" that the writer has challenged on the grounds of its depoliticizing and neutralizing capacities:

> If Morrison can signify upon traditional American values, apparently without alienating her white readership, she does so because she employs traditional, recognizable, often comfortable modes of storytelling, and because much of what she does write eventually leads back to the universal condition of being human. (8)

Heinze sees Morrison's primary audience—those in need of absolution and redemption—as white, while the larger crowd of onlookers is everybody else. Morrison herself asserts, however, that she writes for black people and rejects the notion that her writing is "universal." "If I tried to write a universal novel," she says, "it would be water" (LeClair 1981, 28). From her perspective "there are only black people" (28).

Heinze rejects Morrison's assertions about her target audience, focusing instead on Morrison's success as a public intellectual. The critic presents Morrison as a modern-day Horatio Alger, "unconvinced" and, it seems, unappreciative of the "validity of the system that may have contributed to her success" (7). Rewriting Morrison's life to fit the "quintessential success story" she makes it out to be, Heinze erases what Morrison describes as the "genderized, sexualized, wholly racialized world" that impinges upon the daily life of a black woman writer. Such a reinscription of Morrison's life in terms recognizable and acceptable to the dominant society is characteristic of the liberal gesture to "assume away the difference in otherness," maintaining what David Theo Goldberg calls the "dominance of presumed sameness, the universally imposed similarity of identity" (7). Moreover, Heinze projects her own universalizing imperative onto Morrison's work: "While her intent may be to valorize the black community and ignite both blacks and whites into political action, what she also wishes is to elevate through art the beautiful—and hence reclaimable—in the human condition" (4). By focusing on those broad elements of "human nature" that she insists unite all peoples, rather than those identities that divide politically, racially, culturally, or geographically, Heinze elides the complexities of living in a racist society in the name of the transcendental nature of "great art."

However, to argue that Morrison's acceptance by the academy results from the ways in which her novels reinforce dominant values is to lose sight of how institutions—and departments of English are no exception—appropriate "oppositional" works in order to depoliticize them through a process of reification that renders them as works of profound artistic genius. One has only to recognize that Morrison is first and foremost hailed as an "artist." Accordingly, her novels are most often judged according to the formal aesthetic categories that still dominate literary criticism despite the turn toward theory. To the degree that aesthetic standards alone are used to evaluate Morrison's work, her history, her intentions, and her politics become as irrelevant as they are extratextual.

Heinze points out, however, that not only has the literary establishment recognized Morrison's artistry and genius, but also that Morrison has, by virtue of her position as Random House editor and later as Princeton professor, become part of the establishment. To suggest that one is wholly appropriated by an institution as a result of one's affiliation with it seems to be a rather empty charge, the result of a rather gross romanticization of the margins. Though publishing companies and universities hire minority staff—and I offer this without diminishing the influence that such people wield—few seem willing to address institutional fears and resistance to sharing power even in light of their hiring practices.

However, Heinze's assumption that the dominant culture validates only those texts that reflect the prevailing attitudes and values of the status quo vis-à-vis the literary establishment relies on a notion of power that is as repressive and violent as it is totalizing. Power, as Michel Foucault defines it, is productive; it produces forms of domination and forms of resistance. Thus, rather than assume that the white establishment has the power to repress that which does not conform to its values and practices, one might argue that literary establishment cannot make all black people invisible. Morrison's work—so powerful, so popular, and so vitally important to a variety of minority communities—might be a phenomenon that white society must respond to.

If Morrison can "articulate with near impunity two cultures," as Denise Heinze argues, it is simply because, in her view, she has been "immersed in two distinct ways of life." Missing from Heinze's perspective is an understanding of African American culture as a hybrid culture—a culture separate and distinct from both Africa and white America—and an understanding of double consciousness as a third path, what David Levering Lewis calls a "dialectical solution" to the imperatives of nationalism and integration or cultural chauvanism and assimilation (Lewis 1993, 200). Du Boisian double consciousness acknowledges competing African and American systems of value and links such struggle to the formation of a new self, potentially "gifted" with unique insight or potentially "torn asunder." In characteristic eloquence, Du Bois defines double consciousness in the following terms:

> After the Egyptian and Indian, the Greek and Roman, the Teuton and Mongolian, the Negro is a sort of seventh son, born with a veil, and gifted with second-sight in this American world,—a world which yields him no true self-consciousness, but only lets him see himself through the revelation of the other world. It is a peculiar sensation, this double-consciousness, this sense of always looking at one's self through the eyes of others, of measuring one's soul by the tape of a world that looks on in amused contempt and pity. One ever feels his twoness,—an American, a Negro; two souls, two thoughts, two unreconciled strivings; two warring ideals in one dark body, whose dogged strength alone keeps it from being torn asunder. (214–15)

For Heinze, Morrison's insight has little to do with Du Boisian "double vision," with inhabiting an "unusual point of vantage" in order to bear witness to the contradictions inherent in white American society around questions of freedom, justice, and equality. Instead, Heinze articulates double vision as a manifestation of employing "both the black vernacular and Standard English" (7). What Heinze's model of double consciousness lacks is an understanding of double vision as double critique, the capacity to critique one's own cultural values and practices as well as those of the dominant culture. For Du Bois, the unique position of Negroes in America enables them to see the contradictions in white America's commitment to democracy, freedom, and equality. In a thematically linked essay titled "The Souls of White Folk," Du Bois writes:

> Of them [white folk] I am singularly clairvoyant. I see in and through them. I view them from unusual points of vantage. Not as a foreigner do I come, for I am native, not foreign, bone of their thought and flesh of their language. Mine is not the knowledge of the traveler or the colonial composite of dear memories, words and wonder. Nor yet is my knowledge that which servants have of masters, or mass of class, or capitalist of artisan. Rather I see these souls undressed and from the back and side. I see the working of their entrails. This knowledge makes them now embarrassed, now furious! (1921, 29)

In other words, Heinze's model of double consciousness is pathological; in counterdistinction to Du Bois's, it is cast in exclusively negative terms. She writes, "While this *affliction* requires voluntary participation, double-consciousness is a culturally imposed mind-set in which race . . . 'has become a trope of ultimate, irreducible difference' " (1993, 150, italics mine).

As a marker of "irreducible difference," as Henry Louis Gates suggests, the Du Boisian model poses some difficulty for Heinze. The difference imposed by "a world that looks on with amused contempt and pity" diminishes the degree to which such a world views African Americans as representative of the (Euro)American way of life. The problem becomes evident when African American authors are lauded as "great American writers" in ways that serve to erase their ethnic identifications. To confer "greatness" onto particular African Americans is to simultaneously challenge their ethnic authenticity, given what is perceived to be their accommodation to dominant white American culture. Morrison herself recognizes the fraught nature of such "praise": "When they say I'm a great American novelist, I say 'Ha! They're trying to say I'm not black' " (Caldwell 1994, 243).

Moreover, the irreducible difference of double consciousness problematizes the assimilative thrust behind Heinze's attempts to universalize Morrison's thematics. Related to questions of representation, the appeal to Morrison's universal themes can be seen as another way in which the critic sublimates the author's ethnicity as well as the specificity of her critique of white cultural hegemony. Tied to Heinze's universalistic assumptions is the notion that double consciousness is a state that may be "transcended" rather than a set of tensions that, as a result of the persistence of institutionalized racism among other forces, black Americans must perpetually negotiate.

Double Consciousness as Double Critique

Heinze rightfully asserts that Morrison's appeal to white audiences may be that she does not engage in a politics of demonization in which one race is depicted as "inherently good" while the other is "irrevocably corrupt." However, Morrison's rejection of a such simplistic assessments of good and evil results from a conception of morality that is both complex and context specific, and not from the kind of "accommodation" to white society that Heinze argues. Morrison's refusal to engage in any easy kind of moralizing is implicit in her efforts to challenge and transgress the calcified categories that name the lawful and the unlawful, the good and the evil. Morrison pronounces, "My work bears witness and suggests who the outlaws were, who survived and why, what was legal in the community as opposed to what was legal outside of it" (LeClair 1981, 26).

However, Heinze's assertion that Morrison "subordinate[s] the politi-cal" in order to produce "positive black identit[ies]" is unfair (9). Indeed, such an evaluation seems unlikely in light of criticisms leveled at Morrison for the frequently abject portrayals of black men and women in her novels. As Joy James points out, nowhere does Morrison's work argue for a "perfect Black bliss. Everywhere in her literature there exists the reality of the grim, bizarre and determined struggle of communities which embody the rotting and the purifying" (1995, 217). Part of the overtly political thrust of Morrison's work is her attempt to identify and critically evaluate the ways in which identities, both black and white, get produced in relation to what David Theo Goldberg calls "racist culture." Goldberg defines racist culture as constitutive of a whole way of life, the totality of

> ideas, attitudes and dispositions, norms and rules, linguistic, literary, and artist expressions, architectural forms and media representations, practices and institutions. These cultural expressions and objects embed meaning and values that frame articulations, undertakings, and projects, that consti-tute a way of life. . . . It is made up by the totality of created knowledge—in this case, concerning race(s)—and it involves a set of rules or conventions, a logic or grammar of their relation, and a vocabulary of expression and expressibility. (1993, 8)

David Goldberg's description of what constitutes racist culture provides a useful, descriptive index of those forms, practices, and institutions, particularly the "vocabulary of expressions and expressibility" inflected in cultural, literary, and artistic forms that Morrison critiques and reinvents. What I see at the heart of Morrison's artistic and critical work is a concern for language and how it is employed to both maintain and subvert the apparatuses of racist culture. Focusing on the meanings and values inscribed in the "official" language of the dominant culture, Morrison challenges:

> Official language smitheryed to sanction ignorance and preserve privilege is a suit of armor, polished to shocking glitter, a husk from which the knight departed long ago. Yet there it is: dumb, predatory, sentimental. Exciting reverence in schoolchildren, providing shelter for despots, summoning false memories of stability, harmony among the public. (1993, 5)

Official language, statist language, oppressive language—these are the terms Morrison uses to underscore the institutional and systemic ways in which meaning is reworked through language to benefit the powerful while mollifying the powerless. For Morrison, sexist language and racist language are "policing languages of mastery" that "do not permit new knowledge or encourage the mutual exchange of ideas" (1994, 5). Theorizing the limitations imposed on black artists and critics by the "totality of created knowledges" that constitute white American intellectual history, we see the articulations of double consciousness in Morrison herself. Morrison evaluates her position as such:

> My work requires me to think about how free I can be as an African-American woman writer in my gendered, sexualized, wholly racialized world. To think about (and wrestle with) the full implications of my situation leads me to consider what happens when other writers work in a highly and historically racialized society. For them, as for me, imagining is not merely looking at; nor is it taking oneself intact into the other. It is, for purposes of the work, *becoming*. (4)

Morrison's awareness of herself as an African American woman writer in a dominant white society does not induce a psychopathological state often associated with double consciousness, nor a state of transcendence, as Heinze suggests. Though her characters often suffer from the dissonance between their own definition of self and that imposed on them systemically by a white racist society, double consciousness also produces the potential for what Du Bois called a "second sight," a kind of double vision that enables black Americans not only to identify the contradictions inherent in white society's alleged devotion to the principles of equality, freedom, and democracy, but also to formulate creative strategies for survival and resistance. This becomes most evident in the way Morrison frames the interrelated issues of pedagogy and resistance in her novels.

The Bluest Eye

Critical discourse on *The Bluest Eye* has rightly tended to confer central importance to the primer that serves as a preface to Toni Morrison's first novel. The Dick-and-Jane narrative that uniformly introduces schoolchildren to the world of reading unfolds three times in successively diminishing degrees of intelligibility and familiarity. Critic Phyllis Klotman suggests that the nuanced repetitions of the reader parallel the various life styles explored by Morrison either directly or indirectly in the novel. The first version of the narrative, which is clear, accessible, and unmediated, represents the dominant order. The second version, a run-on, represents the lived experience of the MacTeer children. The last version, distorted and chaotic, represents Pecola Breedlove's world. As the novel proper is divided according to the seasons (autumn, winter, spring, summer), the Dick-and-Jane story is also broken down into seven headnotes for the chapters, further juxtaposing the idealized white world with the material experience of the black families portrayed in the chapters. Raymond Hedin sees Morrison's use of the primer as an interpretive key to the novel. "The seven central elements of Jane's world—house, family, cat, Mother, father, dog, and friend—become, in turn, plot elements, but only after they are inverted to fit the realities of Pecola's world" (Hedin 1982, 123). For Michael Awkward, the relationship between the primer and the text reflects Morrison's attempt to explode the bourgeois myth of the ideal family.

These interpretations of the prefatory material in *The Bluest Eye* offer useful and valid ways of approaching Morrison's views of home and family in relation to the dominant articulations of these structures. I want to extend such analyses by focusing on Morrison's efforts to uncover how a young girl *learns* racial self-loathing. In her afterword to the 1993 Penguin edition of *The Bluest Eye*, Morrison asks the crucial questions: "Who told her? Who made her feel it was better to be a freak than what she was?" In her view, the novel rails against "the damaging internalization of assumptions of immutable inferiority originating in an outside gaze" (210). Though the primer may serve as a metaphor for particular notions of home and the family, a more literal reading of the primer suggests another thematic at work—an exploration of the racism implicit in dominant notions of literacy and the hidden curriculum of formal education. A political and cultural tool as well as an educational tool, the primer reflects the ideological imperatives of the dominant white culture and the institutional authority it wields. The imperative of learning Standard English exemplified in Morrison's primer send black schoolchildren the message that the language they bring to the classroom will be neither valued nor tolerated. Modeled after readers popular in the 1940s (the time of the action), Morrison's primer fosters students' first attempt not only to read words but also to read the world in very class- and culturally specific ways. In a 1981 interview with the *New Republic*, Morrison criticized the language practices that black children learn in elementary school: "It's terrible to think that a child with five different present tenses comes to school to be faced with those books that are less than his own language. And then to be told things about his language, which is him, that are sometimes permanently damaging. . . . This is a really cruel fallout of racism" (LeClair 1981, 27).

Rather than respond to the specific needs of black children, Morrison demonstrates in *The Bluest Eye* that traditional forms of literacy ignore the culture, language skills, and issues that inform and dignify their everyday lives. Morrison's primer is a forceful reminder that the dominant culture and its attendant form of literacy do not simply teach the mechanics of reading and writing; as educational theorist Henry Giroux explains, they also teach young children "how to live passively among alienating structures" (Giroux 1983, 227). Like Giroux, Morrison recognizes the Freirian precept that traditional forms of literacy are not simply repressive and alienating, "they also produce among the oppressed identities and subjectivities that reinforce the dominant ideology's view of them as inferior" and are partly responsible for their degraded position in the hierarchies that organize class, gender, and race relations (Giroux 1983, 226). Morrison depicts the tragedy of the learned self-hatred of schoolboys as they flock around Pecola Breedlove, taunting her blackness:

> They had extemporized a verse made up of two insults about matters over which the victim had no control: the color of her skin and speculations on the sleeping habits of an adult, wildly fitting in its incoherence. That they themselves were black, or that their fathers had similarly relaxed habits was irrelevant. It was their contempt for their own blackness that gave the first insults its teeth. They seemed to have taken all of *their smoothly cultivated ignorance, their exquisitely learned self-hatred, their elaborately designed hopelessness* and sucked it all up into a fiery cone of scorn that had burned for ages in the hollows of their minds—cooled—and spilled over lips of outrage, consuming whatever was in its path. (Morrison 1970, 55, italics mine)

With keen insight Morrison identifies the range of responses of schoolchildren to a formal education that redefines their sense of self-resistance to school knowledge in the form of a "smoothly cultivated ignorance," internalization of an "exquisitely learned self-hatred," and acquiescence expressed in an "elaborately designed hopelessness." Thus, Morrison depicts formal education performing the insidious but efficient task of reproducing relations of inequality.

Internalizing the values and ideals of another culture prove most disasterous for Pecola Breedlove. The longing for a school primer family and a Shirley Temple kind of pretty fuels Pecola's desire for blue eyes in front of which people wouldn't "do bad things." Convinced of her own ugliness, an insight powerfully reinforced by her teacher and classmates, Pecola prays for pretty blue eyes that promise love:

> Long hours she sat looking in the mirror, trying to discover the secret of her ugliness, the ugliness that made her ignored or despised at school, by teachers and classmates alike. She was the only member of her class who sat alone at a double desk. . . . Her teachers had always treated her this way. They tried not to glance at her, and called on her only when everyone was required to respond. She knew that when one of the girls at school wanted to be particularly insulting to a boy . . . she could say, 'Bobby loves Pecola Breedlove! Bobby loves Pecola Breedlove!' (39–40)

In this dramatic projection of the double consciousness of African Americans, Morrison reveals the poisonous intersection of institutionalized racism and the process of identity formation. While Pecola exemplifies the perversion of the will and emotions when they are enslaved by the genteel mores of white society, Pecola's case is not representative of all young girls. Morrison makes this clear in the afterword to the novel: "In trying to dramatize the devastation that even casual racial contempt can cause, I chose a unique situation, not a representational one. The extremity of Pecola's case stemmed largely from a crippled and crippling family—unlike the average black family and unlike the narrator's" (Morrison 1993, 210). Contrary to Heinze's view, Morrison's depiction of double consciousness does not necessarily imply a pathological condition, a model all too frequently used to theorize African American identity formation. Double consciousness also provides the conditions for double critique as well as creative resistance in *The Bluest Eye*.

Claudia MacTeer, the nine-year-old narrator, serves as an interesting counterpoint to Pecola. Unlike Pecola, who has no familial or communal support systems to draw on and who internalizes the values of the dominant culture, Claudia attempts to demystify the ideal of white racial beauty by literally deconstructing it. Given a white doll for Christmas, Claudia attempts to locate the source of alleged white physical superiority:

> I had only one desire: to dismember it. To see of what it was made, to discover the dearness, to find the beauty, the desirability that had escaped me, but apparently only me. Adults, older girls, shops, magazines, window signs—all the world had agreed that a blue-eyed, yellow-haired, pink-skinned doll was what every girl treasured. (20)

Of course, the child's investigation is not without its own set of tensions; Claudia becomes aware of a "truly horrifying thing"—her desire to transfer the same impulses to little white girls. However, Claudia's rather sadistic desires are not the impulses that emerge from a "pathological state" of double consciousness. Rather, they reveal the vulnerability, or "woundability," of what Morrison describes in her afterword to *The Bluest Eye* as "the most delicate member of society": the female child. As such, Claudia learns much later to worship the idea of Shirley Temple, knowing as she learned "that the change was adjustment without improvement" (22).

Though Claudia's "adjustment" to a dominant white society seems to harbor pessimism, she also is enriched by the education she has received from the larger black community of which she is a part. Despite her youth, Claudia is able to identify and draw on the folk traditions of her primary community as strategies not only for survival but also for growth and prosperity. Listening to her mother sing the blues, Claudia recognizes the transformative possibilities of pain:

> If my mother was in a singing mood, it wasn't so bad. She would sing about hard times, bad times, and somebody-done-gone-and-left-me times. But her voice was so sweet and her singing-eyes so melty that I found myself longing for those hard times, yearning to be grown without "a thin di-i-ime to my name." I looked forward to the delicious time when "my man" would leave me, when I would "hate to see that evening sun go down . . ." 'cause then I would know "my man has left this town." Misery colored by the greens and blues in my mother's voice took all of the grief out of the words and left me with a conviction that pain was not only endurable, it was sweet. (24)

With all of the romanticism that accompanies inexperience, Claudia perceives the transformative pedagogical potential—what Albert Murray identifies as "antagonistic cooperation"—of the blues tradition, a resource that will provide her with strategies for growing up in a racist and sexist society (Murray 1973, 39). Claudia's appreciation for the blues and irruptions of "funk" also underscores those aspects of the novel that Morrison regards as major characteristics of a distinctive African American literary tradition.

Tar Baby

If *The Bluest Eye* reveals the racism implicit in forms of early education, *Tar Baby* explores the politics of "higher education." The Farmer Brown character in Morrison's appropriation of Joel Chandler Harris's tar-baby tale is Valerian Street, who inhabits a magnificent, plantation-like home on Isle des Chevaliers with his wife, Margaret, their servants, Ondine and Sydney, and their servants' niece, Jadine, who has become Valerian's protégé. The tar-baby figure in Morrison's novel, Jadine, is a "graduate of the Sorbonne . . . an accomplished student of art history . . . an expert on cloisonné . . . An American now living in Paris and Rome, where she had a small but brilliantly executed role in film" (1982, 116). These are the biographical bits Jadine reads to Son, the Brer Rabbit of the narrative, from the magazine with her face on the cover. And true to the tar-baby folktale, Son is bedazzled. As the narrative unfolds, Son becomes increasingly entangled in the product of a white man's "beneficence." Simultaneously attracted and repulsed by the "exotic Other," Jadine cannot locate Son outside of the catalog of stereo-types about blackness she internalized as part of the process of becoming "educated." She stares transfixed by the mirror reflection of Son's hair behind her "like bundles of long whips or lashes that could grab her and beat her to jelly. And would. Wild, aggressive, vicious hair that needed to be put in jail. Uncivilized, reform-school hair. Mau-Mau, Attica, chain-gang hair" (113). The initial confrontation in Jadine's bedroom foreshadows the ultimate failure of the relationship that develops between Jadine and Son.

That Jadine fails to know Son as a result of the racism perpetuated by the Eurocentric education she has received in a traditional, white institution illustrates Morrison's impatience with dominant notions of what it means to be "culturally literate." Craig Werner argues that by associating Son with "spaces, mountains, savannahs," Jadine endorses the white, Eurocentric logic that links blackness with absence (163). Even Jadine on occasion suspects the value of her elite education: "Too many art history courses, she thought, had made her not perceptive but simple-minded. She saw planes and angles and missed character" (158). Though it is difficult to be sympathetic toward Jadine, who abdicates her responsibility for the aunt and uncle who raised her and rejects black communities in general, Morrison underscores the high price Jadine paid for the material benefits and privileges of the white world she chose not only in terms of her diminished sense of self but also in forfeit-ing "the man who fucked like a star" (292). Speaking of the novel and the cen-trality of the cultural, as opposed to gendered, battle between the two lovers, Toni Morrison comments: "Racism hurts in a very personal way. Because of it, people do all sorts of things in their personal lives and love relationships based on differences in values and class and education and their conception of what it means to be Black in this society" (Wilson 1981, 133).

Contrary to some critics' assumptions, Morrison does not dismiss the importance of higher education. Rather, Morrison insists on a crucial dis-tinction between the education that most black people receive in school and the education that they receive at home, and her work details the ways in which black people's survival depends upon the former not canceling out the latter. Drawing from her own experience, Morrison comments, "There's a difference between the education you get in school and the one you get in the home. I spent years preferring the school's education to the education in the home and then coming back to it and thinking, 'Oh, they're not so stupid, after all.' And in my work they have been the storyteller" (Epstein 1986, 4).

In many ways Margaret and Valerian's absent son, Michael, serves as an interesting foil to Jadine. Valerian describes Michael, a student at Berkeley and the product of a kind of liberal humanist education, as "a purveyor of exotics, a typical anthropologist, a cultural orphan who sought other cultures he could love without risk or pain." (145). It is Michael who challenges Jadine for her decision to study art history at "that snotty school" and for "abandoning [her] history" and "[her] people" (72). In defense of her Sorbonne education, Jadine informs Valerian: " 'Picasso is better than an Itumba mask. The fact that he was intrigued by them is proof of his genius, not the mask-makers.' I wish it weren't so, but . . ." (74). As critic Eleanor Traylor attests, Jadine "has been taught in school what *real* culture is." She is "assured and confident of the fruits of her assumption, her choices, her way of life, and her successes" (Traylor 1988, 141).

Jadine is content in the life choices she has made until an African woman in a canary yellow dress and eggs in hand shatters her confidence by making her feel inauthentic. Jadine's feelings of deep insecurity return with her visit to Son's home, an all-black community in Florida called Eloe. There Jadine is haunted by the images of black women who parade through her dreams. Jadine's hatred of Eloe, Brer Rabbit's briar patch, is symbolic of her rejection of her own African American cultural roots. Jadine "needed air, and taxicabs and conversation in a language she understood. She didn't want to have any more discussions in which the silences meant more than the words did" (Morrison 1982, 259). Jadine's reaction to Eloe is uncannily prophesied by Carter Woodson in *The Mis-Education of the Negro*: "The 'educated Negroes' have the attitude of contempt toward their own people because in their own as well as in their mixed schools Negroes are taught to admire the Hebrew, the Greek, the Latin and the Teuton and to despite the African" (Woodson 1990, 1).

Having agreed to leave Eloe, Son attempts to live in New York City on Jadine's terms, but the concession proves to be too great. Frustrated by what Jadine doesn't know, and the lie of what she does know about him and herself, Son holds her out of their apartment window by her wrists shouting,

> The truth is that whatever you learned in those colleges that didn't include me ain't shit. What did they teach you about me? What tests did they give?

Did they tell you what I was like, did they tell you what was on my mind? Did they describe me to you? Did they tell you what was in my heart? If they didn't teach you that, they didn't teach you nothing, because until you know about me, you don't know nothing about yourself. And you don't know anything, anything about your children and anything at all about your mama and your papa. You find out about *me*, you educated nitwit! (264–65)

Here Morrison provides through Son another way of thinking about what it means to be educated. Challenging the politically mandated absence of discussions of race and the more problematic presences of what Morrison calls Africanism—"the connotative and denotative blackness that African people have come to signify as well as the entire range of views, assumptions, readings and misreadings that accompany Eurocentric learning about these people"—that circulate within the various disciplines in the academy, Morrison insists on the importance of one's roots and one's ancestors (1993, 6–7).

By revealing how knowledge and identities are produced both in educational institutions and in nontraditional sites of learning, Morrison opens up the possibility for a new conception of identity. According to this perspective, identities are constructed, told, spoken rather than simply found. Gideon warns Son, "Yallas [referring to Jadine's light complexion] don't come to being black natural-like. *They have to choose it*, and most don't choose it" (155, italics mine). Emphasizing the instability of black identity psychically, politically, and culturally, Morrison expands the possibilities of critical agency, as bell hooks explains:

Recent critical reflections on static notions of identity urge transformation of our sense of who we can be and still be black. Assimilation, imitation, or assuming the role of the exotic other are not the only available options and never have been. This is why it is crucial to radically revise notions of identity politics, to explore marginal locations as spaces where we can best become whatever we want to be while remaining committed to liberatory black liberation struggle (hooks 1989, 20).

Beloved

Toni Morrison's preoccupation with the relationship between education and identity formation informs her depiction of schoolteacher in the 1987 novel *Beloved*. Having "broke into children what Garner raised into men," schoolteacher was the central reason for the escape that Sethe and the Sweet Home men plotted. Taking notes in the ink Sethe made him while his nephews stole the milk from her breasts, schoolteacher was also the reason that neither Sethe nor her children would return to slavery. The appearance of schoolteacher at 124 Bluestone Road drove Sethe to take the life of her baby girl with a rusty saw, left Baby Suggs holy, bedridden, and waiting to die, and sentenced Denver to eighteen years of isolation with her mother.

Schoolteacher does not only "break" slaves in his efforts to "reeducate" them, but he also teaches his white students the power of domination and its moral justification in Enlightenment rationality and the alleged "neutrality" of racist science. One of schoolteacher's lessons was overheard by Sethe, the subject of a schoolboy's assignment:

> He was talking to his pupils and I heard him say, "Which one are you doing?" And one of the boys said, "Sethe." . . . Schoolteacher was standing over one of them with one hand behind his back. He licked a forefinger a couple of times and turned a few pages. Slow. I was about to turn around . . . when I heard him say, "No, no. That's not the way. I told you to put her human characteristics on the left; her animal ones on the right. And don't forget to line them up." (193)

Like the whipping that schoolteacher gave to Sethe to teach her to be silent, the violence of his pedagogy is again played out on her body: "When I bumped up against the tree my scalp was prickly. . . . My head itched like the devil. Like somebody was sticking needles into my scalp" (193). Morrison provides us with an illustration of the awesome materiality of language and ideology. Schoolteacher's words translate into immediate physical effects.

According to David Goldberg, the process of classification that informs schoolteacher's pedagogy is central to scientific methodology and the epistemological drive to place phenomena in categories. Making the crucial connection between rational scientific discourse and the Enlightenment project of mastery, Goldberg argues that the effect of scientific neutrality, objectivity, and truth was the production of "subjectless bodies" as well as the moral justification for their transformation into "bodies of subjection." He explains:

> The neutrality and objectifying distantiation of the rational scientist created the theoretical space for a view to develop of subjectless bodies. Once objectified, these bodies could be analyzed, categorized, classified, and ordered with the cold gaze of scientific distance. . . . The full weight of eighteenth century science and rationality, philosophy, aesthetics and religion thus merged to circumscribe European representations of others. This reduction of human subjects to abstract bodies had the implication of

enabling their subjection to the cold scientific stare and economic exploitation of Europeans and their descendants. Subjectless bodies were thus dramatically transformed into bodies of subjection. (Goldberg 1993, 50)

Through schoolteacher's pedagogy, Morrison demonstrates the ways in
which the methodologies, classifications, definitions, and discourses of
science and history are played out on the bodies of the black men and
woman. Language in this scenario is neither arbitrary nor objective; it is the
very mechanism of power and authority. When Sixo, one of the Sweet
Home men, attempts to rationalize an act of theft, Morrison writes, "Clever,
but schoolteacher beat him anyway to show him that definitions belongs to
the definers—not the defined" (1987, 190). The "cold gaze of scientific distance" is part of what Raymond Williams once called the "culture of distance," an apparatus that sanctions the worst forms of material and
symbolic violence in the name of objectivity and truth.

Morrison further dramatizes the violence of the oppressor's language in
the critical disjunction between official versions of white male history and
the "dangerous memories" of the slave narrative by recounting the murder
of Sethe's children from the perspectives of the schoolteacher and the sheriff and from Sethe herself. From schoolteacher's perspective, Sethe had
"gone wild, due to the mishandling of the nephew" (149):

> Inside [the woodshed], the two boys bled in the sawdust and dirt at the
> feet of a nigger woman holding a blood-soaked child to her chest with one
> hand and an infant by the heels in the other. She did not look at them; she
> simply swung the baby toward the wall planks, missed and tried to con-
> nect a second time. . . . Right off it was clear, to schoolteacher especially,
> that there was nothing here to claim. The three (now four—because she'd
> had the one coming when she cut) pickaninnies they had hoped were alive
> and well enough to take back to Kentucky, take back and raise properly to
> do the work Sweet Home desperately needed, were not. . . . He could
> claim the baby in the arms of the mewing old man, but who'd tend her?
> Because the woman—something was wrong with her. She was looking at
> him now, and if his other nephew could see that look he would learn the
> lesson for sure: you just can't mishandle creatures and expect success.
> (149–50)

The sheriff interprets these events as "the result of a little so-called freedom
imposed on a people who needed every care and guidance in the world to
keep them from the cannibal life they preferred" (151). Against the official
"objective" portrayal of the ethnographic observer or the historian that

schoolteacher seems to represent and the interpretation of the law, Sethe explains her actions based on the logic of "motherlove:"

> The truth was . . . [s]imple: she was squatting in the garden and when she saw them coming and recognized schoolteacher's hat, she heard wings. Little hummingbirds stuck their needle beaks right through her headcloth into her hair and beat their wings. And if she thought anything, it was No. No. Nonono. Simple. She just flew. Collected every bit of life she had made, all the parts of her that were precious and fine and beautiful, and carried, pushed, dragged them through the veil, out, away, over there where no one could hurt them. (163)

The image of hummingbird beaks stuck through Sethe's headcloth suggests a metaphorical connection to the moment when Sethe overhears schoolteacher instructing his student to put Sethe's "human characteristics on the left; her animal ones on the right." Linking the two scenes is crucial in terms of demonstrating the material effects of schoolteacher's pedagogy as well as his moral culpability in the tragedy that unfolded before him. In combatting the dominant metaphors of the master's narrative—wildness, animality, cannibalism, amorality, and brutality—Sethe "creates a counternarrative that reconstitutes her humanity and demonstrates the requirements of motherlove" (Henderson 1991, 79). Sethe not only effectively changes the plot and meaning of her story, but she also undermines the legitimating discourses of racial oppression—scientific rationality and Enlightened morality.

Moreover, Morrison reveals how the construction of white subjectivity as inherently rational and moral is dependent on the construction of blackness as a negation of these principles. Stamp Paid asserts: "Whitepeople believed that whatever the manners, under every dark skin was a jungle. . . . But it wasn't the jungle that blacks brought with them. . . . It was the jungle whitefolks planted in them. . . . The screaming baboon lived under their own white skin; the red gums were their own" (Morrison 1987, 198–99). In this way, Morrison constructs a pedagogy based not only on the imperatives of self-definition, but also on making whiteness visible as a cultural and political category. Hazel Carby suggests that

> one way to rethink the relationship between the social, political, and cultural construction of blackness and marginality, on the one hand, and assumptions of a normative whiteness within the dominant culture, on the other, is to examine the ways in which that dominant culture has been shaped and transformed by the presence of the marginalized. This means a public recognition that the process of marginalization itself is central to the

formation of the dominant culture. The first and very important stage is . . .
to recognize the cultural and political category of whiteness. It seems obvious to say it but in practice the racialization of our social order is only recognized in relation to racialized "others." (1989, 39)

In revealing the dependence of schoolteacher's knowledge on the presence
of a silent and abiding black population, Morrison shifts the discussion of
difference away from an exclusive preoccupation with the margins, suggesting further that "any analysis of racial identity must include an analysis of
how the dominant Other functions to actively and systematically conceal its
own historical and cultural identity while devaluing the identity of other
racial groups" (Giroux 1992, 127).

Conclusion

Representative of the more defensive responses to Toni Morrison's treatment of larger social practices and institutions, Cynthia Edelberg's position
polarizes Morrison's critical views on dominant forms of education by suggesting that she rejects formal education outright. She comments,

> Morrison posits a kind of primitivism as an answer, as something that coun-
> ters education and work, but primitivism is rhetorical rather than convinc-
> ing. . . . Morrison's values are reduced to wishful thinking. To put it another
> way, she implies that "ancient properties" are better than education and the
> work ethic, but dramatically shows us they are not. (cited in Heinze 1993, 103)

Rather than take seriously Morrison's claims about the ideological nature of
language and literacy, truth and knowledge, Edelberg dismisses Morrison's
critique as "primitivist." Assuming her argument is not meant to carry the
overtly racist connotations of the label "primitive," Edelberg nonetheless
rewrites Morrison's political project as a failed aesthetic, "unconvincing"
and "primitivist."

Contrary to Edelberg and others, I have argued that Toni Morrison's fiction and criticism have much to teach educators and cultural workers about
the deeply political nature of the work they do. In her novels, Morrison not
only engages the process of being that Du Bois called double consciousness,
but also addresses how identities get shaped in relation to a variety of public
spheres: in schools, in higher education, in the mass media, in church—in all
those places where knowledge is produced and deployed pedagogically.
Morrison does not reject educational institutions as much as she is critical of
those rules, practices, and pedagogies that reinforce a culture of domina-

tion. Rather, Morrison offers a counterpedagogy reminiscent of Carter Woodson's proposition: "The education of any people should begin with the people themselves."

References

Awkward, Michael. "The Evil of Fulfillment: Scapegoating and Narration in *The Bluest Eye*." In *Toni Morrison: Critical Perspectives Past and Present*, ed. Henry Louis Gates Jr. and K. A. Appiah. New York: Amistad, 1993

Bell, Bernard W. *The Afro-American Novel and Its Tradition*. Amherst: University of Massachusetts Press, 1987.

Boynton, Robert S. "The New Intellectuals," *Atlantic Monthly*, March 1995, 53–70.

Brenkman, John. "Race Publics: Civic Illiberalism, or Race After Reagan." *Transition* 5:2 (1995): 4–36.

Caldwell, Gail. "Author Toni Morrison Discusses Her Latest Novel *Beloved*." In *Conversations with Toni Morrison*, ed. Danille Taylor-Guthrie. Jackson: University Press Mississippi, 1994, 239–45.

Carby, Hazel. "The Canon: Civil War and Reconstruction." *Michigan Quarterly Review* 28:1 (Winter 1989).

Du Bois, William E.B. *The Education of Black People: Ten Critiques, 1905–1960*, ed. Herbert Aptheker. New York: Monthly Press, 1973

———. *The Souls of Black Folk*. In *Three Negro Classics*. New York: Avon, 1965.

———. *Darkwater: Voices from within the Veil*. New York: Harcourt, 1921.

Epstein, Grace. "An Interview with Toni Morrison." *Ohio Journal* 9:3 (1986): 3–8.

Giroux, Henry A. *Border Crossing: Cultural Workers and the Politics of Education*. New York: Routledge, 1992.

———. *Theory and Resistance in Education*. South Hadley, MA: Bergin and Garvey, 1983.

Goldberg, David Theo. *Racist Culture: Philosophy and the Politics of Meaning*. Oxford: Blackwell, 1993.

Hedin, Raymond. "The Structuring of Emotion in Black American Fiction." *Novel* 161:1 (1982): 123.

Heinze, Denise. *The Dilemma of "Double-Consciousness": Toni Morrison's Novels*. Athens: University of Georgia Press, 1993.

Henderson, Mae G. "Toni Morrison's *Beloved*: Re-membering the Body as Historical Text." In *Comparative American Identities: Race, Sex, and Nationality in the Modern Text*, ed. Hortense J. Spillers. New York: Routledge, 1991, 62–86.

hooks, bell. *Yearning*. Toronto: Between the lines, 1990.

James, Joy. "Politicizing the Spirit: 'African Americanisms' and African Ancestors in the Essays of Toni Morrison." *Cultural Studies* 9:2 (1995): 210–25.

Klotman, Phyllis. "Dick-and-Jane and the Shirley Temple Sensibility in *The Bluest Eye*." *Black American Literature Forum* 13:4 (1979).

LeClair, Thomas. "The Language Must Not Sweat: A Conversation with Toni Morrison."*New Republic*, 21 March 1981, 25–29.

Lewis, David Levering. *W.E.B. Du Bois: Biography of a Race 1868–1919*. New York: Holt, 1993.

Morrison, Toni. "The 1993 Nobel Prize in Literature: Toni Morrison." In *Dictionary of Literary Biography*, ed. James W. Hipp. Detroit: Gale, 1994, 3–8.

————. *Playing in the Dark: Whiteness and the Literary Imagination*. Cambridge: Harvard University Press, 1992.

————. "Unspeakable Things Unspoken: The Afro-American Presence in American Literature." *Michigan Quarterly Review* 28:1 (1989): 1–34.

————. *Beloved*. New York: Plume, 1987.

————. *Tar Baby*. New York: Plume, 1982.

————. *The Bluest Eye*. New York: Washington, 1970.

Murray, Albert. *The Hero and the Blues*. Columbia: University of Missouri Press, 1973.

Traylor, Eleanor W. "The Fabulous World of Toni Morrison: *Tar Baby*." In *Critical Essays on Toni Morrison*, ed. Nellie Y. McKay. Boston: Hall, 1988, 135–49.

Werner, Craig H. "The Briar Patch as Modernist Myth: Morrison, Barthes and Tar Baby As-Is." In *Critical Essays on Toni Morrison*, ed. Nellie Y. McKay. Boston: Hall, 1988, 150–67.

Wilson, Judith. "A Conversation with Toni Morrison." *Essence*, July 1981.

Woodson, Carter G. *The Mis-Education of the Negro*. Nashville: Winston-Derek, 1990 (rpt. 1933).

The Marketplace and the Politics of Inequality

12

A Different Perspective
on Educational Inequality

Stanley Aronowitz

In *There Are No Children Here*, a recent television movie based on Alex Kotlowitz's book, Oprah Winfrey plays a single mother of eight children who live together, on welfare, in a Chicago-area public-housing project.

The project is a dangerous place where the major preoccupation of kids is to escape being shot and where older men offer boys the chance to earn a quick buck doing illegal things. Early in the story, the character played by Winfrey is barred from welfare benefits when officials discover that her estranged husband has claimed child support as a tax deduction. The remainder of the two-hour movie is a diatribe against absent (black) fathers, naming them as crucial agents in the disintegration of the black family and the consequent economic, moral, and life-threatening disasters of segregated ghetto life.

The TV film is, at the same time, a ringing endorsement of schooling as the path out of the calumnies and dangers of impoverished urban communities. Winfrey's two older boys have renounced education for a life of street crime: one goes to jail, and the other leaves his family for the familial protection of a local mobster. But, in the final scenes, the mother's younger kids are planted on the road to success by their outstanding school performances. And the absent father seems to wake up to his own dereliction, even making a feeble attempt to save his son from the grip of evil.

In the United States, we seem to be permanently wedded to the idea that the credentializing system of public and private education is the primary vehicle through which any student, regardless of race, class, gender, or even physical handicap, may succeed in achieving professional or technical status. If not the great leveler, as Lawrence Cremin claims,[1] schools embody, for most Americans, perhaps more than other institutions, the fulfillment of the promise of equality of opportunity. The key institutional variables, according to this common sense, are the extent of public money for schools, the rigor and relevance of the curriculum, and the pertinence and expertise of pedagogy. Tacitly, the underlying assumption of this scenario is that, in the wake of the massive disappearance of production, service jobs are plentiful for the professionally and technically trained, credentialized worker.

Until the 1980s, most educational debates turned on which of these factors was the most important for fulfilling the promise of equal opportunity for working-class and poor kids. "Modern" liberals insisted that student performance—the key variable in occupational mobility—was crucially and causally linked to unequal access of urban schools to resources, both institutional and financial, at least in comparison to private and suburban schools. These schools were often rewarded for their affluence by state laws that allocated money on the basis of enrollment and attendance. Moreover, private and suburban public schools are able to draw money and services from their middle- and upper-class parent organizations. In contrast to most urban schools, in which the voluntarist tradition is typically weak, private and suburban schools can, even with budget cuts and the expansion of women in the paid labor force, count on parents to tutor students in math and reading, attend trips, raise money, and perform a myriad of other unpaid tasks.

Needless to say, the resource imbalance was exacerbated by state fiscal crises that cut deeply into school funds in the 1970s. Conservative educators who rode the tide of the Reagan revolution argued, "You can't solve school problems by throwing money at them." This truism conveniently jibed with the traditional conservative antipathy to social spending and, particularly, to federal support for education. Consequently, in the 1980s, the education debate nearly abandoned funding considerations as the very concept of a federal education policy came under attack.

The superiority of private schools is considered a force of nature, not only because of the profit motive for their proprietors, but also because of their reliance on voluntarism. In turn, even in the wake of a Democratic national administration, the doctrine of privatization shows few signs of abating. Under prodding from the Heritage Foundation, right-wing intellectuals such as Chester Finn, and neo-liberals,[2] curriculum issues partially displaced other considerations. The educational Right demanded a new focus on the three Rs, reinvigorated the almost discredited phonics technology for teaching reading and mounted what, by the mid-1980s, seemed an inexorable campaign to reintroduce "values" into the elementary and secondary curricula, not the least of which were those of work, family, and patriotism.

For the elite, the conservatives insisted on the revitalization of the liberal arts on the premise that, under the sign of antitraditionalism, the 1960s had brought havoc to the curriculum and had resulted in an undereducated middle class. On the cultural front—which spilled over into education—high culture made a roaring comeback. The National Endowment for the Arts and National Endowment for the Humanities were captured by the ideological Right during the Bush administration and, with the Mapplethorpe affair, made clear that some of the crucial innovations of the artistic avant-garde no longer had a place in the pantheon of federal support for the arts, which, in any case, came under sharp attack from critics such as U.S. Senator Jesse Helms.[3]

In the late 1980s the three Rs doctrine was supplemented by a renewed call to focus on the western intellectual tradition, at least in suburban high schools, private colleges, and universities. By contrast, conservative educators and policymakers argued that the tonic for the failed urban public schools was to tie education more closely to the labor market than ever before. For the vast majority, education should be transformed into training in marketable skills. Consequently, corporations should be recruited to sponsor schools and, in the bargain, advise them as to just what marketable skills would be needed by the twenty-first-century economy. The effect of this conservative policy was to widen the *class gap* in education.

But at the beginning of the 1990s the curriculum struggle took an unexpected turn. Having been largely defeated on the fiscal battleground, the educational Left (as distinct from the ideological Left) counterpunched in two directions. First it introduced the "multicultural curriculum," an attempt to broaden the canon to include women and African American and Latino cultures. Accordingly, what may be described as "excluded" literature, history, and popular forms were to be integrated into the canon or, in some perspectives, to replace it. This effort raised the traditional question of high versus low culture, but especially the relative virtues of teaching "universal" western values and culture associated with the work of "dead white men" and what became known as the educational expression of identity politics. Latinos and African Americans posed a new concept—cultural citizenship—against the nationalism of the prevailing political climate and were able to win significant victories, if not complete hegemony. At the same time, conservative attacks against "political correctness" reached a point of near frenzy as the Bush administration came to a close.[4]

The success of multiculturalism, cultural studies, and other movements of the new pluralism may be measured by Irving Kristol's rueful admission that the alliance of conservatives and liberals that had been forged to bring the academy in line with the collapse of communism had, at least at the cultural level, lost.[5] Needless to say, his white flag notwithstanding, the battle goes on: former Reagan speechwriter Pat Buchanan has formed a new group to wage the holy war against the cultural radicals, and a new mood of retrenchment has taken hold within universities, expressed, sometimes, as fiscal restraint. More directly repressive expressions have also emerged, such as the attempt by the University of Minnesota's administration to dissolve its Department of the Humanities and the new assault on the liberal arts that pervades many state colleges and universities, such as the California State University system and New York's City University. Perhaps more sensational have been the budget reductions in the once unassailable University of California system, cutbacks that are likely to result in more restricted opportunities for minority students.

Take the following information as a basis for discussion. Only 50 percent of students entering high school remain to graduate. In some New York, Chicago, and Los Angeles high schools, only about 20 percent graduate; in the middle-class suburbs the range is between 75 and 80 percent. What accounts for the discrepancy?[6]

Many contend that the school performance of kids of color, girls and young women, and, more recently, openly gay and lesbian students is crucially determined by their perception that mastery of school knowledge entails self-estrangement. Consequently, apart from the intrinsic educational value of a broadly based learning regime, one of the essential claims of some who advocate a large-scale effort to amend the established curriculum to include traditionally excluded cultures is that equality of opportunity cannot be fulfilled unless the student can see her/himself in the curriculum. The question before us is whether students "fail" because the curriculum does not engage their perceived needs and interests.

The second trend has been in the relatively neglected area of pedagogy. Movements for educational reform at the local level aimed at arresting or reversing perceived school "failure" have gained new strength as a result of Chicago's massive experiment in school-based management, New York's New Visions initiative, and the spread of elementary education innovations such as "writing across the curriculum," decentralized classrooms, and curricular innovations that place new emphasis on teaching cultural and sexual difference. The basic argument of the new pedagogy is that the interaction of kids and the classroom is the heart of the learning process; following Paulo Freire and other pedagogic theorists, the prevailing conception of knowledge as a bank that saves valuables and dispenses capital to its borrowers is a primary cause of student turnoff.[7] Contrawise, it is claimed, an *interactive* classroom in which students produce their own knowledge and, *mutis mutandis*, their learning, may reverse the trend of large dropout rates among many city kids, especially from high school. We are still in the midst of this controversy. In this education regime, the teacher is primarily engaged in dialogue with students and their culture rather than acting as a transmitter of the prevailing tradition. Of course, in the most intellectually rigorous versions of this pedagogy, the term *dialogue* presupposes that the teacher is actively engaged in the process and has something of significance to say. But he or she is also a keen listener and is prepared to learn from students.

Educational conservatives, who include a considerable chunk of modern liberals, insist that the multiculturalists are imposing politically "correct" curricular criteria, while those who favor the curriculum of inclusion insist that the old universal curriculum privileged a specific version of the European cultural tradition, seeing it as universal truth or at least identical with civilization *as such*. This tradition was forged in its victory over what became subordinated cultures.[8] Having defeated them, it retroactively excluded them. Interestingly, education innovators include among their number some who would otherwise consider themselves free marketeers. For the hallmark of some curriculum reform is the goal of encouraging the individuality of the student by offering choices to replace the standard approach that places responsibility upon the school and the teacher to deliver a body of inherited knowledge for which students are also accountable.

Whereas in the late 1960s and early 1970s the critique emanated from the Left, it has passed decisively to the Right. In recent years, the religious Right and other conservatives have consistently interrogated the standard curriculum. In the wake of the fundamentalist attack against the exclusive focus of the biology curriculum on genetics and evolution, and conservative critiques of the alleged "leftward" drift of social studies textbooks—some have presented race, gender, equality, and peace issues in a favorable light— liberals have found themselves, paradoxically, as in the abortion debate, in the stance of defenders of the status quo. Thus, the task of deconstructing and otherwise interrogating school knowledge from the Left has fallen on hard times. Apart from the multicultural curriculum, the "Left" has had almost nothing to say about the nature and the direction of school knowledge.

From the perspective of the school counselor, psychologist, or social worker, as well as a large segment of the administration, the task in city schools is to find the keys to "motivating" the learner to master the essentials of the curriculum. Most conventional educators who accept neither the contentions of various school reformers nor biological explanations for student failure such as race and its twin, intelligence, believe that, given a relatively level playing field in purely educational terms, the problem of succeeding rests squarely on the learner. In this view, which remains the dominant one, the fundamental thesis of the conservatives that the culture of poverty—chiefly the absence among poor people of strong families and the work ethic—explains the inability of poor children to master school knowledge.

Tacitly, this explanation has already linked school knowledge to a style of life associated with the job culture. It presupposes what needs to be explored: Are we still ensconced in the industrializing era that designates paid work as the marker of self-worth and social dignity? For, if the job culture proves to have been a historically situated way of measuring value, then the ethical basis of contemporary life requires re-examination and, with it, the goals and purposes of schools.

The distinctly social and economic orientation of school reform movements in the 1960s considered educational performance less a straightforward measure of individual talent, initiative, or imagination, and more the outcome of a complex of individual and environmental determinants such as the degree to which children and their families had a measure of economic security or were subject to the relentless degradations of systemic racism and sexism. Contrary to such considerations, the resurgence of individual psychology coupled with a new version of the culture of poverty thesis to account for educational performance is surely distressing. What unites new proposals for school reform—whether focusing on curriculum, pedagogy, or school funding—is a rather tired version of autonomous individualism and an unwavering commitment to the American dream.

In the context of education, the dream may be described as a tacit understanding that no long-term economic barriers to class mobility exist because the U.S. economy is sufficiently supple to weather various storms. Put bluntly, education policy assumes long-term, job-producing economic growth as a given. Therefore the crucial issue is *opportunity* structure, of which access to education is a central component.[9] On this assumption, racism and other forms of discrimination, bad school organization, arcane curriculum and pedagogy, and the unfortunate results of intergenerational poverty are seen as formidable obstacles preventing individual kids from doing well in school. But the proposal that the social structure of U.S. society is a zero-sum game is simply not entertained by educators, legislators, or almost anyone else—except many high school students.

To account for the high, even alarming dropout rates among African American, Latino, Asian, Italian, and, indeed, most working-class youth requires at least three kinds of analysis: historical, contemporary economic, and educational; all are issues that bear on schooling itself as a discourse.

Historical

Before the advent of compulsory public schooling and its enforcement by the turn of the twentieth century, relatively few children of working-class families completed or expected to complete high school, much less go on to post-secondary schools of various sorts. During the industrializing era of American capitalism, which spanned the century after the Civil War, most working-class kids got working-class jobs in factories, in transportation, and, after World War I, in manual, clerical, and sales jobs in retail and wholesale services. Many dropped out of school at the legal minimum age, but were often considered delinquent well before then. With a factory job waiting, most teenagers could scarcely tolerate eight years let alone twelve years of schooling. Since all but the most skilled industrial work required little or no knowledge of reading, writing, and calculation, working-class kids—black and white—typically resented compulsory schooling; with the usual exceptions, they correctly perceived these years as a form of detention.[10]

For these kids, white as well as black, schooling was a life chore one *endured*, but few expected to learn much or to enter careers that might be opened up by acquiring cultural capital. Paul Willis's superb description of how working-class kids "fail" school in Britain pertains today for a very large segment of working-class kids of color, but also for many who are coded as "white," especially students of Appalachian, southern European, and eastern European heritage.[11] Willis's ethnographic investigation discovered that what is coded as school "failure" is actually resistance by kids to the authority of school knowledge, the administration, and teachers. Although their rejection of the curriculum condemns them to working-class existence, many view the price of rising above their class as too high for the promised rewards. Though industrial labor may not always be pleasant, it was, until recently, fairly well paid—at least compared to many subprofessional jobs such as teaching, social work, and nursing—and strong unions provided protection against arbitrary discharge and the unfair exercise of managerial prerogatives against labor.

More to the point, mastering school knowledge almost invariably entails leaving family and community; the world of relatives and close peer relationships must be surrendered, even renounced, in a favor of the new world of professionalism. As a professional, the kid becomes a different kind of social individual; he must dress differently, consort with new people, and observe an entirely new set of rules. Few working-class girls are even afforded the option of escaping their fate of the double shift: housework and paid work. In contrast, for kids reared in middle-class homes, the transitions between family, school, and work are fairly seamless during an era when work defines the self. However strict the parental upbringing, the "modern" family within the ranks of professionals and managers typically fosters the autonomous development of the child; family resources provide the basis for a wider range of choices at an earlier age than are available to working-class kids. Although school remains, for many, a ritual performance, as Peter McLaren has forcefully argued,[12] the student is prepared to endure its boredom and the rote learning required for the acquisition of cultural capital.[13] For the goal of professional status helps the middle-class student endure the regimentation that marks everyday school life, regardless of how innovative the curriculum may be. The promise of becoming a doctor, lawyer, or computer programmer provides a rational basis for adapting to what may be perceived, at the student's level of experience, as knowledge abstracted from her contemporary concerns. In short, for the middle-class kid, the experience of schooling may or may not be better than it is for working-class kids. What matters is: Schooling for what?

In the wake of urbanization and industrialization, some school reformers sought to attract children of working-class backgrounds to school knowledge by measures that democratized the classroom; this is, provided spaces for kids to *participate* in the production of their own knowledge. John Dewey and his associates provided a theoretical framework for this strategy by insisting on the ineluctable link between cognition and practice.[14] Dewey did not argue that people "learn by doing"; rather, his central claim is that practical concerns provide the context for theoretical reflection because, for him, theory is generalized practice. Dewey, George Herbert Mead, and later Harold Rugg, William Kilpatrick, and others developed curricula, advanced new pedagogic notions, and proposed a major shift in the architecture of the classroom to reflect a child-centered, rather than teacher- or curriculum-centered, learning environment. The object of all this was not to assist students in obtaining the credentials necessary for professional and technical jobs; Dewey's aim was to transform public education into sites for citizenship, to prepare students to take possession of the political, if not the economic, system. For Dewey and his associates, keeping immigrant and migrant urban kids in schools had broad social aims, not vocational aims. In fact, Dewey's concept of occupational education was that learning practical skills such as gardening were better routes than purely book learning to acquiring a theoretical knowledge of biology. Contrary to popular myth, he did not advocate the vocationalization of schooling.[15]

Of course, the fundamental function and the goals of schooling have been in contention for as long as education has been universal. Recall that many public school advocates, especially in the middle of the nineteenth century, preferred schools to child labor or day prisons as a way of dealing with the roving gangs of children and teenagers who roamed and pillaged every important city and town.[16] In this mode, schools are conceived as *aging vats* when not constituted as training sites to provide the discipline required by the social order, including, but not limited to, the labor market. Others wanted a much more dedicated vocational curriculum for most working-class students. This objective is embodied in trade high schools, but also commercial tracks and the whole concept of "home" work, the imposition of a regimen according to which the school day extends from classroom to the home.

In the context of these debates at the turn of the twentieth century, Dewey's ideas were little short of revolutionary, because his whole aim was to provide a positive philosophy and series of goals and strategies for school knowledge that addressed the problems of industrial society by reference to democratic, not market or juridical, considerations. Schools would address social disorder by preparing students, whatever their occupation or socioeconomic station, to address the new problems of modernity: science and technology, mass culture, the massification of politics and the consequent subversion of democratic processes. For Dewey, the labor movement, not schools, was the best vehicle to deal with the economic problems of working-class kids. The role of schools was to foster knowledge that could be used fruitfully in dealing with a panoply of life problems, of which work was only one. And the goal of education was certainly not identical with the specific needs of the labor market. Until well into the 1960s Dewey's ideas, although never dominant among educators, succeeded in creating a vocabulary according to which the student was the normative subject of education.

Economic

Two massive developments conspired to turn the attention of schools from some version of this social mission to close identification with labor market outcomes. The first was the GI Bill of Rights, which provided to literally millions of returning veterans the ability to complete high school and college through substantial grants for tuition and living expenses. University and college administrations welcomed this development for a variety of reasons, among them that through veterans' benefits the federal government provided substantial aid to higher education. But the credentializing process, which in the last analysis remains the primary business of schooling, was given a big push by the concomitant expansion of public sector jobs that, in many cases, sorted candidates on the basis of these credentials; and by the expansion of managerial, professional, and technical occupations in the private sector, an expansion that was also fueled by the tremendous growth of health and education services after the war.

After the war all kinds of paid work grew. A work force of 60 million expanded to more than 90 million people by 1970; the public sector expanded from 3 million jobs just before the war to 15 million in 1970, about 15 percent of all jobs. In the midst of this exponential growth, factory employment rose only arithmetically, from about 20 million at the war's end to 25 million by 1970. From 50 percent of the work force, industrial and other blue-collar labor declined to about a third by 1970, and factory workers accounted for an ever smaller proportion of the labor force. The big winners were clerical, professional, and technical workers. Many of the new entrants into the labor force were women.

During the war, hundreds of thousands of blacks and Latinos got well-paid factory jobs, and many others were able to work in services other than domestic work for the first time. As farm work declined, even as food production multiplied owing to incredible technological change, black sharecroppers and share-tenants, Latino farmers, and farm workers were thrown off the land and migrated to cities, where they found work in factories, services on trucks, and blue-collar jobs in the public sector, the great majority of which did not require credentials of any kind. Even so, blacks finished high school in greater numbers and, especially in the civil rights decade of the 1960s, gained access to universities.

Consider New York in the 1940s and 1950s. It was the world's garment center, with nearly 200,000 jobs in the men's and women's sections of the needle trades—the third-largest machine tool and metal fabricating market. The New York area led in the production of pharmaceuticals and cosmetics; it was the biggest port in the country, a major trucking and rail center, and a leader in electrical and chemical manufacturing. Working-class kids, especially but not exclusively whites, had plenty of places to work after they graduated or dropped out of high school. Similarly, Detroit was the world car-producing capital, and Chicago, in Carl Sandburg's words, was the hog butcher of the world and a leading farm equipment, steel, and electrical manufacturing center, but it also had considerable metals fabricating and men's clothing industries.

Certainly, many employers discriminated by refusing to hire black workers or relegating them to the lower-paid and dirty jobs. And in the building trades and skilled metal trades, such as tool and die, sheet metal, and others, blacks to this day have difficulty getting hired or obtaining apprenticeships. However, the period between 1940 and 1970 was marked by the entrance of literally millions of once-excluded African Americans into industrial plants where, abetted by union protection, they built up considerable seniority and, therefore, job security.

The contemporary economic situation may be expressed in the phrases "restructuration" and "deindustrialization," which have affected the entire country but have had particular significance in large cities such as New York and Detroit, where low- and intermediate-technology plants such as garment and metal fabricating have moved away or been forced out of business by, among other factors, international competition. In the 1980s the United States lost nearly 6 million factory jobs, and another 2.5 million disappeared in the early 1990s. Capital flight has had a disastrous effect on all workers, but to the extent that it has wiped out unskilled and semiskilled jobs, black and Latino workers, their families and communities have suffered severe losses. For, since the 1960s, the urban industrial labor force has been largely black and Latino. In the cities, the new jobs that were created in the wake of capital flight required bureaucratic or clerical skills and, in many cases, academic credentials in order to qualify for employment. For many young people, the 1970s and 1980s were disastrous, except for the group that was able to obtain clerical jobs and entry-level technical jobs in the burgeoning financial services such as banking and brokerage, a boom that lasted less than a decade. For example, at least half of the 400,000 jobs that were lost in New York between 1988 and 1993 were in clerical and administrative occupations, most of which were in financial services.

Compounding the economic shift was the fiscal crisis produced by the drying up of federal aid to cities and reduced tax revenues consequent upon capital flight and the low-wage service industries that replaced them. Today, high school dropouts who would have entered these jobs—and graduates who would have worked in the tens of thousands of public sector jobs created between 1965 and 1980—have absolutely no employment prospects. The unemployment rate for workers between sixteen and twenty-one is 20 percent, nearly three times the national average. Only 15 percent of New York high school students have steady part-time employment during the school year, although more than 60 percent of them would gladly accept such jobs. And black and Latino unemployment for workers aged twenty-one to thirty-five remains more than 40 percent in most large cities, including New York.

Even where the economy is relatively vital, such as in computer services and financial services, new jobs are not being created because, responding to uncertain economic forecasts, employers prefer to pay overtime to existing workers rather than to acquire the burdens of added health, pension, and other costs associated with hiring new employees. Jobs for professional and technical categories are drying up, as well as those for clerical and administrative workers. Moreover, in the past two decades, new technologies such as computers, fax, and photocopying machines have been widely introduced and have had an enormous impact on nearly all workplaces.

In colleges and universities, just as in public administrative and corporate offices—relatively labor-intensive operations—such technologies as personal computers, voice mail, and answering machines have eliminated many jobs, but not clerical functions. Now the professoriate and administrators assume most of these tasks, and secretaries, file clerks, and receptionists are not hired. And with the major reorganization of retail trades, a change that resulted in the bankruptcy of Alexander's, the sharp curtailment of Macy's branches, especially in suburban shopping malls, and the closing of dozens of department stores or branches of large chains, one of the major sources of employment for unskilled and semiskilled young people has been foreclosed.

Considerable shortages persist in nursing and some technical categories of work in the health industry. But teaching jobs at all levels are tight; computer programmers are being laid off as banks and brokerage houses merge, consolidate their businesses into fewer locations, and introduce labor-saving technologies that eliminate technical labor; unemployment among attorneys and legal workers is beginning to erode this once-safe profession; and computer-aided design and drafting have all but eliminated the technical job of draftsperson, as engineers can perform this work with the help of a computer program and are thus freed by three-dimensional computer graphics to engage in the work of design.

In sum, there is little or no work in the above-ground economy, and the kids know it. Among the sources of profound paradox among the school systems of large urban centers is that, at a time when the links between education and work are radically decoupled, administrators and educators are pressing for a closer tie with business on the mistaken assumption that the problems of student motivation could be greatly alleviated if schools aligned themselves in every way with the labor needs of major employers. As a result, there is a new drive toward vocationalization, such as a renewed emphasis on co-op education, and revisions of the curriculum directed toward courses that train students for specific occupations.

Internships, apprenticeships, and the like have much to recommend them. Students get a chance to learn something about the world of work and, most importantly, get out of the stifling and confining environment of the classroom for a few hours a day. But no evidence exists—except for a small number of students who respond to innovative and exciting teachers and programs linked to traditional professions such as social work and teaching—that occupational programs have had a significant effect in improving employment chances for the larger student population. Indeed, dropout rates are still very high. Many, if not most, students recognize that school knowledge has little or nothing to do with their lives, either present or future. For them, as well as for prior generations of children of the working and nonworking poor—a growth population in big cities—buying into the curriculum has little or no point, especially since the outcomes are more than indeterminate.

Educational

The Center for Cultural Studies at City University of New York (CUNY) conducted in 1995 preliminary studies in high schools of majority African American and Latino student populations. We found that most students who graduate from "at risk" high schools—those designated by the Board of Education as having low daily attendance and high dropout rates, lower than average academic achievement, and serious social and economic problems—are from middle-class and stable working-class families. Their parents work in the construction trades, own small businesses, or have steady, well-paying jobs in the health industry and in education. These have been among the occupations that have survived budget cuts relatively well and resisted industrial migration. More than three-quarters of graduates from these schools go on to undergraduate schools, a proportion parallel to that in suburban high schools.

In short, school knowledge is perceived to be relevant, or at least tolerable, only by those students raised in families who have, in one degree or another, middle-class expectations and the resources to support their kids. Educators can sometimes overcome the deep-seated economic/cultural expectations that students bring to schools, but cannot successfully motivate students when they know, as most educators do not, that a high school diploma accumulates less cultural capital than ever before unless it reflects a fairly rigorous academic course of study. In order to gain admission to most universities and colleges, students are required to demonstrate that they have met breadth requirements in science, math, and languages. Many city schools do not have adequate offerings in these subjects and, indeed, do not have working laboratories or course offerings in languages other than English. But perhaps of equal importance, many bright students contrive to "fail" because they have rejected the implications of mastering school knowledge. Put succinctly, the street culture is their only community. It may be dangerous, but, in contrast to the boredom and rote learning characteristic of the secondary school curriculum, it offers friends, sometimes a way of making a living, and even some excitement.

So school failure is pre-eminently a form of resistance to school knowledge, class, and other forms of social mobility and, most important, is an affirmation of the youth street counterculture that has once more become a subject of political and professional rumination. What is striking and perhaps more distressing to mavens of social mobility for minorities and working-class white kids is that street culture has become increasingly attractive to students who would, in previous years, have readily entered the fast track. Students are aware that they must separate themselves from their peers in order to master the curriculum. This is neither new nor is it unexpected from the historical perspective. What is different is this: rejecting the curriculum and other aspects of school authority no longer purchases entrance into working-class or many middle-class jobs. More to the point, kids are likely to remain unemployed or find "work" in various sectors of the underground economy—drugs, sex work (prostitution), but also subminimum wage production of garments, toys, and small electrical parts. Some turned to the military until the recent budget cuts reduced recruitment. With high rates of unemployment among youth, the armed services have raised educational and physical qualifications for admission. The lack of a high school diploma is already a barrier for many who would otherwise find a life in the progressively shrinking armed forces. Within a decade, we may expect that the pared-down armed services may require some postsecondary credentials as a prerequisite for enlistment.

The alternative to an even more frenzied attempt to make schools acceptable to businesses that have no room for school leavers is to re-examine the mission of schools. I suggest that educators ask whether schools can—or should—have anything to do with the job market. School should be a place where the virtues of learning are extolled (a) for their own sake and (b) for the purpose of helping students become more active participants in the civic life of their neighborhoods, their cities, and the larger world. If these proposals sound utopian, they are so only relative to the current myopic educational climate. Yet if educators, parents, and kids are concerned at all with what has been termed "literacy," all of the successful contemporary examples of countries that have achieved this goal are revolutionary or at least radical reformist societies. Despite profound economic and political differences, a number of countries have achieved a level of literacy exceeding that of the United States: the Soviet Union (now deceased), Israel, Nicaragua, Israel, Sweden, and China. Moreover, literacy among the perpetrators of the American Revolution was quite high; most acquired their letters through an assiduous reading of the Bible, an activity that qualifies as ideological and even political in the context of the struggle for religious freedom in the eighteenth century. At their national inception, Israelis read Zionist literature, and Russians read socialist and communist literature as a means to master language and achieve solidarity with the profound social changes that were under way. And until the 1980s, Chinese children and adults pored over Mao's Little Red Book on the road to acquiring the scientific, technical, and bureaucratic knowledge needed to build their society. These readings were, in various ways, linked to a more or less clear vision of the good life and, in the cases of the infant United States and Israel, of a democratic society.

Certainly, the good life embodied economic as much as social and cultural elements. In these developing societies knowledge was clearly fused with power over nature, over the hardships associated with a new society, and over the human adversary, often an interloper, an exploiter. Which is not to deny the degree to which schools in communist and developing societies were often obliged to purvey the ideological orthodoxies of the prevailing rulers. But even if democratic aspirations were cruelly betrayed in many of these societies, education was closely linked to the rhetoric of political, civic, and economic citizenship.

The problem with a scenario of democratic education in the context of the decline of ideological clarity in contemporary politics is that none of the *alternatives* to professionalism, vocational education, and entrepreneurship—the troika of the current emphasis on education for jobs and business—seems credible. After all, the movement for participatory democracy is, in some ways, at a low ebb. Nevertheless, I have no doubt that even the mild-sounding but profoundly subversive demand for democratic participation as the goal of schooling is better than either the ritualistic adherence to a curriculum that was out of date twenty-five years ago or the business-oriented educational reforms of the current era.

Meanwhile, those of us involved in alternative schools, new pedagogies, and the curriculum of inclusion could ponder some aspects of our practice(s). For example, no high school can be said to have broken with curriculum centeredness unless students are involved in governance, including setting learning goals, selecting courses, and having their own, autonomous organizations, including a free press. Nor can the new schools and programs ignore the imperative of citizenship, not primarily through the electoral system, but through discussions of social movements, a community-based curriculum in science and technology, and issues of class, race, sexuality, and gender as forms of power and subordination.

For example, if Brooklyn communities Brownsville or Williamsburg-Greenpoint have some of the highest pollution rates in New York and, consequently, a high incidence of cancer, asthma, emphysema, and other respiratory diseases the high school science program within these areas might initiate student-centered investigations of the nature and extent of these diseases and treatment programs for them. In Ocean Hill-Brownsville, students might learn the history of toxic-waste dumping, which has contributed to the high sickness rates. In Williamsburg-Greenpoint, they might address the city government's garbage disposal plan to build an incinerator on the Brooklyn Navy Yard site. This inquiry would require students to know basic biology and physiology, interview and survey techniques, and how to use health statistics and other sources of information. Moreover, they would have to learn how to use the library, not in a hypothetical way, but in order to complete their project(s). They might decide to participate in the debate on the Navy Yard proposal.

Of course, what students would learn in the course of such investigations might get them interested in knowing more about science and even point them in an academic direction. More important, it might foster civic engagement; students might learn how power works and how to confront it. And this could be the most important outcome of an innovative course of study, even if they remain in the community and do not take the path to professionalism right out of high school.

Our schools have no social or historical vision today. Neither the established authorities nor the reformers possess a way to describe the relationship between education and any possible challenge to the existing economic, social, and political order. At best—and only sporadically—some education reforms articulate alternative cultural visions whose reference is to nationalism and populism, the twin pillars of identity politics. Though these efforts are surely necessary as a tool of engagement, they are by no means sufficient because, at the end of the day, the curriculum of inclusion refuses to address class issues. It cannot or will not speak to the contradiction between the now surpassed elements of the largely middle-class American dream that undergirds the appeal to school knowledge and the legitimate demands of African Americans, Latinos, gays and lesbians, and other oppressed groups to see *themselves* as subjects in the canon and the curriculum.

Perhaps more profoundly, educators remain tied to a doctrine according to which schooling is the core socializing instrument for the established order. Thus, when mainstream educational institutions agree to innovation, this becomes a strategy for achieving the old goals of public education. It may be naive to suppose that schools can be change agents, that they can address the reality of the formative contexts of student lives. If this is the case, we need many more naive but clearheaded educators, parents, and students to demand the impossible.

Notes

1. Lawrence Cremin, *The Transformation of the School* (New York: Random House, 1969).
2. Chester Finn, a professor of education at Vanderbilt University, was assistant secretary of education for research and policy in the Bush administration. During the late 1980s and

early 1990s, he became a powerful voice for the proposition that throwing money at schools was not the answer to their problems, and he instead advocated returning to a strong emphasis on the "basics" in school curricula as the most efficacious school policy. Since the Bush and Reagan administrations opposed federal aid to public schools on the belief that school funding was a local matter, Finn's influence was mainly ideological.

3. The Humanities and Arts Endowments were established to provide federal financial support to artists, writers, and academics for a plurality of cultural and intellectual expressions. Congress's intent was explicitly opposed to government interference in the arts and scholarship. Although money for these agencies was cut in the Reagan years, Bush, who could not have cared less about cultural issues, publicly criticized, under pressure from his own right wing, performance artist Karen Finley and others for their explicitly sexual politics. And Humanities Chair Lynn Chaney openly proclaimed the agency's commitment to promoting only mainstream intellectual and cultural expressions and, in the midst of the presidential campaign, withdrew funds from a controversial conference on genetics and violence. That the Bush era may not be quite over is demonstrated by the difficult time a Senate committee gave Sheldon Hackney, President Clinton's nominee for the Humanities Endowment Chair, during July 1993 hearings. Among his several moral misdemeanors, Hackney has been accused of bowing to political correctness on the University of Pennsylvania campus of which he is president.

4. The concept of "political correctness" may best be defined as the fear of being *perceived* as being racist, sexist, or homophobic. In its crudest form, to be politically correct means to restrict "hate" and other types of objectionable speech. However, its historical roots lie elsewhere: it was used as an ironic term to describe some of the orthodoxies of the New Left of the late 1960s. But mockery has a way of becoming cant, as the debates of the early 1990s amply show.

5. Irving Kristol, "Comment on Francis Fukuyama's End of History," *The National Interest*, May 1989.

6. Board of Education of the City of New York, "Annual Report on Project Achieve," Spring 1992.

7. Paulo Freire, *The Pedagogy of the Oppressed* (New York: Seabury, 1971).

8. See especially Arthur Schlesinger Jr., *The Disuniting of America* (New York: Basic Books, 1992) for a conventional New Deal liberal's alarm at the emergence of identity politics and multiculturalism.

9. Perhaps the most influential treatise on the economic significance of education is Gary Becker, *Human Capital with a Special Reference to Education* (Chicago: University of Chicago Press, 1963). The accepted view, that growth is an ineluctable feature of the United States and other advanced industrial economies, is shared by liberal and conservative economists alike, indeed by the Marxist tradition as well. Economic crisis is regarded as cyclical, periodic, occasional, but stagnation cannot be considered a permanent condition of capitalist economies. For an exception to this prevailing view, see Paul Baran and Paul Sweezy, *Monopoly Capital* (New York: Monthly Review Press, 1966).

10. Michael Katz, *The Irony of Early School Reform* (Chicago: University of Chicago Press, 1971).

11. Paul Willis, *Learning to Labor: How Working Class Kids Get Working Class Jobs* (New York: Columbia University Press, 1981).

12. Peter McLaren, *Schooling as a Ritual Performance* (London: Routledge, 1991).

13. For a brilliant exposition of the concept of schooling as an instance of the accumulation of cultural capital, see Pierre Bourdieu and Jean Passeron, *Reproduction in Education, Culture and Society* (London and Beverly Hills: Sage Publications, 1977).

14. John Dewey, *Democracy in Education* (New York: Putnam, 1916).

15. For a discussion of the issue of vocationalization in relation to Dewey's educational theories, see Stanley Aronowitz and Henry Giroux, *Education Still Under Siege* (Westport , MA: Bergin and Garvey, 1993).

16. Herbert Asbury, *The Gangs of New York* (New York: Greenwood, Putnam, 1968 [1928], provides an extraordinary account of Irish and other immigrant gangs, many of which were youth groups, and their involvement in organized vandalism throughout the nineteenth century. Taken together with Katz's account of school reform in the same period, one has a radically different perspective on the rationale for public schools than that which links them to employment. Schooling for six years was a demand of the labor movement and educational reformers, but compulsory secondary education is clearly linked to getting teenagers off the streets.

17. CUNY Center for Cultural Studies, "A Student Profile of Five New York City High Schools," Report to the Council of Supervisors and Administrators and the United Way, New York, 1993.

13

Let Them Eat Skills

Douglas D. Noble

Over a decade ago I had occasion to respond to a published essay by Marc Tucker titled "Readying Future Workers to Move from Challenge to Challenge." In that article, Tucker, then director of something called the Project on Information Technology and Education, offered speculations about the implications of a high-technology economy for education. He argued that if the United States is to compete with low-wage competitors and still maintain high-wage jobs, it would require an entire nation of workers who "think for a living," who are continually on the "cutting edge" of technological innovation, whose expertise perpetually adds value to custom-designed, "state-of-the-art" products. "We need a labor force that is creative, knowledgeable and flexible," wrote Tucker, with workers "who can move from challenge to challenge." A consequence was that students and workers would need far better education and training than ever before. Tucker concluded, "It is now very important to think about our education and economic policies in tandem. If we do not, we will have to decide how to share among ourselves a swiftly declining national income."

At the time, I found Tucker's contentions both preposterous and dangerous. His fanciful scenario of an entire work force on the cutting edge smacked of the most simpleminded high-tech futurism. Furthermore, he seemed to be pinning the economic woes of American corporations on the inadequate skills of American workers at precisely a time when thousands of highly skilled workers were being laid off, thousands of college graduates couldn't find meaningful work, workers' rights and protections were being undermined at every turn, technology was being introduced to deskill and routinize once challenging jobs, and the jobs being created were decidedly low-tech, low-skill, nonunion, and precarious. I saw precious little connection between worker skill, training, and education, on the one hand, and the availability of secure, high-wage employment, on the other. And I had little reason to believe things would improve, so long as multinational corporations could shut down plants, go offshore, bust unions, and deskill or automate jobs without constraint. Yet Tucker seemed oblivious, choosing a dubious high-tech patriotism over an ominous workplace realism, which he labeled defeatist. Meanwhile he seemed to be blaming the victims—workers and students—for the nation's economic malaise while ignoring a more obvious explanation: wanton corporate abandonment, with government complicity, of the social contract.

Apparently, though, Tucker was a messenger expounding the right message at the right time. For just when his article appeared, the Carnegie Corporation, which had been funding Tucker's work, set up its multimillion-dollar Carnegie Forum on Education and the Economy, with Tucker as its new executive director and Ray Marshall, Carnegie trustee and former secretary of labor, on its advisory council. The objective of the forum was to link educational policy with economic competitiveness. In 1986 the forum released its report *A Nation Prepared: Teachers for the 21st Century*. The promotion, publicity, and elite consensus orchestrated by Carnegie for this report catapulted Tucker into national prominence. The report was premised on the assumption that a reinvented school system was the critical factor in preserving the country's standard of living. It called for full-scale restructuring of public schools and teacher education, and for the establishment of a National Board of Professional Teaching Standards, the first of what would be many such calls for national standards.

The Carnegie Foundation, after all, had been pivotal throughout this century in establishing educational standards for high school and college, as well as for medical, engineering, law, and teacher education (Legemann 1983). Henry Pritchett, founder of the National Bureau of Standards and the Carnegie Foundation's long-term first president, was eager to reform American education on a German model. Although Andrew Carnegie established a generous pension fund for college teachers, Pritchett used the fund as leverage to shape the standards of high school and college, from the size and qualifications of faculty to course requirements ("Carnegie unit"). Subsequently, the Carnegie Corporation was instrumental in establishing the Educational Testing Service to insure the ubiquity of standardized tests. Years later, Lewis Branscomb, another former head of the National Bureau of Standards, became the pivotal player in the Carnegie

Forum's standardizing efforts, as chairperson of the report on teaching standards.

The year after *A Nation Prepared* appeared, Tucker established the independent National Center on Education and the Economy in Rochester, New York, with money from the Carnegie Corporation, Rockefeller Brothers Fund, and New York state to carry on the forum's agenda. The National Center quickly became a strategic focus of national education reform, brokering and promoting consensus among elite corporate and political leaders. Among the luminaries on the center's board were Ray Marshall, David Rockefeller Jr., Govs. James Hunt and Thomas Kean, the CEOs of Kodak and Xerox, Hillary Rodham Clinton, and, as chair, John Sculley, who then was CEO of Apple Computer. Through such contacts the National Center has strongly influenced federal initiatives in education, first within the National Governors Association and the Bush administration, and more recently and far more directly within the Clinton administration. Meanwhile the National Center has formed the New Standards Project, with millions of dollars from major foundations, to establish national examinations and performance standards; and the Alliance for Restructuring Education, with millions from Apple Computer and from the corporate-funded New American Schools Development Corporation, to further corporate-style, technology-based restructuring of schools across the country.

In 1989 the National Center, with additional Carnegie funds, established the Commission on the Skills of the American Workforce. The commission was chaired by Ira Magaziner, later Clinton's health care reform czar, with Marshall and Hillary Clinton on its board. The commission's report, *America's Choice: High Skills or Low Wages!*, carries forward the scenario of Tucker's original article and has become the blueprint for Clinton's education and training agenda. Its recommendations are being implemented in states across the country, and it is the basis for significant education legislation now before Congress.

America's Choice is the subtext for Tucker and Marshall's book *Thinking for a Living*, which should be read more as a fleshed-out blueprint for a national policy of education and economic reform than as a work of scholarship. The arguments and recommendations in the book must be taken very seriously, if not for their coherence then for their already considerable influence on policy. A critique of this book is at the same time a critique of accepted policy wisdom linking education and the economy.

Thinking for a Living

"The thesis of this book is simple," we are told by the authors of *Thinking for a Living*: "The key to productivity and competitiveness is the skills of our people and our capacity to use highly educated and trained people to maximum advantage in the workplace." In order to organize a population as a "learning system," in order to forge a society of workers "thinking for a living," economic policy, labor-market policy, and education policy must be linked into an integrated strategy they call "human resource capitalism." This strategy calls for a coordinated transformation of the workplace, of schools and training systems, and of family and community services, into a "seamless web" of continual learning and renewed productivity.

The book is in five parts. The first is a brief historical account of early twentieth-century industrial mass production and the mass-produced education that supplied its labor. The focus is on Taylorist industry, designed to extract thinking from labor within hierarchical organizations, and on an anti-intellectual education system designed to produce a reliable if unthinking work force for industry.

Part I sets the stage for the new realities taken up in Part II, which outlines recent changes in global economic competitiveness, technological innovation, and sophisticated consumer demand. These changes, the authors tell us, necessitate new, less hierarchical forms of work organizations, with an emphasis on quality, flexibility, customized production, continuous improvement, labor-management cooperation, and highly skilled labor. The economic "miracles" of key U.S. competitors Germany and Japan are offered as countries modeling these required workplace transformations. The authors point to the strong national consensus in social policy in those countries that ensures full employment, centralized labor participation, employment security, high wages, and constraints on employers, without which, they argue, new "high-performance" workplaces are impossible. Also pivotal to workplace transformation are such "external forces" as universal health care, high-quality education systems, and sophisticated training systems, all necessary for a highly educated labor force. With these elements in place, the authors tell us, "Germany and Japan have become societies whose members think for a living."

But not so America. So Part III addresses the book's central challenge to an America "on the precipice." Curiously, here the focus is entirely on inadequacies in education and work-force skills although, by their own account, these were hardly the pivotal ingredients in Germany and Japan's successes. Echoing A Nation at Risk a decade earlier, the authors warn of a "skills crisis"—"a crisis of the same proportions that our defeated foes faced after the war." The authors depart from earlier hyperbolic claims (made by Tucker and others in the 1980s) about a critical "skills gap" between employers' needs and workers' skills. This is because the National Center's Commission on Workforce Skills found that 95 percent of

America's employers still use Taylorist production methods requiring of most workers less than an eighth-grade education and minimal training. The authors argue, however, that "if the vast majority of employers *were* to embrace high-performance work organizations, there *would be* a shortage of skilled labor of epic proportions [italics mine]." In preparation for that eventuality, and as an incentive to employers to transform their workplaces, the authors challenge America either to recognize the crisis in skills, training, and education at the heart of our economic malaise, or else be reduced to a Third World standard of living. After reciting a now-familiar litany of the comparative inadequacies of our education system, the authors note as hopeful signs: Bush's America 2000 education goals, the labor department's codification of workplace skills, and the education initiatives of the Business Roundtable.

Part IV, the bulk of the book with eight chapters, spells out the authors' proposed "New American System: Strategies for High Performance." It starts off with a chapter on the "total quality management" successes at Xerox and Motorola, among the handful of American companies that have achieved "high performance" workplaces—thanks, in this account, to the patient determination of visionary executives and their emphasis on (often mandatory) training of front-line workers. The authors then ask what incentives would transform the 95 percent of American companies still unchanged. They concede that most companies can continue "to meet the competition by keeping wages down, contracting out, automating jobs, [and] exporting production offshore," but that such measures "are disastrous for the country." Since what is good for American companies might not be good for the American people, how then can these corporations be persuaded to do the right thing? Unfortunately, "the European solution of tough legislative programs enacted by labor governments is out," the authors tell us, so they propose that "this country can begin by committing itself to a policy of high wages and full employment" as "overarching social goals." Beyond this rather empty appeal, given current economic conditions, the authors propose raising the minimum wage, requiring employers to invest 1 percent of salaries and wages in worker training (though they doubt it can be done), and, "most important" (and least threatening to business), establishing an extension system to advise, inform, and hold employers' hands as they experiment with new approaches.

Astonishingly, such is the extent of Tucker and Marshall's plan to get American employers to change their ways, which are detrimental to American society, though not necessarily to themselves. The authors rush instead to remind us that "if this effort [to transform employers and workplaces] . . . succeeds, it will provoke a crisis . . . in skilled workers." So most of the remainder of the book turns to students, teachers, schools, and training systems, leaving this reader wondering how they got there from here.

They first discuss school "restructuring," the effort to get school districts to model their organization after (the precious few) "high-performance" companies. The authors tell the story of the lackluster accomplishments of Tucker's National Center in its efforts since 1987 to restructure Rochester city schools for "high performance," using the Xerox model of quality organization. Tucker originally considered the innovative Rochester schools the "perfect laboratory" for school reform; here, he blames the lack of progress in the center's efforts on "public-school staffs [who] . . . choose to sit on their hands." Despite such failure, the book blithely insists that "America's challenge is to restructure the entire system for public education, from the Federal government to the classroom." Remarkably, as Tucker has proved, if your chosen laboratory doesn't fly, go advise the president instead.

Restructuring is very difficult, we are told, but there are no shortcuts. Using a borrowed critique, the authors reject the claim that vouchers and private school "choice" offer a quick fix for schools via the market. Although they reject vouchers, the authors still favor market incentives, choice, and the "discipline that competition for customers brings," but only among the public schools, envisioned as "entrepreneurial units." Such competition, the authors argue, would provide badly needed incentives for complacent public school personnel to shape up.

Students, too, need incentives, say the authors; they must be motivated to work hard in school through "a system driven by standards," the topic of the subsequent chapter. In the Carnegie tradition, the authors propose "world class" standards of mastery and performance, encompassing every stage of education, from sixth, eighth, tenth grades to high school graduation to college admission to college graduation. They go further to include professional standards for public school and college teachers, curriculum standards for high school and college courses, and technical competency standards for every imaginable occupation. There is here a veritable frenzy of standardization, upon which Tucker and others have launched a minor industry developing national tests, certificates, and standards boards.

The really hard questions of day-to-day curriculum and instruction, and of equal opportunity to ensure all students are equally prepared, receive only lip service amid the din. The tone throughout is one of get-tough accountability, emphasizing systematic, transparent performance assessment that would enable teachers, employers, and others to readily determine the qualifications of potential employees. A streamlined "human resource" delivery system, no muss, no fuss. "If the United States combines such a system of performance standards with the restructuring agenda," insist the authors, "and greatly reduces poverty among its children, it can have the finest educational performance in the world."

The next chapter turns, then, to poverty of children and the family ("the quintessential learning system"). Following closely the lead of the National Commission on Children, the authors offer such recommendations as child tax credits, earned income tax credits, child-support enforcement, higher minimum wage, a single-payer national health insurance system, family leave, and a national system of affordable, high-quality day care. These are all worthwhile recommendations, constituting what the authors call an expedient "system of family and youth policy to serve as a firm foundation for an economy based on the quality of our human resources."

Only fifteen pages are devoted to this "foundation," however; the authors' priorities are clearly on "human resource" development, not on poor children and their families. And their recommendations target not just poor but also middle-class and rich families because "like it or not, the country will not do what must be done for its [poor] children until everyone's children benefit." This surrender of moral highmindedness to perceived political and cultural realities is perhaps the foremost characteristic of this book. The goal is to achieve through instrumental, consensual policy what will not otherwise happen through moral decency and fairness. Thus, while the rhetorical challenge to employers is perhaps most vigorous here, the authors emphasize that "such policies [are] not a matter of compassion, but rather of self-interest," underscoring economic benefits and vigorously dispelling possible concerns about a potential "welfare state."

Next is an innocuous, anecdotal chapter devoted to the importance of rebuilding the community fabric as another foundation for "human resource" development. There are no specific recommendations. This chapter stands in ironic contrast to the oft-noted disengagement of Tucker's National Center from the Rochester community where it resided until recently. "Human resource" development, the theme of the book, is addressed more directly in the remaining two chapters in Part IV, which discuss job training and a revamped labor-market system. Since high performance workplaces require sophisticated workers, "the economic future of the United States depends mainly on the skills of the front-line work force." Borrowing from Japan, Sweden, Germany, and Denmark, the authors therefore recommend a system of vocational education and occupational training for non-college-bound youth, comparable in status to the college-bound track. Students around sixteen would all have to achieve academic Certificates of Initial Mastery, after which they would choose a college preparatory program, go directly into the work force, or pursue vocational training. The last one would involve a modular training curriculum to ensure flexible skills within broad occupational areas. A national system of occupational certificates and standards for all trades and occupations would be set by "high-performance" employers. And youth centers for "dropout recovery" would be established, to provide a second chance to enter the system.

At this writing, considerable effort is being expended to codify occupational skills and standards; the key problem, though, is employers' reluctance to commit to recognizing such standards, without which, all agree, this is an empty exercise. Tucker and Marshall fail to address this pivotal issue. Another issue they don't address is this: with so few jobs available, the concoction of occupational standards serves both as make-work for redundant researchers and as the erection of new qualification barriers by which to sort hordes of luckless job candidates.

The chapter on labor-market reform focuses on the need for an "active labor market" modeled on Sweden's, which includes a sophisticated training system, computerized job matching (with mandatory job listings), living stipends and relocation subsidies for trainees, sophisticated career counseling, and subsidized transitional employment. Such a system would be implemented through an arrangement of federal, state, and local employment and training boards. All of this would, of course, require a political commitment to full employment, in contrast to the haphazard, ineffectual government programs currently in use.

The book concludes with Part V, whose sole chapter identifies how the authors propose to pay the $100 billion of additional federal spending they estimate their "human resource" system would cost. Their recommendations include a slightly more progressive income tax, a national value-added (VAT) tax, and the transfer of funding from the military and other agencies. They would, however, greatly reduce corporate income taxes, to ensure the availability of capital to businesses. They conclude with a plea for a "new politics" of consensus, one in which everyone gives up something in order to adopt their mixed agenda of both conservative and liberal proposals. *Thinking for a Living* is, after all, a blueprint in Realpolitik, a flurry of proposals from left and right that we are urged to endorse somehow as a totality, as a system. All or nothing, take it or leave it, high skills or low wages. Lest we begin to think, as I shall try to do in what follows.

Critique

Many of the points made in this book are familiar to those who have been following the rhetoric and politics behind business-led school reform and the corporate quality management "revolution" over the past decade. While the book offers some cogent analysis and some laudable recommendations, the whole is far less than the sum of its parts. Its lack of prima facie credibility, its absence of argument and evidence at crucial points, and its logical incoherence leave one to wonder: if this is the best their promoters can do, why have such ideas become so popular among policymakers? We'll return to that question later.

The most significant economic problem in this country is a labor *surplus*. This is true as well in Japan and Germany (Beauchamp 1991; Sengenberger 1992; Taira and Levine 1992). This country has a dire shortage of decent jobs, not a shortage of skilled labor. More than 2,000 workers, most of them highly skilled and experienced, are being laid off each day, with no end in sight (Richman 1993). The wages and job security of those still employed are steadily eroding, as organized labor has been all but destroyed, and most new jobs are in the low-wage, temporary, part-time service sector, requiring minimal skill (Mishel and Teixeira 1991; Mishel and Bernstein 1993). Meanwhile, extensive government retraining programs have provided few workers with decent jobs, raising for knowledgeable analysts the central question: Training for what? (Jackson 1992; Gans 1993).

And yet, despite this relentless deterioration of quality work and a general disregard for the plight of workers, skilled and unskilled alike, we are somehow deluged, at the very same moment, with a delirious new celebration of human capital (Hornbeck and Salamon 1991), renewed commitment to work-force skills and training, and urgent calls, as in this book, for "a renaissance in human capacity." Education reform (aka "human resource development") takes on a shiny new significance as the engine of economic progress, its meaning and its mandate tied increasingly to a glorious, high-performance world of work.

What we have here, in part, is denial. A decade or so ago, latter-day postindustrial ideologues began to pontificate about the educational implications of a high-technology economy, with its elevated intellectual requirements (Noble 1990). Soon it became clear that new jobs were increasingly coming in low-end, low-skill areas, not in high-tech, high-skill areas. It also became clear that the organization of work, not technology, was the key factor in determining skill requirements and work quality (Zuboff 1988). Based on a handful of corporate success stories (as told by their CEOs), the movement for "total quality management" (TQM) and organizational restructuring took off, with as-yet checkered results. But even within high-tech companies' with restructured organizations, researchers began to find no concomitant rise in academic skill requirements for workers (Brown, Reich, and Stern 1990; Finnan, Levin, and Rumberger 1990). The presumed links between a high-technology economy, a high-performance workplace, and a "high-skill" education were no longer obvious.

Yet Tucker, Marshall, and other champions of the education/economy link, such as Clinton's Secretary of Labor Robert Reich (1991), ignore such subtlety; to them "high technology" and "high performance" still mean, simply, "high skill." (It is appalling, by the way, that a book ostensibly about worker "skill" and "thinking" on the job never begins to unpack the meaning of these terms, in any of their complexity and controversy. Here, they serve merely as convenient catch phrases for policymakers.)

Proponents of the link between education and the economy aren't merely identifying new skill requirements for a new economy, of course. They are pinning the rap for a bum economy on education and workers. Tucker and Marshall recognize that 95 percent of employers will have to radically change their ways before an educated labor force can be utilized, if at all. And they concede that a social compact of policies dictating high wages, strong labor, and employment security—as in Japan, Germany, and Sweden, and utterly absent here—is a prerequisite to transformed workplaces. Yet they choose to focus their energies (and their exasperation) further down the food chain, on schools and training, while paying mere lip service to "high wages" and "full employment," and merely holding the hands of recalcitrant employers. Curiously, almost no mention is made of organized labor here, in a book ostensibly praising the potential of the American worker as the backbone of the economy. Marshall, former secretary of labor, stressed in his book *Unheard Voices* (1987) the essential contribution of strong labor unions and full worker participation to economic success; yet here the voices of workers have been silenced, leaving only their shell, "human resources."

On its face, any link between educational achievement and the nation's economic strength is a tenuous one, mediated as it must be by a host of factors, among them adequate jobs, appropriate management, a strong labor presence, and a committed employment policy. Given their (often perfunctory) acknowledgment of these factors, such books as *Thinking for a Living* and Reich's *Work of Nations* are pervaded by denial and logical incoherence in their insistence on skills and education as the key to economic prosperity. At times, Tucker and Marshall contend that strong training and education will enable and encourage management to transform work and to create quality jobs; Reich argues that a highly skilled work force will attract corporate investment, creating quality jobs. In each case, they stretch logic to the limits, putting the cart before the horse by insisting on the primacy of education and training. One wonders what is really going on here.

Of course, the massive industry of education reform, led by Tucker and others, depends on such skewed logic for continued support from corporate and government resources. Education reform, after all, provides a relatively risk-free domestic agenda for governors, senators, and presidents, while appearing to be addressing economic problems at the same time (they have no ideas or political will to create jobs). Corporate leaders have been prominent in recent education reform, too, emphasizing the contribution of "human capital" and "human resources" to economic viability. Some critics argue that "education-first" promoters such as Tucker and Marshall concentrate on education as a scapegoat for rampant mismanagement by these corporate/government elite whom they ultimately represent (Gorz 1989; Jackson 1992; Gans 1993; Weisman 1993). The insistent focus on human resources, education, and skills is thereby a convenient distraction from economic disasters caused by myopic managers with their relentless downsizing in the name of productivity. (Interestingly, many of the key corporate players in federal education policy, among them John Akers of IBM, Kay Whitmore of Kodak, and John Sculley of Apple, have lost their jobs in the past several years amid desperate management and massive layoffs. Sculley and Whitmore have been key board members of Tucker's National Center.)

Gorz (1989) argues that the corporate focus on "human resources" is more strategic than mere distraction. Capital, he observes (68), has brought about the disintegration of the working-class and the trade union movement by "adopt[ing] the values of the utopia of work as its own": technical control by workers over the means of production, full individual development, the importance of skill, and a professional ethic. "Insofar as it corresponds in large part to the ideal of the sovereign, multi-skilled worker . . . the employers' discourse, and the strategy concealed within it, have brought about the most serious crisis in the history of the trade union movement." Here the corporate focus on human capital, training, and skills is largely a ruse, a device to win over labor through a false promise of worker empowerment. To the extent this promise is genuine, its target is the steadily diminishing core of stable workers, amid a growing mass of peripheral and unemployed workers (Mishel and Bernstein 1993).

The celebration of education and skill can go hand in hand with the ongoing deterioration of work for the vast majority of people so long as a visible few reap the rewards of the new celebration and the rest strive to be among them. This is precisely the situation in Japan, where "lifetime employment" applies to a dwindling core of workers, while the harsh realities of the "peripheral work force," which constitutes up to 75 percent of the Japanese labor force, reflect "the other Japan" we hear almost nothing about (Steven 1988; Chalmers 1989). Yet Tucker and Marshall, ironically enough, point to Japanese lifetime employment as a model for the "great majority" of America's "front-line workers." In this country, too, we hear about the massive layoffs and outsourcing that set the stage for this belated attention to "human resources." Meanwhile, unions and others who have promoted the training and development of workers now find themselves outflanked by corporate leaders who mandate company training as a sign of corporate loyalty and as a means of skill-based pay schemes (as happens at Tucker and Marshall's nonunion model of high performance, Motorola [Brown, Reich, and Stern 1990; Weisman 1993]).

The corporate usurpation of the discourse and subversion of the practice of progressive unionists and educators leads to such statements as this by Marshall and Tucker (82): "What employers need now are workers who bring the kinds of skills that [progressive] educators have always said they wanted to develop in their students. . . . The demand for a highly skilled work force is in fact a call for educators to realize what have always been their highest aspirations" (82). Such sleight of hand, arrived at along a path of undefined terms, twisted logic, and denial of reality, is the source of the title "thinking for a living." It is also the source of bewilderment among those who mistrust the messenger but who are seduced by the appeal, considering its opposite: mindless work, abandoned schools. How, then, might an educator proceed?

A Note on Pedagogy

The value of education clearly must be addressed independent of its alleged links to the economy and to the workplace. The automatic link between education and economic competitiveness is dubious, and the supposed skills required in the "high-performance" workplace of the future, though codified in one official list after another, can just as well be taught when, or if, that future arrives. Some of the items on such lists, including team-based, "hands-on," "real-life," project-oriented pedagogy that encourages decision making and clear thinking, are simply good pedagogy and need not be linked to the workplace to be considered important. There is more to real life than what goes on in the workplace.

Of course, the working world should be made part of the curriculum so that students of all ages might know what goes on there. But such integration of work and education is typically skewed toward "career education," offering a distorted, employer-friendly image of workplace realities, or else toward vocational education, with a terrible record over the past century for tracking students and being disconnected from relevant jobs (Grubb and Lazerson 1981). The current trend toward vocationalizing academics and toward emphasizing "tech prep," apprenticeship, and career academies also depends excessively on the atypical good will of employers, to whom educators are beholden for the success of their programs; not infrequently, the programs are exploitative of students rather than providing educative work opportunities (Roditi 1992).

All too often, the emphasis in such programs is on preparing students with appropriate "employability" skills, attitudes, and personal attributes sought by potential employers seeking loyal employees. Little room is allowed for questioning and debating such workplace issues as personal experiences of work, labor unions, health and safety, power relations, and the changing nature of work in society. Only a handful of work-related programs encourage such independent thinking, in part for fear of losing employer contacts, in part from career educators' own lack of a broader vision, and in part from the secondary role played by labor unions in such pedagogical efforts (in contrast to German and Swedish models typically noted). One excellent example of critical work-related pedagogy available to educators is the curriculum developed by Canadian educators, titled *Learning Work* (Simon, Dippo, and Schenke 1991).

An excessive attention to standards and performance is characteristic of much recent school reform. The primary impulse behind this effort, as illustrated in this book, is to motivate students and teachers to become more productive. This argument is premised on the needs of the economy, a claim that, as we have seen, makes little sense. Its promoters also appear to view the nation's entire school system as deficient, and the entire population of students as somehow ill-prepared for work. Clearly, this is hardly the case, as the vast number of capable high school and college graduates unable to find decent jobs would attest. The energies of the standardizers would perhaps be better spent on the very real educational deficiencies of many poor, black, Hispanic, or otherwise "at-risk" students through, among other things, a struggle for equity in educational finance (which receives one passing mention by Tucker and Marshall).

Although a full treatment of the standards debate cannot be taken up here, the question of standards and examinations for motivation is worth considering in light of Japanese education and training, which is used as a model by Tucker and Marshall and by many others. According to recent studies conducted by the Department of Education in conjunction with the Japanese Ministry of Education, much of what has passed as true about Japanese education is mythology (Leestma 1992).

In fact, promotion from grade to grade in Japan is automatic and not dependent on academic achievement until grade ten. Recent researchers have begun to question what, if any, are the academic standards for high school graduation, and reliable recent evidence suggests that a large number of Japanese high schoolers have severe reading problems and are seriously behind in basic subjects. And though the average achievement rate is higher in

Japan, researchers strongly suggest that this results less from formal schooling than from traditional family and cultural values (Dore and Sako 1989; Leestma 1992), which make possible a very high intensity of schooling. The examinations administered in the tenth year are tied closely to future employment in large Japanese companies, which motivates Japanese students, for cultural reasons, far in excess of their slim chance to be among the winners. The intense examination system also leads to a student population who rarely read for pleasure, and whose creativity and initiative are diminished by stressful examination preparation (Dore and Sako 1989). An American system of examinations and standards, disconnected from job-related guarantees and used as a template over a school system in disarray, is unlikely to contribute significantly to a desirable form of student achievement and motivation.

Also doubtful is the theory that mandated employer training of workers, conforming to occupational standards and certificates envisioned by Tucker and Marshall, could match the Japanese workplace training model the authors desire to emulate. This is because very little formal training occurs in Japanese companies, despite the mythology to the contrary (Dore and Sako 1989; Taira and Levine 1992). Instead, Japanese companies rely almost exclusively on job rotation and team-related informal training and skill acquisition. Requiring already reluctant employers to spend 1 percent or more of wages and salaries on formal worker training, as Tucker and Marshall (and the Clinton administration) endorse, benefits only those Tucker-led consortia articulating occupational standards to which such training would be expected to conform.

Tucker and Marshall's favorite example of workplace training is Motorola, a nonunion company that has instituted a battery of academic and technical skills tests it expects its employees to pass through extensive company training. According to a recent study, often nonessential training and testing, assumed to be important by Motorola management, is used to determine pay rates and even to downgrade job placement of otherwise highly skilled, seasoned employees. The requirement of academic and technical proficiency not necessarily related to job performance is thereby used as a weapon against workers in this highly touted paragon of high performance and human resources (Brown, Reich, and Stern 1990; Weisman 1993). For unionists promoting worker training, this usurpation of the training prerogative raises very serious questions about the control, content, and value of proposed workplace training (Davis et al. 1989). Training and "lifelong learning," in the hands of management, are not necessarily good for workers, and formal workplace training, conforming to a new array of standards and certificates, is not necessarily appropriate for skills acquisition or improved job performance.

According to thoughtful observers, we are at a critical historical moment, one in which the place of work in an advanced industrial society must be reconsidered (Gorz 1989; Gans 1993). The downsizing of industry is most likely a permanent trend, as capital uses technology and reorganization to accelerate its diminishing dependence on skilled labor (Richman 1993). Around the globe, and certainly here in the United States, millions of highly educated and skilled people have given up trying to find a decent job. Many in Europe, and increasingly here as well, are recommending work sharing as the only reasonable approach to addressing the very real crisis of a burgeoning labor surplus. Perhaps the supreme irony of Tucker and Marshall's book is that it trots out work as the pivotal source of student motivation and as the principal purpose of education at precisely the time when the nature and availability of work itself is so up in the air. Never mind thinking for a living; the people I know will do anything for a living. And there's precious little thinking going on about how to proceed from here.

References

Abraham, K. G., and Houseman, S. N. 1993. *Job Security in America: Lessons from Germany*. Washington, DC: Brookings Institution.

Brown, C., Reich, M., and Stern, D. 1990. *Skills and Security in Evolving Employment Systems: Observations from Case Studies*. Berkeley: University of California.

Chalmers, N. J. 1989. *Industrial Relations in Japan: The Peripheral Workforce*. London: Routledge.

Davis, J., et al. 1989. *It's Our Own Knowledge: Labour, Public Education, and Skills Training*. Toronto: Our Schools/Our Selves Education Foundation.

Dore, R. P., and Sako, M. 1989. *How the Japanese Learn to Work*. London: Routledge.

Evans Jr., R. 1991. The contribution of education to Japan's economic growth. In E. W. Beauchamp, ed., *Windows on Japanese Education*. New York: Greenwood.

Finnan, C., Levin, H. M, and Rumberger, R. 1990. Escalating skill requirements or different skill requirements. Unpublished paper, Stanford University.

Gans, H. 1993. Making jobs. *The Nation* 257(8): 270, 295–296.

Gorz, A. 1989. *Critique of Economic Reason*. London: Verso.

Grubb, W. N., and Lazerson, M. 1981. Vocational solutions to youth problems: The persistent frustrations of the American experience. *Educational Analysis* 3(2): 91–103.

Hornbeck, D. W., and Salamon, L. M. 1991. *Human Capital and America's Future*. Baltimore: Johns Hopkins University Press.

Hart, H. 1991. The Swedish labor unions. In M. Maccoby, ed., *Sweden at the Edge*. Philadelphia: University of Pennsylvania Press.

Henkoff, Ronald. 1992. Where will the jobs come from? *Fortune*, October 19, 58–64.

Jackson, N., ed. 1992. *Training for What? Labour Perspectives on Skill Training*. Toronto: OurSchools/OurSelves Education Foundation.

Legemann, E. C. 1983. *Private Power for the Public Good: A History of the Carnegie Foundation for the Advancement of Teaching.* Middletown, CT: Wesleyan University Press.

Leestma, R. 1992. Further research: Needs, possibilities, and perspectives. In R. Leestma and H. J. Walberg, eds., *Japanese Educational Productivity.* Ann Arbor: University of Michigan Press.

Maccoby, M. 1991. Introduction. In M. Maccoby, ed., *Sweden at the Edge.* Philadelphia: University of Pennsylvania Press.

Marshall, R. 1987. *Unheard Voices.* New York: Basic Books.

Marshall, R., and Tucker, M. 1992. *Thinking For A Living: Education and the Wealth of Nations.* New York: Basic Books.

Mishel, L., and Bernstein, J. 1993. The joyless recovery: Deteriorating wages and job quality in the 1990s. Briefing paper. Washington, DC: Economic Policy Institute.

Mishel, L., and Teixeira, R. A. 1991. *The Myth of the Coming Labor Shortage.* Washington, DC: Economic Policy Institute.

National Center on Education and the Economy. 1990. *America's Choice: High Skills or Low Wages!* Rochester, NY: National Center on Education and the Economy.

Noble, D. 1990. High tech skills. In S. London et al., *The Re-education of the American Working Class.* New York: Greenwood.

Reich, R. 1991. *The Work of Nations.* New York: Knopf.

Richman, L. S. 1993. When will the layoffs end? *Fortune,* September 20, 54–56.

Roditi, H. F. 1992. High schools for docile workers. *The Nation,* March 16, 340–43.

Sengenberger, W. 1992. Vocational training, job structures, and the labor market— an international perspective. In N. Altman et al., eds., *Technology and Work in German Industry.* London: Routledge.

Simon, R., Dippo, D., and Schenke, A. 1991. *Learning Work: A Critical Pedagogy of Work Education.* New York: Bergin and Garvey.

Steven, R. 1988. The Japanese working class. In E. P. Tsurumi, *The Other Japan.* Armonk, NY: M. E. Sharpe.

Taira, K., and Levine, S. 1992. Education and labor skills in postwar Japan. In R. Leestma and H. J. Walberg, eds., *Japanese Educational Productivity.* Ann Arbor: University of Michigan Press.

Weisman, J. 1993. Skills in the schools: now it's business's turn. *Phi Delta Kappan,* January, 367–69.

Zuboff, S. 1988. *In the Age of the Smart Machine.* New York: Basic Books.

14

Fighting Academic Agoraphobia

Self-Help Books for Cultural Studies' Fear of the Marketplace[1]

Kakie Urch

> Where solitude ceases the market place begins; and where the market place begins the noise of the great actors and the buzzing of the poisonous flies begins too. In the world even the best things amount to nothing without someone to make a show of them: great men—the people call these showmen.
>
> —Nietzsche, *Thus Spoke Zarathustra*

Advertising *schools* people, in both senses of the word. It is at once the bene-volent schoolmarm of society that it purports to be, disseminating impor-tant hand-washing information and, with it, new lists of germs that can be killed by Listerine. But advertising is also the player in the game who cold outmoves you and drives, despite all your arm waving, directly to the base line and the easy lay-up. Desire has been created, and you have been *schooled*. It is this arm-waving, passed-by, helpless feeling that the cultural critics on the Left seem to be avoiding when they, in their writing, accept the attitude that advertising—the literal and overt cultural stuff of the marketplace, the rhetoric of the showmen, and of the spectacle—is too poi-sonous to touch. Advertising proper, addressed in cultural studies work, is mostly presented as an example of something too ludicrous to be taken seriously, or as something so evil that only its name, not its specific slogans, may be uttered.

This "agoraphobia," or textual "fear of the marketplace," which is often manifested in the quick dismissal of advertising either because of its "trivial" nature or stance of address, or because of its direct and unrepentant con-nection with the ethic of consumption (and thus the female consumer), is disabling to cultural studies' power. The way to defend against the player who outmoves you is not to refuse to show up to the game, but rather to *study the moves*.

In this article, I want to provide both a theoretical study of the basis of this problem in cultural studies and brief reviews of a new, fearless wave of books produced within what Stuart Hall calls the "New Times" of post-Marxism. These books take into account the idea put forth by Frank Mort that "to fail to recognize that marketing taps something of our pleasures and aspirations as consumers is to ignore the how and why of its success" (1990, 167). The piece seeks first to examine the genealogy of cultural studies' "agoraphobia"—fear of the marketplace—as it makes an argument for a new conception of the *pedagogical* function of advertising, moving beyond the earliest work in cultural studies of advertising. This work, despite its initially important research strides, tends in its rhetoric of presentation to demonize markets and the consumers who inhabit them (Ewen and Ewen 1992). These important early works that figure advertising as a demonic force within political economy are indeed cornerstones for the argument that advertising must be included in serious cultural critique in all its specificity. However, many of the ways in which they have been taken up establishes for the Left (and for the individual leftist) the continuance of a Utopian positionality *outside* of the hegemonic influence of markets—the Emersonian/Thoreauvian "solitude" that Nietzsche hopes for in the quotation above.[2] This utopian stance, this article takes as its premise, is an impossible position in post-Fordist postmodern New Media; neither leftists nor the producers of ads, or the producers of "art" can be outside the marketplace.[3]

Within New Media, a new pedagogy of advertising is a rich way to examine the specificities of construction of race, gender, class, and region in order to understand and build alternative hegemonies under late capitalism. Underpinning this look at the (non)representation of advertising in cultural studies is the idea that the "trivial" is aways a gendered category, and the further conclusion that the rejection of the everyday is a way in which gendered value judgments are deployed. In concluding, I offer a view to some recent critical works that are useful for this approach to advertising as a pedagogy and as part of a cultural pedagogy—one that necessarily includes the everyday, the trivial, and the "poisonous."

Historical Rejection on the Left

In 1935, the proto-cultural critic Kenneth Burke addressed the American Writers' Congress, a group of Left writers who gathered at Madison Square Garden "to extend the reach of the John Reed Clubs by providing the basis for a much broader organization of American writers" (Lentricchia 1983, 21). Burke directly invoked agency advertising (in 1935, only some twenty-five years after its formal inception, many advertisers fretted that American women still needed to be taught how to use the refrigerators they had pur-chased [Woodward 1938, 6^4]) as a powerful pedagogy of desire. Burke told the Writers' Congress:

> "Adult education" in capitalist America to-day is centered in the efforts of our economic mercenaries (our advertising men and sales organizations) to create a maximum desire for commodities consumed under expensive conditions—and Hollywood appeals to the worker mainly by picturing the qualities of life in which this commercially stimulated desire is gratified. The question arises: Is the symbol of the worker accurately attuned to us, as so conditioned by the reactionary forces in control of our main educational channels? (Burke 1968, 269)

In the Writers' Congress speech, Burke presaged Baudrillard's work by some forty years when he told the Left audience, "In a sense a myth that works well is as real as food, tools, and shelter are. As compared with the reality of material objects, however, we might say that the myth deals with a *secondary* order of reality" (267).

Operating under this assumption, Burke told his audience, which included the radical writer Granville Hicks as well as Joseph Freeman, Michael Gold, Friedrich Wolf, and Martin Russak, that the Left might do well to pay attention to the specificities of desire and identification created by advertising and invoke the term "the people" in place of the traditional term of "the worker" as used in the texts of Marx. Burke said, "In suggesting that 'the people,' rather than 'the worker,' rate highest in our hierarchy of symbols, I suppose I am suggesting fundamentally that one cannot extend the doctrine of revolutionary thought among the lower middle class without using middle-class values" (269).

As Frank Lentricchia points out in *Criticism and Social Change* (1983, 31), Burke's comments to this Congress animated Gramscian notions of cultural hegemony that contemporary cultural studies employs in its cri-tique, although Gramsci was still imprisoned by Mussolini at the time, and thus the *Prison Notebooks* and *Cultural Writings* were not available to Burke.

What is most significant for our consideration here, though, is not that Kenneth Burke put forth several of the major premises of postmodern cul-tural study in 1935 but the way in which the Left reacted. Burke was reviled, rebuffed, attacked, and termed a "traitor" (Selzer 1996) for addressing the practical deployment of mythological mass desire toward the ostensible goal of the Congress—how to spread the influence of the John Reed Clubs and their "cooperative"[5] message. The variance from what Lentricchia calls the "sacred texts" (1983, 33) of Marx was one reason for the Left's strong reaction; the other reason, apparently, is the attachment of Marxist tenets to the practices of promotional culture,[6] which continue to be characterized by most on the Left as a dismissable poison.

Burke's defense of his point to the Congress was, "I think that we are all agreed that we are trying to defend a position in favor of the workers, that we are trying to enlist in the cause of the workers. There is no issue about that. The important thing is: how to make ourselves effective in this particular social structure?" (1968, 279). In 1935, when capitalism was most obviously failing the majority of Americans, and the Left had in fact a good opportunity to enact widespread change, Kenneth Burke recognized that the "particular social structure" of capitalism, even in advertising's infancy, only thirteen years after the first commercial radio broadcast and a full two decades before the era of television, was built on a foundation of desire created mythologically. Burke's simple heresy was that any counter-structure must take that mythological foundation and its promotional culture methods of dissemination firmly into account.[7]

Meet the *New Times*—Same as the Old Times?

Flashing forward to 1996, to post-Fordist, postmodern, post-Birmingham School "New Times," as they are termed by Stuart Hall and Martin Jacques in their influential essay collection by the same title, we can see an analogy to the 1930s, both economically and culturally. As Henry Giroux points out in his recent *Fugitive Cultures*, contemporary social and economic conditions (technological change, unemployment, lost hopes, downsizing, etc.) serve as a premise for the need to look at all popular culture, including advertising, as an important site in the dream work, the desire, and the "schooling" of American youth. Giroux notes that the "emergence of the electronic media, coupled with a diminishing faith in the power of human agency, has undermined the traditional visions of schooling and the meaning of pedagogy" (1996, 47). Giroux notes the way in which the very site of education has shifted from print to electronics, from a single locus of a modernist school to a multiple intersection of media intervention (his main examples are Disney, talk radio, films depicting Generation X and Generation *Malcolm* X, and the hyperviolence of such films as Tarantino's *Pulp Fiction* and *Reservoir Dogs*). Giroux thus challenges education to take up cultural studies. Within this challenge, he in other works[8] has included the cultural pedagogy of advertising in his definition of "culture" and takes "talk radio" seriously as a pedagogical medium. The Left's attitude toward "talk radio" mirrors its view on advertising, as it is dismissed as too "trivial" or "ludicrous" for concern, despite the sheer power of the Nietzschean replication of Rush Limbaugh's "Dittoheads."

The recommendations of Kenneth Burke in 1935 and the call by Giroux in 1996 seek to address questions raised by Gramsci in 1920, when he wrote:

> This revolution also presupposed the formation of a new set of standards, a new psychology, new ways of feeling, thinking and living that must be specific to the working class, that must be created by it, that will become "dominant" when the working class becomes the dominant class.... Do elements for an art, philosophy and morality (standards) specific to the working class already exist? ... The working class, therefore, has its own "metaphysical needs" which are proper to it alone. Even a bourgeois can conceive the world from the standpoint of the class struggle, but since he cannot but imagine this struggle as perpetual, he does not ask himself, "And after the abolition of classes?" (1985, 41)

This passage can be read as a direct support of the type of purist imagery of "the worker" that the 1930s Left sought in its strong reaction against Kenneth Burke's call to vary the aesthetic of its rhetorical terminology.[9] Or it can be read as an intersection that leads toward the current enactment of Giroux's categories of "Fugitive Cultures," cultures with an aesthetic, with standards and a philosophy, all created by the fugitive classes who inhabit them.[10] The latter view is the one in which the working class has agency, is able to pick and choose its own aesthetic, philosophy, and standards. And it is quite possible that the working class has always interacted with mass promotional culture in this way, that only the *analyses* of these reactions have privileged a monologic sender-receiver model of relationship to public marketplace messages of desire.

Burke, for his own part, realized two important points about working-class agency. First, although the working class indeed has its own standards, the "metaphysical needs" of a working class might be constructed as a hybrid that deploys imagery "sampled" from the dominant culture of advertising. Secondly, Burke understood that advertising's "Democracy of Goods"[11] had already created, in some sectors of American culture, the strong myth that the abolition of classes *had already occurred*. Burke's simple proposal of a change in terminology sought to work between the interstices of the hegemony that was in place—what he called "this particular social structure."

Bringing Burke's career-long focus on psychological and rhetorical "identification" forward into late capitalism,[12] the social and political stakes of the observation in *New Times* that advertisers are "intermediaries who construct a dialogue between the market on the one hand and consumer culture on the other."

> Marketers will tell you that this is a two-way process; it doesn't simply come from above. Product design and innovation, pricing and promotion, are shaped by noises coming from the street. Market research is the business of collating these noises and shaping them into consumer profiles. The net result, is, of course contradictory. (Mort 1990, 167)

Thus cultural studies steps into a world of advertising that is perhaps ahead of its critics in its self-reflection. But as boundaries between post-modern advertising media and genres blur,[13] understanding the historical and contemporary specificities of practices of advertising becomes crucial to understanding identity. The promotional professional class understands that identities are multiply constructed and that many of these multiple sites are constructed by promotional media. (The folk practice of American teenage girls, who paste together collages of advertising slogans as gifts for their best friends—in which the slogans represent the interests, desires, and activities of each girl and interactions between the two—comes to mind as one of the most vivid ways in which youth is consciously and literally constructing self *of* media.)

Taking the multiple cultural traces of advertising as Foucauldian markers of constitutive power across social groups allows cultural studies to investigate structures of repression and structures of resistance, and just how identity is taught and learned, "address(ing) issues and speaking from spaces in which people reflect daily on their lives" (Giroux 1996, 155). Susan Bordo's work in *Unbearable Weight*, for example, works through texts of advertising in articulating the way in which women are taught "womanness." In a chapter titled "Hunger as Ideology," Bordo argues that

> more than a purely profit-maximizing, ideologically neutral, Madison Avenue mentality is at work in these ads. They must be considered as gender ideology—that is, as specifically (consciously or unconsciously) servicing the cultural reproduction of gender difference and gender inequality, quite independent of (although at times coinciding with) marketing concerns. (1993, 110)

Bordo's comment here demonstrates that the traditional Left view to markets—that is, that they simply maximize capitalist profits—is inadequate in a market in which identity, identification, ideology, and actual bodies are legislated. When we consider the necessary element of desire—lack, however it is rhetorically created—markets take on a new meaning socially. Chantal Mouffe points out that this lack is not necessarily a problematic "separation" from a truthful origin (let's recall the original figures of the "pure" workers with which the 1930s Left hounded Kenneth Burke), but a productive place on which identity is built through a "dialectic of subversion and over-determination," in which "whatever identity s/he has can be constituted only through acts of *identification*" (1992, 11). This, of course, is precisely what Kenneth Burke told the Left in the 1935.

I for one, on the Left, and quite without a prepostmodern subjectivity (having been born at practically the instant that John F. Kennedy was assassinated), am ready to take the capitalist acts of *identification* that have never not been part of the U.S. cultural art, philosophy, and standards[14] as the player who has the strongest moves. Rather than give up, take my ball, and go home to Walden woods, I aim to study this player's moves, even if time and again I am beaten by some fast break, for in the beating is the power.

"How is advertising an evil temptress (*pace* Baudrillard) threatening to engulf our pure selves in some fearsome labial quicksand of capital and lip gloss?" is an outmoded and gendered question, which nonetheless continues to be imbricated in cultural studies' assumptions.[15] "How does advertising make this move of *producing* desire, and how does it interact with audiences *as* identity?" is the new question that becomes relevant in New Times.

To address the new question, we can look at any number of a new grouping of videos, books, and articles that take advertising seriously as a producer of political and social identity. This grouping of texts ranges from the archival investigation to theoretization; the key thing is that advertising as a popular cultural form in these works is accorded an investigation that takes into account the depth of its influence and penetration into the media, personal, social, and political elements of identity formation. (In hands-on pedagogy, this might be effected by devoting entire courses within cultural studies programs to the analysis of advertising history and production— though this is problematic because these courses are now part of a "how-to" curriculum in business or journalism/communications departments.)

One reason, in fact, that cultural studies has valorized cultural genres such as film, television, music video, and performance art over the more pervasively public advertising culture may lie in the disciplinarity of advertising and the disciplinarity of the fields that have been the home courts of cultural study. Since its beginnings, advertising has attached its dream work to the scientism of sociology, and demography, and the "top-down" psychology of behaviorism (it had yet to invent the term "market research" for itself).[16] Thus advertising desire becomes part of the more scientific fields of business or psychology, rather than part of a humanities emphasis, though the humanities are squarely focused upon imaginary production of desire in all other areas of investigation. But these disciplinary factors of contemporary academe are not the sole reason for agoraphobia in cultural studies; the strongest force behind it is the long-held deep mythologies of the Left, which continue from its American heyday in the 1930s to the present.

Daniel Miller, in his introduction to *Acknowledging Consumption: A Review of New Studies* (a collection of works that looks at desire from a "macro" political economy stance), offers the best summary of some Left attitudes toward markets that seem to underpin the fear of the marketplace. He identifies several key macro myths held by the Left that, in my view, result in the "micro" rejection of advertising as a powerful player. The main myths that Miller identifies are (in summary): (1) mass consumption causes global homogenization; (2) consumption is opposed to sociality; (3) consumption is opposed to authenticity; and (4) consumption creates particular kinds of social beings who are keyed to emulation (Miller 1995, 21).

Paul Gorman, in an important new study of the Left and popular culture in the early century, observes the same tendency on the part of leftists who sought to theorize the close cousin of advertising—popular entertainments.

> Their considerations of mass culture typically started from preconceptions about the public's passivity, suggestibility, or lack of imagination that made its interactions with entertainments seem dangerous by definition. . . . Intellectuals assumed that entertainments were literal embodiments of particular values and that they produced direct and immediate effects on their audiences. (1996, 10)

In some senses, when the Left accepts what these myths present as the top-down influence version of advertising as an Evil Influencer, it is reproducing advertising's own best copy: We Can Gauge and Make Desire, and We Know *How* We Do It. Advertising has located its own training and self-study in business, whereas cultural studies draws faculty and students primarily from more humanistic disciplines such as English, film, sociology, philosophy, political science, and education. But in fact, advertisers of Kenneth Burke's era and of our era are still, despite their scientific study of populations and of reactions of desire, not clear on precisely *how* desire is created, which yields the space of relevance for investigation by the humanities.

With this said, below is listed a cross-section of works, each with a brief summary of the approach and content, that take a view to advertising in the spirit of productive cultural study, offering either theoretical, historical/ archival, production-oriented, or aesthetic looks at advertising.

Note on the one hand that my goal is not to build a better Barbie, nor is it to emplace advertisers as "heroes" or "heroines" in place of the "devil" they have been made by traditional Marxist thought. Advertisers' current and historical problematics should be exposed in all their specificity. As a superstructure, advertising has at times in its history been indeed a racist, sexist, anti-Semitic, xenophobic, homophobic entity; we should bear this always in mind as we ask the new question of: What is advertising as a legitimate and strong shaper of identity and of social groups, who may "sample," hybridize, and articulate it in ways that are anything *but* racist, sexist, anti-Semitic, xenophobic?

She's Not *My* Aunt: Advertising and Race, New Figures, New Tropes

Clearly one true crime of advertising, in its dream-work pedagogy, is the unrelenting brutality with which it has historically entered into the American imaginary on the issue of race—in other words, how this pedagogy of ideology has taught Americans (of all races) "blackness." So, publications that work with race, taking into account a rehistoricized view of race, will lead our list of texts, since this new work is perhaps most important to offer to students of all races. First, Marlon Riggs's *Color Adjustment*, a film by the late award-winning filmmaker about the way in which race is made in advertisements, is central to this canon. Second are two books that raise the issue of race in regard to the creation of markets and how those markets are perceived as social groups. The first of these, *Watching Race: Television and the Struggle for "Blackness"* by sociologist Herman Gray, takes up the issue of "authenticity" of representation of blackness on 1980s television, and cross-fades this look with consideration of the construction of the "underclass" as a "pure" category by the Reagan administration. The book includes chapters that address *The Cosby Show, A Different World, Frank's Place,* and others and how the discourses of blackness distinguish different viewing groups for the shows. The second book is *Racism, Culture and Markets* by British thinker John Gabriel. Gabriel's work has British culture as its referent, and so might be difficult for some U.S. students to work with, but it provides a wide-ranging view, moving from solid theoretical considerations about the construction of race to particular instances in the British public sphere, including the issue of interracial adoption and the complexities of the post-Rushdie division of Islamic and Christian Britain over the publication of the *Satanic Verses*.

Those interested in rehistoricizing the period of the 1920s in which advertising first grew up will find a strong resource in Ann Douglas's 1995 604-page monument, *Terrible Honesty: Mongrel Manhattan in the 1920s.* Douglas attempts to put race (and immigrant culture) back in the picture in the history of the period, and provides an extraordinary bibliographic essay for further research. An outstanding article by Maurice Manring appears in the fall 1995 issue of *Southern Cultures* (a new journal by Duke University Press) in which he outlines the construction of Aunt Jemima by the J. Walter Thompson advertising agency. Manring uses archival material to provide a specific and historical unmasking of this figure that has been such a problematic point in advertising. This article is an example of some of the strongest analysis of precisely how, historically, the representation and desire for a particular figure of female blackness was created for markets.

Perhaps the strongest text in providing ways to rethink race in terms of the representations of advertising is Kobena Mercer's *Welcome to the Jungle: New Positions in Black Cultural Studies.* Though Mercer's work ranges widely across the production of images and selves in film, hair style, gay communities, and under postmodernism in general, his presentation of the specificity of identity production is most relevant to the issues facing students who would approach advertising representations theoretically.

Truth and Lie in an Ultra-Modern Sense: The Nietzschean Myth

One book reorganizes all thinking on advertising study, and though this essay seeks to engage recent looks, this one in all likelihood will not be superceded in its significance: Roland Marchand's pivotal *Advertising the American Dream: Making Way for Modernity 1920–1940*, published in 1985. In painstaking historical detail, Marchand retells the story of American advertising as organized around the type of Nietzschean mythologies that guide identities and ideologies (as opposed to the mythologies so often invoked by Left critics of advertising who use the word "myth" as simply a synonym for "not true," the Platonic lie). With numerous plates of actual ads from the 1920s to the 1940s (the Jazz Age through the Great Depression and WWII), Marchand looks at the specificities of production of the advertisements that shaped "modern" American working, middle, and ruling classes, exploring a variety of audiences and audience responses to different ad appeals, which changed with historical need. (For example, the Left wasn't the only producer that sought to have "pure" and "realistic workers" in the 1930s—advertisers sought to use this appeal as well. Significantly, it was not successful for them either.[17]) Marchand's work is particularly strong in tracking the developments of different types of product lines and different types of audience markets; he includes several chapters and chapter sections on marketing to women. This text alone could serve as an introduction to a productive cultural study of advertising for advanced undergraduate or graduate courses.

Jackson Lears's 1994 *Fables of Abundance: A Cultural History of Advertising in America* builds on Marchand's work and presents the kind of justified caution about the power of advertising that a truly historicized look brings forth. Lears's work is theoretically situated in the opening chapter and proceeds through an extraordinarily interdisciplinary examination of the history of advertising, ending with a look at the fictional autobiographical settling of oneself into one's market niche in the novel *A Fan's Notes*. Lears's book is most interesting in its examination of the complex relationship between advertising and high culture in chapters titled "The Courtship of Avant-Garde and Kitsch" and "The Pursuit of the Real."

Andrew Wernick's *Promotional Culture* offers an important theoretical bridge (and a highly useful term in the title) between what he identifies as an earlier theoretical view (of the top-down variety) that he held at first and a later view (of the productive identity variety) at which he arrived after specific study of promotional techniques. Wernick includes an interesting chapter investigating the marketing campaign of his own institution, Trent University in Canada.

New Markets/New Histories

Works that seek to investigate not the history of advertising but the history of particular markets for cultural ideas that were spread through advertising are also quite useful in this investigation. Joan Shelley Rubin's *The Making of Middlebrow Culture* builds on the important work of Janice Radway and offers a very strong history and analysis of the creation in the 1930s, 1940s, and 1950s of the "banal" market for culturally commodified icons of taste, including literature, art, and philosophy. This work is highly useful in providing a look at the way in which ideology *per se* can be advertised and sold.

Less useful, because it is written in more general terms and does not specifically trace ideologies to their particular marketing campaigns, is Stephanie Coontz's best-selling *The Way We Never Were*, which debunks the myths of American Family that are built up through advertising. Susan Willis's *A Primer For Daily Life* and Rachel Bowlby's *Shopping with Freud*, which are oriented to actual and literary experiences of shopping and selling, are quite productive, especially Willis's chapter titled "I Shop, Therefore I Am" and Bowlby's chapter "*Lolita* and the Poetry of Advertising," which identifies the fear of the American mass market as literally embodied in Nabokov's *Lolita*.

Among recent feminist looks at advertising, Naomi Wolf's work (*The Beauty Myth*) is highly readable and addresses specific ad campaigns, but it is highly problematic in its continuance of the feminist equivalent of the Left's fear of the marketplace—the top-down approach.[18] On the other hand, Susan Bordo's groundbreaking *Unbearable Weight: Feminism, Western*

Culture, and the Body, grounded in the work of Foucault, engages the productive power of advertising as Bordo takes up some of the most problematic contemporary examples of the "training" of the female body to slimness. Though Bordo's work in many ways does not embrace the "hybridity" of the postmodern in its critique, it does offer a view to mass media that gives the audience (girls, working class, etc.) the possibility of agency when engaging advertising matter. Bordo's current attention is turned toward advertising's increasing focus on the construction of a hard (and hyperphallic) masculinity; she has published article-length studies on this topic.

These texts, which specifically engage the history and construction of advertising and markets, when combined with theoretical readings by Baudrillard, Horkheimer, Adorno, Judith Butler, Paul Virilio, E. Ann Kaplan, Teresa De Lauretis, and perhaps, because of the close fit of the semiotic method with rhetorical analysis of visual images, Roland Barthes, offer the possibility for undergraduates and graduate students in cultural studies to break their replication (no matter how well meaning and Left-leaning) of the advertisers' own public relations line: that *they*, not the agency of markets, create and control desire. Advertisers, we may be sure, are not sure, or they would not continue their intensive study of subjectivity. Desire controls desire, or desire unleashes desire, or lack unleashes desire, and no one (despite Freud, Lacan, Cixous, and all rereaders to date) has yet found, bottled, labeled or sold that which, unleashes lack.

So the important move for cultural studies pedagogy is to be certain that the approach is one that does not simply seek to "uncover lies" told by advertisers, or in other words go looking for the "origin" of lack by quickly labeling a particular appeal "pathetic" or "based on fear" or, that is to say, associated with the reviled feminine. Cultural studies workers must examine *in particular* how markets (which both are themselves and are composed of social groups [LaClau and Mouffe 1985] of human subjects) constitute and produce identity, both within the hegemony of these "lies" and within alternative hegemony. For as the Left stands out of bounds— swatting poisonous flies and trying to uncover the authentic, purified, true representation of the worker—or out of whatever we are under New Times, desire fakes right and scores.

There's nothing to be afraid of. We're already soaking in it.

Notes

1. Thanks to Jack Selzer, Debra Hawhee, Andrew Alexander, Pat Shannon, Henry Giroux, Susan Searls, and the Philosophy I.M. Basketball Team (D. Conway, S. Grass, J. Lee, B. Lewis, J. Lindsey et al.) of Pennsylvania State University, and to Virginia Blum,

Ellen Rosenman, Greg Waller and Steven Weisenburger of the University of Kentucky for their help in preparing this article.

2. Nietzsche was strongly influenced by the works of Emerson (see Stack 1992). Emerson, of course, was involved in Thoreau's Walden experiment in solitude, making this market-free utopia possible by paying Thoreau's rent on his tract of land, and by frequently having Thoreau to Concord for dinner. Thoreau, thus, could step out of the "poison" of the marketplace only by attaching himself to ruling-class support.

3. This immanence, so central to the work of Adorno, seems slippery when Horkheimer and Adorno actually address specific cultural creations, such as the Hollywood cinema. When the distasteful (and often feminized) cultural object comes near, all of a sudden "immanence" is not so close to its analytic object, and the Left culture critic can move aside with gendered disdain.

4. Woodward, who was one of the first women to work in advertising, wrote prolifically about the experience, publishing several books on the topic. Note the direct identification of the pedagogical goal of advertising, and the present tense (1938) used in relation to these goals: "Advertising has jobs to do. Women, for instance, haven't learned how to use new stoves and iceboxes; they haven't caught up with domestic labor-saving appliances. Here there's still legitimate work to be done in what advertising calls consumer education" (6).

5. In most of his writings, Burke uses the term "cooperation" as a direct euphemism for "communism."

6. This term, from Andrew Wernick's work in 1991 on ideology and symbolic expression, is extremely useful, encompassing advertising and the associated promotional practices that attend to it, such as product tie-ins with movies.

7. The strong reaction against promotional culture on the Left has been preserved in Horkheimer and Adorno's "culture industry" thesis, so central to much work in cultural studies, but in many ways a continuance of the "trivializing" and "poison-painting" of issues that were folded into working-class consciousness from 1921 forward. Baudrillard, though a leading theorist of the simulacral, in his early (1970) work on consumer society and in his later work consistently rhetorically presented the mass market as an evil (female) seducer. In fact he uses the French term *medussé* from "Medusa" to indicate what was translated into English as "stupefied." The translator found the usage so problematic as to include the original French for the reader despite moves in the later work to blur the early conflation of women/consumption/evil, Freud famously conflates directly with the female genitalia in the 1922 essay "Medusa's Head").

8. "Bennetton's 'World Without Borders': Buying Social Change." Giroux also discusses the recent tie-ins to Disney movies that re-created every Burger King in the country as an ideology stand.

9. This "purified" worker's alignment with a pure Platonic hierarchy of forms, clearly a ruling-class metaphysical preference of categories, is instructive.

10. Michel de Certeau's *The Practice of Everyday Life* (1974) holds that we "must first analyze its manipulation by users who are not its makers. Only then can we gauge the difference or similarity between the production of the image and the secondary production hidden in the process of its utilization" (xiii).

11. Roland Marchand applies this term as one of the leading "mythologies" of advertising in his *Advertising the American Dream: Making Way for Modernity 1920–1940*.

12. In Proposition 10 of his "Twelve Propositions on the Relations Between Economics and Psychology," first published in *Science and Society* in 1938 and later collected in *The Philosophy of Literary Form* in 1941, Burke said, "Style is an aspect of identification. . . . Even a materially dispossessed individual may 'own' privilege vicariously by adopting the 'style' (or 'insignia') of some privileged class. . . . Consideration of such 'symbolic boasting' offers an excellent instance in support of our contention that the analysis of aesthetic phenomena can be

extended or projected into the analysis of social and political phenomena in general. We see a petty clerk, for instance, who can 'identify' himself either by 'owning the style' of the workers or by 'owning the style' of his boss" (309–10).

13. An interesting look at the practices of New Media and the interplay between what is "really" an ad and what isn't can be found in Solomon and English, "Reality Engineering: Blurring the Boundaries Between Commercial Signification and Popular Culture." *Journal of Current Issues and Research in Advertising*, Fall 1994.

14. Whether embodied in the figure of F. Scott Fitzgerald (along with John Barrymore) in a Woodbury soap ad as the judge of the "loveliest" woman using Woodbury soap, or in the figure of high modern mystic poet Hart Crane, who began "The River" in *The Bridge* with direct reference to advertising slogans created by the advertising agency he worked for in 1923 (J. Walter Thompson), the year of the poem's composition, or in the "portrayal" of the culture of "color-matched" bathrooms or the Books of the Month (Radway), twentieth-century American art has never not defined itself either via, in opposition to, or complicitly with promotional culture.

15. Andreas Huyssen's *Beyond the Great Divide* addresses the way in which theorists of modernism and modernity, including Horkheimer and Adorno (and, I would argue, most postmodern theorists who base their work on culture industry theses) view the expanding mass commercial market of advertising and any association with it as feminine, a great Medusa Head to be feared, and so on.

16. The "father of behaviorism," John B. Watson, left a position at Johns Hopkins University to take up a vice presidency at the J. Walter Thompson advertising agency, where he, working with the "father of the MBA," Paul Cherington, who was instrumental in creating the notion of "market research." (JWT Archives)

17. Consider also that the Left was not as "purified" from advertising in these early days as it would have liked to portray. Helen Woodward writes: "There has been a great deal of wailing on the part of advertising clients lately because so many copy writers seem to have interests which they consider subversive. The ad-writers since they have to supply brains and imagination and seldom get the biggest money, are inclined to the left. They are such traitors as to like Roosevelt, and some of them are even for the American Labor Party. There are Communists among them, and Socialists, but these keep very quiet. Advertising clients try to fight these 'vicious tendencies,' but they creep out. If the copy writer is good, the agency will overlook his radical opinions and keep them a secret from the client" (1938, 28–29).

18. The feminist version of the Ewen-style early work in the study of advertising, which nonetheless simply reproduces an uncomplicated top-down relation, is best represented by the work of Jean Kilbourne, whose readings of advertisements for messages about sex indeed find those sexual images, but often do not make the further move of extrapolating from this "sex" to the power of "desire" and how it is marshaled.

Works Cited

Baudrillard, Jean. *Selected Writings*. Edited and with an introduction by Mark Poster. Trans. by Jacques Mourrain. Stanford, CA: Stanford University Press, 1988.

Bordo, Susan. *Unbearable Weight: Feminism, Western Culture, and the Body*. Berkeley: University of California Press, 1993.

Bowlby, Rachel. *Shopping With Freud*. New York: Routledge, 1993.

Burke, Kenneth. *Counter-Statement*. Berkeley: University of California Press, 1968. (First published 1931.)

————. *Permanence and Change: An Anatomy of Purpose*. Third edition with a new afterword. Berkeley: University of California Press, 1985. (First published 1935.)

Certeau, Michel de. *The Practice of Everyday Life*. Trans. Steven Rendall. Berkeley: University of California Press, 1984. (First published in French in 1974.)

Coontz, Stephanie. *The Way We Never Were: American Families and the Nostalgia Trap*. New York: Basic Books, 1992.

Douglas, Ann. *Terrible Honesty: Mongrel Manhattan in the 1920s*. New York: Farrar, Straus, Giroux, 1995.

Ewen, Stuart, and Elizabeth Ewen. *Channels of Desire: Mass Images and the Shaping of American Consciousness*. Minneapolis: University of Minnesota Press, 1992. (First published in 1982 by McGraw-Hill).

Freud, Sigmund. "*Medusa's Head*" (1940 [1922]). In *Freud on Women: A Reader*, 272–273. Edited and with an introduction by Elisabeth Young-Bruehl.

Gabriel, John. *Racism, Culture, Markets*. New York: Routledge, 1994.

Giroux, Henry. "Benetton's 'World Without Borders': Buying Social Change." *The Subversive Imagination*. 187–207.

————. *Border Crossings: Cultural Workers and the Politics of Education*. New York: Routledge, 1992.

————. *Fugitive Cultures: Race, Violence, and Youth*. New York: Routledge, 1996.

Gorman, Paul R. *Left Intellectuals and Popular Culture in Twentieth-Century America*. Chapel Hill: University of Norton Carolina Press, 1996.

Gramsci, Antonio. *Selections from Cultural Writings*. Edited by David Forgacs and Geoffrey Nowell-Smith. Trans. by William Boelhower. Cambridge: Harvard University Press, 1985.

Gray, Herman. *Watching Race: Television and the Struggle for "Blackness."* Minneapolis: University of Minnesota Press, 1995.

Hall, Stuart, and Martin Jacques, eds. *New Times: The Changing Face of Politics in the 1990s*. New York: Verso, 1990.

JWT Archive. Special Collections Library, Duke University. Durham, North Carolina.

LaClau, Ernesto, and Chantal Mouffe. *Hegemony and Socialist Strategy: Towards a Radical Democratic Politics*. London: Verso, 1985.

Lears, Jackson. *Fables of Abundance: A Cultural History of Advertising in America*. New York: Basic Books, 1994.

Lentricchia, Frank. *Criticism and Social Change*. Chicago: University of Chicago Press, 1983.

Manring, Maurice M. "Aunt Jemima Explained: The Old South, the Absent Mistress, and the Slave in a Box." *Southern Cultures* 2(1) (Fall 1995): 19–44.

Marchand, Roland. *Advertising the American Dream: Making Way for Modernity 1920–1940*. Berkeley: University of California Press, 1985.

Mercer, Kobena. *Welcome to the Jungle: New Positions in Black Cultural Studies*. New York: Routledge, 1994.

Miller, Daniel, ed. *Acknowledging Consumption: A Review of New Studies*. London: Routledge, 1995.

Mort, Frank. "The Politics of Consumption." In Hall, Stuart and Martin Jacques, eds. *New Times: The Changing Face of Politics in the 1990s*, 160–172. New York: Verso, 1990.

Mouffe, Chantal, ed. "Democratic Politics Today." In *Dimensions of Radical Democracy: Pluralism, Citizenship, Community*, 1–17. London: Verso, 1992.

Nietzsche, Friedrich. *Thus Spoke Zarathustra: A Book for All and None*. Translated and with a preface by Walter Kaufmann. New York: Modern Library, 1995.

Riggs, Marlon, and Vivian Kleiman. *Color Adjustment: Blacks in Prime Time*. California Newsreel/Media at Work/Resolution, 1991.

Rubin, Joan Shelley. *The Making of Middlebrow Culture*. Chapel Hill: University of North Carolina Press, 1992.

Selzer, Jack. *Conversing With the Moderns: Kenneth Burke, 1915–1931*. Madison: University of Wisconsin Press, 1996.

Stack, George J. *Nietzsche and Emerson: An Elective Affinity*. Athens, Ohio University Press, 1992.

Willis, Susan. *A Primer for Daily Life*. London: Routledge, 1988.

Wernick, Andrew. *Promotional Culture: Advertising, Ideology and Symbolic Expression*. London: Sage, 1991.

Wolf, Naomi. *The Beauty Myth: How Images of Beauty Are Used Against Women*. New York: W. Morrow, 1991.

Woodward, Helen. *It's an Art*. New York: Harcourt, Brace, 1938.

Pedagogy, Education, and Cultural Studies

15

Is There a Place for Cultural Studies in Colleges of Education?

Henry A. Giroux

With the last decade, cultural studies has become something of a boom industry. Bookstores have scurried to set up cultural studies displays that house the growing collection of texts now published under its theoretical banner. Within universities and colleges, cultural studies programs appear with growing frequency in traditional disciplinary departments and in new inter-disciplinary units as cultural studies becomes the "umbrella of choice" among younger academics.[1] Large crowds attend cultural studies symposiums at academic conferences. Moreover, as the favored sites of cultural studies have shifted from England to Australia, Canada, Africa, Latin America, and the United States, it has become one of the few radically innovative fields to have traveled across multiple borders and spaces, loosely uniting a diverse group of intellectuals who challenge conventional understandings of the relationship among culture, power, and politics. Far from residing in the margins of a specialized discourse, cultural studies has more recently attracted the interest of both the popular media and established press.

Given the lavish attention that cultural studies has received, many critics have dismissed it as simply another academic fashion. More serious criticism has focused on its Eurocentric tendencies, its narrow academic presence, and what some have called its political fuzziness. I believe that, despite its popularity and the danger of commodification and appropriation that its growing influence and appeal pose, cultural studies is a field that holds enormous promise for progressives who are willing to address some of the fundamental problems of our times. But whether that promise is realized will depend not only on the relevance of the challenges, contexts, and problems that cultural studies addresses but also on the willingness of its practitioners to enter into its interdisciplinary discourses less as a journey into sacred theoretical ground than as ongoing critical interrogation of its own formation and practice as a political and ethical project. This raises as many questions for those who practice cultural studies as it does for educators who might be interested in applying its insights to educational theory and practice, especially with respect to reforming colleges of education.

Given the popularity of cultural studies for a growing number of scholars, I have often wondered why so few academics have incorporated cultural studies into the language of education reform, particularly as it applies to colleges and schools of education. In part, this indifference may be explained by the narrow technocratic models that dominate mainstream reform efforts and structure many education programs. Other considerations would include a history of education reform overly indebted to practical considerations that often support a long tradition of anti-intellectualism. Within such a tradition, management issues become more important than understanding and furthering schools as democratic public spheres. Hence, the regulation, certification, and standardization of teacher behavior is emphasized over creating conditions for teachers to undertake the sensitive political and ethical roles they might assume as public intellectuals educating students for responsible, critical citizenship. Moreover, the dominant tradition favors containing and assimilating cultural differences rather than treating students as bearers of diverse social memories with a right to speak and represent themselves in the quest for learning and self-determination. While other disciplines have appropriated, engaged, and produced new theoretical languages in keeping with changing historical conditions, colleges of education have maintained a deep distrust of theory and intellectual dialogue.[2]

Cultural studies is largely concerned with the relationship among culture, knowledge, and power. Consequently, it is not surprising that mainstream educators rarely engage it except to dismiss it as another theoretical fashion. The refusal on the part of such educators can, in part, be understood against the background of their claim to being professional, scientific, and objective.

In opposition to this alleged "view from nowhere," cultural studies challenges the self-ascribed ideological and institutional innocence of mainstream educators by arguing that teachers always work and speak within historically and socially determined relations of power. Education is a site of ongoing struggle and contestation, shaped in the intersection between social and cultural reproduction, on the one hand, and the disruptions produced through competing, resisting, and unsettling practices and discourses on the other. As institutions actively engaged in forms of moral and social regulation, schools presuppose fixed notions of cultural and national identity. As agents in the production, circulation, and use of particular forms of cultural and symbolic capital, teachers occupy an inescapably political role.[3]

By virtue of its refusal to decouple the dynamics of politics and power from schooling, cultural studies is often dismissed as being too ideological; or, by virtue of its conviction that education generates a privileged narrative space for some students and a space that fosters inequality and subordination for others, it is simply ignored. Embodying dominant forms of cultural capital, schooling often functions to affirm the Eurocentric, patriarchal histories, social identities, and cultural experiences of middle-class students while either marginalizing or erasing the voices, experiences, and cultural memories of so-called minority students. For many students, schooling means either experiencing daily forms of classroom interaction that are irrelevant to their lives or bearing the harsh reality of discrimination and oppression expressed through tracking, policing, harassment, and expulsion.[4]

Traditionally, schools and colleges of education in the United States have been organized around either conventional subject-based studies (e.g., math education) or disciplinary/administrative categories (curriculum and instruction). Within this type of intellectual division of labor, students generally have few opportunities to study larger social issues through a multi-disciplinary perspective. This slavish adherence to structuring the curriculum around disciplines is at odds with the field of cultural studies, whose theoretical energies are largely focused on issues regarding gender, class, sexuality, national identity, colonialism, race, ethnicity, cultural popularism, textuality, and critical pedagogy.[5] The resistance to cultural studies may also arise from its emphasis on understanding schooling as a mechanism of politics embedded in relations of power, negotiation, and contestation.[6] By offering educators a critical language through which to examine the ideological and political interests that structure conservative reform efforts such as nationalized testing, standardized curriculum, and efficiency models, cultural studies incurs the wrath of mainstream and conservative educators who often are silent about the political interests that underlie their discursive practices and reform agendas.

Cultural studies also rejects the notion of pedagogy as a technique or set of neutral skills and argues that pedagogy is a cultural practice that can be understood only through considerations of history, politics, power, and culture. Given its concern with everyday life, its pluralization of cultural communities, and its emphasis on knowledge that is "between or among the disciplines without being reducible to any or all of them,"[7] cultural studies is less concerned with issues of certification and testing than it is with how knowledge, texts, and cultural products are used. Pedagogy becomes, in this instance, the terrain through which students critically engage and challenge the diverse cultural discourses, practices, and popular media they experience in their everyday existence. Indeed, such a pedagogy would examine the historical, social, economic, and political factors that impel the current concern with issues of certification. From this perspective, culture is the ground "on which analysis proceeds, the object of study, and the site of political critique and intervention."[8] This in part explains why some advocates of cultural studies are increasingly interested in "how and where knowledge needs to surface and emerge in order to be consequential" with respect to expanding the possibilities for a radical democracy.[9]

Within the next century, educators will not be able to ignore the hard questions that schools will face regarding multiculturalism, race, identity, power, knowledge, ethics, and work. These issues will largely define the meaning and purpose of schooling, what it means to teach, and how students should be taught to live in a world that will be vastly more globalized, high tech, and racially diverse than ever before. As capitalist globalization integrates financial systems, mobilizes worldwide communication and consumption networks, and increasingly divides a post-Fordist labor force between "core" and "periphery" workers, cultural studies will need to recognize that the politics and space of globalization is one of struggle and contestation, and not merely a space of domination.[10]

Cultural studies offers some possibilities for educators to rethink the nature of educational theory and practice as well as what it means to educate future teachers for the twenty-first century.[11] In what follows, I want to chart the diverse assumptions and practices defined loosely under the theoretical banner of cultural studies that might inform a transformative pedagogical project. I will conclude by suggesting how this field might have important consequences for reforming schools and colleges of education. I will also take up how progressive educators might address or theorize cultural studies as part of a larger discourse of social and political reconstruction.

The Space of Cultural Studies

Within the past decade, the field of cultural studies has developed a broad following in the United States.[12] In the most general sense, cultural studies signifies a massive shift away from Eurocentric master narratives, disciplinary knowledge, high culture, scientism, and other legacies informed by the diverse heritage of modernism. The parameters and cartography of this shift include but are not limited to three important assumptions.

First, cultural studies is premised on the belief that the traditional distinctions that separate and frame established academic disciplines cannot account for the great diversity of cultural and social phenomena that has come to characterize an increasingly hybridized, postindustrial world. The university has long been linked to a notion of national identity that is largely defined by and committed to transmitting traditional western culture.[13] Traditionally, this has been a culture of exclusion, one that has ignored the multiple narratives, histories, and voices of culturally and politically subordinated groups. Challenging this legacy, disparate social movements have emerged, arguing for a genuinely multicultural and multiracial society. Movements organized largely by feminists, radical students of color, and gay and lesbian activists have contested how subordinate groups are often prevented from drawing upon their own histories and cultural experiences in order to challenge how knowledge is organized and legitimated within higher education. Moreover, the spread of electronically mediated culture to all spheres of everyday intellectual and artistic life has shifted the ground of scholarship away from the traditional disciplines designed to preserve a "common culture" to the more hybridized fields of comparative and world literature, media studies, ecology, society and technology, and popular culture.

Second, advocates of cultural studies have argued strongly that the role of media culture—including the power of the mass media, with its massive apparatuses of representation and its mediation of knowledge—is central to understanding how the dynamics of power, privilege, and social desire structure the daily life of a society. This concern with culture and its connection to power has necessitated a critical interrogation of the relationship between knowledge and authority, and of the historical and social contexts that deliberately shape students' understandings of representations of the past, present, and future. But if a sea change in the development and reception of what counts as knowledge has taken place, it has been accompanied by an understanding of how we define and apprehend the multitude of electronic, aural, and visual texts that have become determining features of media culture and everyday life in the United States. By analyzing the full range of assorted and densely layered sites of learning such as the media, popular culture, film, advertising, mass communications, and religious organizations, among others, cultural studies expands our understanding of the pedagogical and its role outside of school as the traditional site of learning.

At stake here is the attempt to produce new theoretical models and methodologies for addressing the production, structure, and exchange of knowledge. This approach to inter- and postdisciplinary studies is invaluable because it addresses the pedagogical issue of organizing dialogue across and outside of the disciplines. It does so in order to promote alternative approaches to research and teaching about culture and the newly emerging technologies and forms of knowledge. For instance, rather than organize courses around strictly disciplinary concerns arising out of English and social studies courses, colleges of education might organize courses that broaden students' understanding of themselves and others by examining events that evoke a sense of social responsibility and moral accountability. Such courses might focus on scholarship that addresses a multiplicity of contexts in which issues concerning identity formation, language, work, cultural production, and social responsibility intersect. For instance, the politics of health care could be linked to analyzing public attitudes toward communities in which class and race have a strong influence on shaping public schooling. The question of national identity and education could be analyzed through the ways in which various Hollywood films combine narrative and spectacle to glorify colonial power and imperialism from the dominant perspective. Similarly, such narratives can also be analyzed through forms of cinematic counter-telling provided by Third World films such as *The Battle of Algiers, Hour of the Furnaces,* and *The Official Story.*

Equally important is the need for educators to appropriate the critical insights provided by cultural studies and incorporate them into pedagogical projects that provide political resources for students to understand the dynamics of practical politics and active citizenship. Whether through historical inquiry, public service, or analyses of larger public events, educators can provide students with the opportunity both to engage problem-solving projects that teach the lessons of civic education and to interact with diverse groups that engage social issues within specific public arenas. For example, the relationship between racism and schooling can be analyzed through forms of antiracist education conducted by diverse groups in the larger community. Students can meet with such groups in order to understand how different views of racial justice are brought to bear on the issue of racism and reflect on how such views might inform their historical and social formation as teachers and the pedagogies they use in their classrooms.

Third, in addition to broadening the terms and parameters of learning, cultural studies rejects the professionalization of educators and the alienating and often elitist discourse of professionalism and sanitized expertise. Instead, it argues for educators who self-consciously produce knowledge and power-related discourses that must be examined in relation to both "the conditions of their construction and their social effects."[14] In this view, teachers must be accountable in their teaching to the ways in which they take up and respond to the problems of history, human agency, and the renewal of democratic public life. Cultural studies strongly rejects the assumption that teachers are simply transmitters of existing configurations of knowledge. Academics are always implicated in the dynamics of social power and knowledge that they produce, mediate, and legitimate in their classrooms. In this perspective, intellectual work is incomplete unless it self-consciously assumes responsibility for its effects in the larger public culture. Hence, cultural studies raises questions about what knowledges are produced in the university and how these might extend and deepen democratic public life. Equally important is the issue of how to democratize schools so as to enable those groups largely divorced from or simply not represented in the curriculum to be able to produce their own self-images, tell their own stories, and engage in respectful dialogue with others.

Doing Cultural Studies:
An Agenda for Colleges of Education

The current drive in the United States toward the vocationalization of colleges of education is evident in the ascendancy of reforms emphasizing efficiency and applied learning. Lost from this reductionistic emphasis on the practical is any broader sense of vision, meaning, or motivation regarding the role that colleges of education might play in expanding the "scope of democracy and democratic institutions."[15] The moral bankruptcy of the new vocationalization is increasingly matched by that of state legislatures and others seeking to further mandate the current emphasis on the technical training of prospective teachers. Cost efficiency, restructuring, and downsizing have become code words to tie education more closely to the ideological and economic imperatives of the labor market. This is evident, for instance, in the current conservative assessment of liberal arts programs as ideologically expendable and economically unfeasible. In many universities, including the University of Minnesota and Yale, critical programs within the humanities focusing on ethnicity, feminism, and literary studies have been eliminated or drastically reduced in size.

Corporate influence in the university can be seen in the funding of endowed chairs, research projects, and policy institutes organized around conservative ideological interests, and training programs that promise future employment in the new global order. Whereas higher education might have once applauded educating students for occupations that revitalize public life, such as health care, teaching, and social work, the new emphasis is on educating students for work in technical and managerial fields, such as computer and financial services. The MBA has become the degree of choice in higher education, and the ideological considerations that legitimate it have become the model for evaluating other college and university programs.[16]

In opposition to this view, I believe that cultural studies can define and provide the institutional space and practice needed to educate teachers and administrators to play a vital role in renewing civic life. Joe Murphy, former chancellor of the City University of New York, has captured the spirit of what it means for teachers to address such a project. He argues that teachers should "give students sensibility to understand economic, political, and historical forces so they're not just victims of these forces but can *act on them with effect*. Giving [students, especially the poor] this power is a threatening idea to many. But it is essential to the health of a democratic society."[17]

Broadly conceived, cultural studies can become the theoretical matrix for producing teachers at the forefront of interdisciplinary, critically engaged work. Central to such an approach would be a number of identifying themes that would organize lectures, seminars, research projects, academic programs, and collaborative work among both faculty and students. A number of theoretical elements could shape the context and content of a cultural studies approach that would address reforming schools and colleges of education. What follows is my own partial list of considerations.

First, by making culture a central construct in our classrooms and curricula, cultural studies focuses the terms of learning on issues relating to cultural differences, power, and history. In order to make a difference, cultural studies needs to analyze these issues as part of a wider struggle to extend the possibility for dialogue and debate about the quality of democratic public life. In this perspective, both the construction of curriculum knowledge and pedagogy provide narrative space for the understanding and critical analysis of multiple histories, experiences, and cultures. Cultural studies offers education theorists a transnational approach to literacy and learning. By pluralizing the concept of literacy, cultural studies provides fertile theoretical ground for taking up pedagogy as an act of decentering, a form of transit and border crossing, a way of constructing an intercultural politics in which dialogue, exchange, and translation take place across different communities, national boundaries, and regional borders. Cultural studies has been traditionally concerned with culture as something that is unfinished, incomplete, and always in process. In this approach, the study of culture is grounded in a continual analysis of local, national, and global conditions as they enable or prevent possibilities for human dignity and critical agency in others. Knowledge and beliefs are not rendered legitimate or useful by virtue of their production within specific disciplines nor to their indebtedness to what is alleged to be western culture, but mix and merge with different cultural histories and environments both within and outside of the United States.

Second, cultural studies places a major emphasis on the study of language and power, particularly in terms of how language is used to fashion social identities and secure specific forms of authority. In this instance, language is studied not as a technical and expressive device, but as a historical and contingent practice actively engaged in the production, organization, and circulation of texts and institutional powers. The implication here is that educators can address the diverse ways in which different discursive practices constitute a formative rather than merely expressive force. The pedagogical challenge for cultural studies is to analyze how language functions to include or exclude certain meanings, secure or marginalize particular ways of behaving, and produce or prevent certain pleasures and desires. Language in this sense is analyzed through the various ways in which it actively produces and mediates the context and content of students' lives within and across numerous public arenas and sites of learning. The link between language and the construction of individual and social identities is evident, for instance, in the way in which language is used to privilege representations that exclude subordinate groups. It is evident in the ways in which the discourse of testing, assessment, and management is given priority over the language of politics and ethics when dealing with the purpose and meaning of schooling at all levels. And, of course, it is evident in the assumption that Standard English rather than, for example, an Afro-American idiom is the proper way to speak and write in schools. Historical analysis of the relationship between power and language can be addressed by analyzing how different discourses have been privileged over time to legitimate and regulate institutional sites such as schools, the justice system, the workplace, unions, media culture, and other sites of learning. But the study of language must not fall prey to what Stuart Hall has called an overwhelming textualization. Cultural studies cannot run the risk of constituting "power and politics as exclusively matters of language and textuality."[18] Material forces and institutions have a social gravity that can be understood only through language but cannot be reduced to a representational practice. Students can learn that the critical value of language is based not merely on its possibilities for expanding the range of textual literacy but on understanding how people and social groups use language as a way of mobilizing resistance, challenging dominant forms of cultural authority, and creating democratic social relationships.

The relationship between language and literacy must extend beyond its pedagogical importance as vehicle of interpretation; it should also be understood as a site of social contestation. As part of a broader struggle over signs and social practices, language cannot be abstracted from the power of those institutional forces that use it as part of a systematic effort to silence, exclude, and dictate the voices of subordinate groups. As a discourse of possibility, language must be understood as both a politics of representation and a social practice through which identities are refigured, struggles produced, and hopes mobilized. Hence, the study of language becomes crucial for understanding how structures of inequality and oppression work in schools and through the larger society. For educators, the study of language becomes essential for revealing how power functions as a condition for and a form of representation. Educational politics and pedagogical practices are impossible to grasp critically without focusing on how language works in deploying the machinery of power, discipline, and regulation.

For many cultural studies advocates, the study of language is also important for redefining the relationship between theory and practice. The language of theory is crucial to the degree that it is grounded in real life experiences, issues, and practices. Theory must begin to address the range of complex issues and events that give meaning to everyday life. Theory needs to be translated into practice that makes a difference, that enables people to live out their lives with dignity and hope. At the same time, considerations of the practical cannot take place without a detour through theory. Everyday life does not privilege the pragmatic over theory, but views it as being both informed by and transformative of reflective theoretical considerations. As a pedagogical issue, theory is not only a matter of students learning other people's discourses. It is also about students doing their own theorizing around historical undertakings and contemporary issues. Theory has to be *done*, it has to become a form of cultural production and not merely a storehouse of insights drawn from the books of the "great theorists."

Third, cultural studies places a strong emphasis on linking the curriculum to the experiences that students bring to their encounter with institutionally legitimated knowledge. For cultural studies advocates, texts cannot be understood outside of the context of their historical and social production. Nor can such texts be removed from the experiences and narratives of the students that engage them. The pedagogical implication here is that schools and colleges of education should take the lead in refiguring curriculum boundaries. In part, this suggests reformulating the value and implications of established disciplines and those areas of study that constitute mass culture, popular culture, youth culture, and other aspects of student knowledge and the contested terrain of common sense. This is not a matter of abandoning high culture or simply substituting it for popular culture. It is, rather, an attempt to refigure the boundaries of what constitutes culture and really useful knowledge in order to study it in new and critical ways.

Teachers and future teachers need to be educated about the viability of developing context-dependent learning that takes account of student experiences and their relationships to popular culture and to the terrain of pleasure. Despite the growing diversity of students in both public schools and higher education, few examples exist of curricula sensitive to the multiplicity of economic, social, and cultural factors bearing on a student's educational life. Even where programs such as ethnic and black studies proliferate in higher education, these are marginalized in small programs far removed from the courses organized around history, science, and the humanities. Cultural studies at least provides the theoretical tools for allowing schools and colleges of education to recognize that the crucial culture war today is between education institutions that do not meet the needs of a massively shifting student population and students and their families for whom schools are perceived as merely one more instrument of repression.[19]

Fourth, cultural studies is committed to studying the production, reception, and situated use of varied texts and how they structure social relations, values, particular notions of community, the future, and diverse definitions of the self. Texts in this sense do not refer merely to the culture of print or the technology of the book, but to all those audio, visual, and electronically mediated forms of knowledge that have prompted a radical shift in the construction of knowledge and the ways in which knowledge is produced, received, and consumed. Contemporary youths do not rely simply on the technology and culture of print to construct and affirm their identities; instead, they are faced with the task of finding their way through a decentered cultural landscape no longer dominated largely by print culture, closed narrative structures, or the certitude of a secure economic future. The emerging technologies that construct and position youths represent interactive terrains that cut across "language and culture, without narrative requirements, without character complexities. . . . Narrative complexity [has given] way to design complexity; story [has given] way to a sensory environment."[20] I don't believe that educators and schools of education can address the shifting attitudes, representations, and desires of this new generation of youths within the dominant disciplinary configurations of knowledge and practice. On the contrary, youths are constituted within languages and cultural practices that intersect differently across and within issues of race, class, gender, and sexual differences. Consequently, the conditions through which youths attempt to represent themselves must be understood within the context of their struggles and the shared language of agency that points to a project of hope and possibility. This language of difference, specificity, and possibility is precisely what is lacking from most attempts at educational reform.

Fifth, cultural studies also argues for the importance of analyzing history not as a unilinear narrative unproblematically linked to progress, but as a series of ruptures and displacements. History in this sense becomes decentered, more complex, and diffuse. Rather than taking up history within the confines of a rigid and narrowly defined tradition, teachers can name and address the multiple traditions and narratives that constitute the complex and multilayered constructions, deployments, and uses of national identity. The pedagogical benefit of such an approach is that it makes available to students those narratives, local histories, and subjugated memories that have been excluded and marginalized in dominant renditions of history. Through the lens of cultural studies, history can be read from a transnational and intercultural perspective.[21] In part, history becomes a critical reading focused on the local and global relations that the United States has constructed over time with other countries. Historical learning in this sense is not about constructing a linear narrative but about blasting history open, rupturing its silences, highlighting its detours, and organizing its limits within an open and honest concern with human suffering, values, and the legacy of the often unrepresentable or misrepresented.

History is not an artifact, but a struggle over the relationship between representation and agency. James Clifford is insightful in arguing that history should "force a sense of location on those who engage with it."[22] In other words, history is not merely about looking at facts, dates, and events. It is also about critically examining one's own historical location amid relations of power, privilege, or subordination. Similarly, cultural studies strongly supports the notion that the work of theory, research, and practice must, in part, be approached through historical undertakings and struggles around nationhood, ethnicity, race, gender, class, youth cultures, and other contestations over culture and politics.

Sixth, the issue of pedagogy is increasingly becoming one of the defining principles of cultural studies.[23] Teachers must expand the definition of pedagogy in order to move beyond a limited emphasis on the mastery of techniques and methodologies. This should enable students to understand pedagogy as a configuration of textual, verbal, and visual practices through which people understand themselves and the possible ways in which they relate to others and their environment. Pedagogy represents a form of cultural production implicated in and critically attentive to how power and meaning help construct and organize knowledge, desires, values, and identities. Pedagogy in this sense is not reduced to the mastering of skills or techniques. Rather, it is defined as a cultural practice that must be accountable ethically and politically for the stories it produces, the claims it makes on social memories, and the images of the future it deems legitimate. As both an object of critique and a method of cultural production, pedagogy refuses to hide behind claims of objectivity and works vigilantly to link theory and practice in the service of expanding the possibilities for democratic life.

Though this list is both schematic and incomplete, it points to a core of theoretical considerations that offer a beginning for advancing a more public vision for schools and colleges of education. I hope it suggests theoretical tools for constructing new forms of collaboration among faculty, a broadening of the terms of learning for teachers, and new approaches toward interdisciplinary research that address local, national, and international concerns. The potential that cultural studies has for developing forms of collaboration that cut across national boundaries is enormous.

But cultural studies also needs to be interrogated so as to expand its theoretical reach and pedagogical possibilities. Given the interdisciplinary nature of educational work, the space it provides for linking theory and practice, and the important role that teachers play as public intellectuals, I want to suggest that education theorists can make a major contribution to how cultural studies is taken up by deepening and expanding three major considerations central to the intersection of pedagogy, cultural studies, and a project for political change.

First, while cultural studies has multiple languages, histories, and founding moments, its underlying commitment to political work has not been adequately developed as part of a wider project for social reconstruction and progressive change. As cultural studies has moved from its earlier emphasis on adult literacy, class analysis, and youth subcultures to concerns with feminism, racism, popular culture, and identity politics, it has failed to unite its historical undertakings under a comprehensive democratic politics and shared notion of public struggle and social justice. While issues of racism, class, gender, textuality, national identity, subjectivity, and media culture must remain central elements in any cultural studies discourse, the issue of radical democracy must be located at the center of its politics.

Progressive educators can amplify and build upon the various ways in which cultural studies has broadened our understanding of how politics and power work through institutions, language, representations, culture, and across diverse economies of desire, time, and space. But in enabling this vast reconceptualization of power and resistance, cultural studies has failed to provide a clear sense of what these sites have in common. Educators can address this issue by emphasizing the importance of radical democracy as a political, social, and ethical referent for rethinking how citizens can be educated to deal with a world made up of different, multiple, and fractured public cultures. Cultural studies provides theorists, educators, and others with an opportunity to develop a new ethical and political language to map the problems and challenges of a newly constituted global public. It is within this postmodern politics of difference and the increasingly dominant influence of globalization that cultural studies and the field of education need to become more attentive to restoring the language of ethics, agency, power, and identity as part of the wider revitalization of democratic public life.

At stake here is the necessity for progressive educators' studies to provide some common ground in which traditional binarisms of margin/center, unity/difference, local/national, public/private can be reconstituted through more complex representations of identification, belonging, and community. Critical educators must address how cultural studies can continue to develop new theoretical frameworks for challenging the way we think about the dynamics and effects of cultural and institutional power. This suggests the need for a discourse of ruptures, shifts, flows, and unsettlement, one that functions less as a politics of transgression than as part of a concerted effort to construct a broader vision of political commitment and democratic struggle. Cultural studies in combination with progressive education theory can further expand its theoretical horizons by addressing the issue of radical democracy as part of a wider discourse of rights and economic equality. In this context, cultural studies as a pedagogical discourse offers the possibility for extending the democratic principles of justice, liberty, and equality to the widest possible set of social relations and institutional practices that constitute everyday life. Under the project of radical democracy, critical educators can rewrite the possibilities for cultural studies to forcefully assert its own politics by affirming the importance of the particular and contingent while acknowledging the centrality of the shared political values and ends of a democratic society.

Second, cultural studies both reinvigorates intellectual work through its transdisciplinary and transcultural scholarship and also echoes Walter Benjamin's call for intellectuals to assume responsibility with regard to the task of translating theory back into a constructive practice that transforms the everyday terrain of cultural and political power. Unlike traditional vanguardist or elitist notions of the intellectual, cultural studies advocates that the vocation of intellectuals be rooted in pedagogical and political work tempered by humility, a moral focus on suffering, and the need to produce alternative visions and policies that go beyond a language of critique. On one level this means that cultural studies is important because it takes on the task of establishing and struggling over institutional spaces and practices that might produce public intellectuals. What critical educators need to stress is the need for cultural workers to struggle not only for the institutional space necessary for public intellectuals to have a voice, but also for a cautious pedagogical regard for striking a critical balance between producing rigorous intellectual work, on the one hand, and exercising authority that is firm rather than rigid, self-critical and concretely utopian rather than repressive and doctrinaire, on the other. Rather than denouncing authority, those who engage in cultural studies must use it to organize their cultural work; but at the same time they must allow their own forms of authority to be held up to critical scrutiny.

This suggests rejecting both the notion of the educator who speaks as the "universal intellectual" as well as the specific intellectual who speaks exclusively within the often essentializing claims of identity politics. Cultural studies needs to rethink the role of educators as both public and border intellectuals. If the universal intellectual speaks for everyone, and the specific intellectual is wedded to serving the narrow interests of specific cultural and social formations, the border intellectual travels within and across communities of difference working in collaboration with diverse groups and occupying many sites of resistance while simultaneously defying the specialized, parochial knowledge of the individual specialist, sage, or master ideologue. By connecting the role of the intellectual to the formation of democratic public cultures, critical educators can argue for a version of cultural studies that provides an ethical referent for cultural workers who inhabit sites as diverse as the arts, religious institutions, schools, media, the workplace, and other spheres. As border intellectuals, educators can articulate and negotiate their differences as part of a broader struggle to secure social justice, economic equality, and human rights within and across regional, national, and global spheres.

Third, cultural studies has played an important role in providing theoretical frameworks for analyzing how power works through the popular and everyday to produce knowledge, social identities, and maps of desire. Crucial here is the ongoing pedagogical work of understanding how social practices that deploy images, sounds, and other representations are redefining the production of knowledge, reason, and new forms of global culture. Cultural studies has been enormously successful in making the objects of everyday life legitimate sources of social analysis; now it faces the task of investigating how technology and science combine to produce new information systems that transcend high/low culture dichotomies. Virtual reality systems and the new digital technologies that are revolutionizing media culture will increasingly come under the influence of an instrumental rationality that relegates their use to the forces of the market and passive consumption. Critical educators can make clear that popular culture must be addressed not merely for the opportunities it provides to revolutionize how people learn or become cultural producers, but also for the role it can play in guaranteeing human rights and social justice. This suggests the need for a new debate on reason, Enlightenment rationality, technology, and authority.

Colleges of education are uniquely suited to developing a language for rethinking the complex dynamics of cultural and material power within an expanded notion of the public, solidarity, and democratic struggle. What cultural studies offers educators is a conception of the political that is open yet committed, respects specificity without erasing global considerations, and provides new spaces for collaborative work engaged in productive social change. Critical education, on the other hand, makes pedagogical practice a central aspect of cultural studies and reminds us of the multiplicity of settings in which learning takes place as part of a broader struggle to provide students with the knowledge, skills, and resources they need to participate effectively in the shaping of democratic public life.

Notes

1. I have borrowed this phrase from Lawrence Grossberg, "Toward a Geneology of the State of Cultural Studies," in *Disciplinarity and Dissent in Cultural Studies*, ed. Cary Nelson and Dilip Parameshwar Gaonkar (New York: Routledge, 1996), 132.

2. I take this issue up in detail in Henry A. Giroux, *Schooling and the Struggle for Public Life* (Minneapolis: University of Minnesota Press, 1988), and in *Living Dangerously* (New York: Peter Lang, 1993).

3. This is discussed in Paul Smith, "The Political Responsibility of the Teaching of Literatures," in *Margins in the Classroom*, ed. Kostas Myrsiades and Linda S. Myrsiades (Minneapolis: University of Minnesota Press, 1994), 64–73.

4. The literature on this issue is too abundant to repeat here, but examples can be found in Lilia Bartolome, "Beyond the Methods Fetish: Towards a Humanizing Pedagogy," *Harvard Educational Review* 64(2) (Summer 1994): 173–94; Michelle Fine, *Framing Dropouts* (Albany: State University of New York Press, 1991); Stanley Aronowitz and Henry A. Giroux, *Education Still Under Siege* (Westport, CT: Bergin and Garvey, 1993); Donaldo Macedo, *Literacies of Power* (Boulder, CO: Westview, 1994); Stephan Nathan Haymes, *Race, Culture, and the City* (Albany: State University of New York Press, 1995); and Sharon Sutton, *Weaving a Tapestry of Resistance* (Westport, CT: Bergin and Garvey, 1995).

5. For representative examples of the diverse issues taken up in the field of cultural studies, see Lawrence Grossberg, Cary Nelson, and Paula Treichler, eds., *Cultural Studies* (New York: Routledge, 1992); and Simon During, ed., *The Cultural Studies Reader* (New York: Routledge, 1993).

6. The relationship between cultural studies and relations of government are looked at in Tony Bennett, "Putting Policy Into Cultural Studies," in Grossberg, Nelson, and Treichler, *Cultural Studies*, 23–34.

7. Peter Hitchcock, "The Othering of Cultural Studies," *Third Text* 25 (Winter 1993–1994), 12.

8. Cary Nelson, Paula Treichler, and Lawrence Grossberg, "Cultural Studies: An Introduction," in Grossberg, Nelson, and Treichler, *Cultural Studies*, 5.

9. Bennett, "Putting Policy Into Cultural Studies," 32.

10. The notion of globalization as a space of struggle is taken from Lawrence Grossberg, "The Space of Culture, the Power of Space: Cultural Studies and Globalization," in *The Post-Colonial Question*, ed. Iain Chambers and Lydia Curti (New York: Routledge, 1996), 169–88. See also Stuart Hall, "Culture, Community, Nation," *Cultural Studies* 7(3) (October 1993): 349–63.

11. I take up these issues in more detail in Henry A. Giroux, *Border Crossings* (New York: Routledge, 1992), and in *Disturbing Pleasures: Learning Popular Culture* (New York: Routledge, 1994).

12. For a history of cultural studies in the United States and England, see Stanley Aronowitz, *Roll Over Beethoven: The Return of Cultural Strife* (Hanover, MA: Wesleyan

University Press, 1993). Also see Lawrence Grossberg, "The Formations of Cultural Studies: An American in Birmingham," in *Cultural Studies: Developments in Theory and Research*, ed. Valda Blundell, John Shepard, and Ian Taylor (New York: Routledge, 1993), 21–66. For a shorter analysis, see the introduction to *Cultural Studies* by Nelson, Treichler, and Grossberg, and Stuart Hall's "Cultural Studies and Its Theoretical Legacies," in Grossberg, Nelson, and Treichler, *Cultural Studies*, 277–86.

13. Anyone who has been following the culture wars of the last eight years is well aware of the conservative agenda for reordering public and higher education around the commercial goal of promoting economic growth for the nation while simultaneously supporting the values of western civilization as a common culture, allegedly under siege by those educators calling for equity and multiculturalism. For a brilliant analysis of the conservative attack on higher education, see Ellen Messer-Davidow, "Manufacturing the Attack on Liberalized Higher Education," *Social Text* 36 (Fall 1993): 40–80. Also see Jeffrey Williams, ed., *PC Wars: Politics and Theory in the Academy* (New York: Routledge, 1995); and John K. Wilson, *The Myth of Political Correctness* (Durham, NC: Duke University Press, 1995).

14. Douglas Crimp, "Portraits of People With AIDS," in Grossberg, Nelson, and Treichler, *Cultural Studies*, 126.

15. Cornel West, "America's Three-Fold Crisis," *Tikkun* 9(2) (1994), 41.

16. For an example of this, see Alisa Solomon, "Lower Education: Is CUNY Abandoning Its Mission to Educate the Poor?" *The Village Voice*, 14 December 1993; 11–18.

17. Joe Murphy quoted in Solomon, "Lower Education," 18.

18. Hall, "Cultural Studies and Its Theoretical Legacies," 286.

19. This issue is taken up in Aronowitz and Giroux, *Education Still Under Siege*, especially in the introduction, "Beyond the Melting Pot—Schooling in the Twenty-first Century."

20. Walter Parkes, "Random Access, Remote Control: The Evolution of Story Telling," *Omni*, January 1994, 50.

21. Paul Gilroy is very instructive on this point. He writes:

> There is a plea here that further enquiries should be made into precisely how discussions of "race," beauty, ethnicity, and culture have contributed to the critical thinking that eventually gave rise to cultural studies. . . . The emphatically national character ascribed to the concept of modes of production (cultural and otherwise) is another fundamental question which demonstrates the ethnohistorical specificity of dominant approaches to cultural politics, social movements, and oppositional consciousness. . . . I want to develop the suggestion that cultural historians could take the Atlantic as one single, complex unity of analysis in their discussions of the modern world and use it to produce an explicitly transnational and intercultural perspective.

See Paul Gilroy, *The Black Atlantic: Modernity and Double Consciousness* (Cambridge, MA: Harvard University Press, 1993), 9, 15.

22. James Clifford, "Museums in the Borderlands," In *Different Voices*, ed. Carol Becker, James Clifford, Henry Louis Gates Jr., Amalia Mesabains, John Tchen, Irene Winter, and Tomas Ybarra-Frausto (New York: Association of Art Museum Directors, 1992), 129.

23. See Henry A. Giroux and Peter McLaren, eds., *Between Borders: Pedagogy and the Politics of Cultural Studies* (New York: Routledge, 1993).

16

The Fine Art of Teaching

David Trend

Increasingly in recent years painters, filmmakers, writers, and performers have abandoned conventional galleries, journals, and theaters to work in education contexts. To popularize their efforts, these well-meaning artists have taken their expertise into schools, community centers, hospitals, and other nonart venues, thereby rejecting notions of art as a substance set apart from daily life. This exodus from the gallery is more than a sociological exercise, for it implicitly challenges established economies of knowledge, cultural worth, and the institutions that support them. Moreover, it is almost always directed toward some disempowered group (young people, the poor, the infirm, the aged), thus suggesting a redistribution of cultural capital.

The political implications of this new approach to cultural work have caused considerable uproar, as evidenced in controversies over artistic patronage and censorship. Indeed, many of the debates over the National Endowment for the Arts (NEA) have hinged as much on questions of what counts as art as they have on matters of content. Like education, art is customarily seen as something that is found only in certain places and under certain conditions. To question these conventions is to throw into doubt an entire system of professional certification and disciplinary separation. Shift the emphasis to communities outside the so-called mainstream, and conservative anxieties are exacerbated.

In theoretical terms, most of these debates were cast until relatively recently in terms of a modernist western center struggling to maintain itself in a world increasingly destabilized by groups on the unassimilated margins. This monoculture versus multiculture model is useful as far as it goes, but it obscures the complex and often contradictory ways that power and identity are constituted. Specifically, this crude dichotomy fails to account for how difference can be co-opted by the very interests it confronts. Writing in a recent issue of *Harper's Magazine*, David Rieff points out that big business has adopted a multicultural approach to product development and distribution that perfectly complements its drive to market segmentation and transnational expansion.[1] This is manifest both in the "friendly" colonialism of enterprises such as The Body Shop and the disingenuous pluralism proffered in the "United Colors of Benneton." In both cases a seemingly friendly nod is given to the premise of cultural diversity, but only within the larger interests of corporate profiteering and public relations. Such token gestures do little to obviate the effects of international terrorism, hunger, or ecological devastation.

Within the art world, a similar appropriation of difference has occurred in the seemingly innocuous entry of artists into educational contexts. The process began in the 1970s, when large metropolitan museums first felt the monetary effect of suburban "white flight."[2] With changing economic and racial demographics (and the recognition of the growing irrelevance of European culture to urban communities of color), many museums began to develop education programs—previously thought to be mere frills. In recent years this turn to community education has trickled down to smaller arts organization. In an age of decreasing resources and continual assaults from the political Right, arts organizations—especially avant-garde groups—have adopted community and education programming to reach fresh audiences, attract added funding sources, and establish a more resistant rationale for their existence. This move to education is embraced by many groups because it is perceived not as an abandonment of aesthetic vanguardism but as a "new" extension of it. Here the previously esoteric impulses of conceptual and performance art meld with the practical imperatives of public approval and the political motives of progressive activism. Who could ask for a better package?

Nowhere is this emerging form of community artwork more in evidence than in the San Francisco Bay Area. In the past few years the region has seen dozens of alternative educational initiatives address such issues as immigration, gang violence, gentrification, drug abuse, and homelessness. This is partly attributable to the progressive and generally "tolerant" political atmosphere in the Bay Area. But it is also due to San Francisco's historic commitment to nonobject art. Since the golden age of what was termed "California Conceptualism" in the 1960s and 1970s, the Bay Area has been home to scores of nonprofit experimental arts organizations, including Artspace, Capp Street Project, New Langton Arts, The Lab, and Southern Exposure. In fact, San Francisco ranks second only to New York City in the number of such groups funded by the NEA.[3]

This essay will review a sampling of recent community art education projects sponsored by San Francisco organizations: "Boulevard of Dreams" at Southern Exposure Gallery, "Utopia in the Teen Age" at Capp Street Project, and "The Voice of Citizenry" at the San Francisco Art Institute.[4] The appearance of such projects generally is and should be seen as a positive development, for it signals a dramatically more democratic role for arts organizations. At the same time, however, these educational initiatives can present problems if they are pursued uncritically, as I intend to show in this paper.

These problems can be addressed by taking a hard look, first of all, at the social positions of the parties involved. Who are the artistic groups, educational constituencies, and audiences involved? Does each of them understand the projects in the same way? Who gains from the efforts and how in terms of knowledge, programming, artistic statement making, grants, and publicity? Finally, what are the long-term effects of projects for those involved? Was the endeavor part of a larger program? How consistent was the project with the world view and practical needs of those involved?

As suggested above, that all of these undertakings were sponsored by alternative nonprofit groups is not coincidental. One unifying theme among the three efforts was their presumption of radical innovation. At Capp Street the "Utopia in the Teen Age" project was organized through the organization's "Experimental Projects" program; Southern Exposure characterized "Boulevard of Dreams" as a component of its "lab approach" to art making; the San Francisco Art Institute placed its "Voice of Citizenry" exhibition within the context of "controversial themes." To the three institutions, then, these projects represented more than simple acts of benevolence for the disempowered ("teens" at Capp Street, "at-risk youth" at Southern Exposure, and "marginalized" communities at the San Francisco Art Institute). They were *aesthetic* and *social* interventions, and in each case these quite different purposes confused each other.

Are You Being Served?

"The Voice of Citizenry: Artists and Communities in Collaboration" was more than a typical show at the San Francisco Art Institute. It was the school's special "annual" exhibition devoted to showcasing the Bay Area's "leading contemporary artists." More to the point, this explicitly educational exhibition marked a departure for a college historically identified with the detached aestheticism associated with such faculty members as Linda Connor, Ernie Gehr, Tony Labat, and Paul Kos.

"The best defense against social marginalization is a cultural offensive," read the opening wall label, adding that "a culture that proactively asserts its development is a culture that best defends itself against prejudice, divisiveness, fear, and isolation." With these words viewers were introduced to installations by groups ranging from the AIDS awareness collectives to a theater workshop for inmates at the county jail. Aside from the socially oriented character of the show, the most striking element of the "The Voice of Citizenry" was the degree of artifice involved in bringing this work into the art gallery. Clearly *any* exhibition of works by "nonartists" presents curatorial challenges in both formal and didactic terms. How can an object done in a therapeutic session be dressed up for gallery consumption? What types of explanatory material are needed to ensure that the object is understood? Indeed, how important is the original context, anyway?

In some instances these questions were addressed at "The Voice of Citizenry" through accompanying videos that either documented the production of the work or provided background on the group involved. By far the most compelling of these was the presentation of "Cultural Odyssey: The Media Project," the three-year-old improvisational drama project conducted by Rhodessa Jones at the San Bruno Correctional Facility for women. An altar-like installation of artifacts relating to the program—including items like posters, news clippings, snapshots, and costuming—provided a multilayered introduction to the project, which was accompanied by a videotape of the classes Jones conducts. In the tape, the women inmates re-enacted the often brutal circumstances that led them to break the law. But rather than focusing on their prostitution or drug dealing, the tape emphasized the women's personal histories and the methods they developed for overcoming racism, sexism, and economic exploitation. As an ensemble, the installation and tape offered a densely cross-referenced image of the Cultural Odyssey project from the perspectives of its director, the inmates, and the community (outside the jail) in which the productions are seen.

In stark contrast was the ambiguous presentation of sketches by clients of Oakland's St. Mary's Community Center. The display consisted of drawings from the "No Place to Stay" project conducted by artist Roxanne Hills with seventy homeless senior citizens, accompanied by a brief wall label attesting to project's "empowering" intentions. In a crayon rendering by Milas Hackett, a stick figure stands between welfare hotel and a sign for the bay bridge. The caption reads: "Mentally ill and homeless. Help me." Beyond the evidentiary value of this image as the work of homeless person, the viewer is left to speculate on the conditions and purposes of its making, as well as the social or psychiatric reasons for its maker's complaint. As a consequence the display served only to mystify the program.

This latter example highlights the inherent difficulty in bringing such works into the gallery. Without questioning the value of projects such as "No Place to Stay" to their original constituents, clearly a great deal was lost in its translation into the gallery. This might have been due to the fact that the St. Mary's Center was the only group in the show without direct ties to the local gallery community, or it might have been evidence of a reluctance to "package" its social service programs for an arts audience. Regardless of intention, when detached from their original contexts, efforts by groups like the St. Mary's Center can become little more than curiosities of an inexplicably "childlike" or "insane" population. This was certainly the case at the San Francisco Art Institute. As such the display did little to help the homeless population or to inform gallery goers of the dimensions of their plight. What it did was provide an assortment of inexplicably strange and brightly colored images for the gallery wall.

This practice of transforming cultural "otherness" into material for artistic display has an unfortunately long history, dating at least to the colonial empires of Europe. The impulse among artists to become "inspired" or to appropriate the motifs of foreign peoples has two significant consequences. Obviously there is a tendency to misrepresent the "outside" culture according to the needs of the representer, as otherness becomes a fictional text. Additionally, this process throws the dominant culture into relief, thus creating an equally unrealistic representation of the colonizer.[5]

Such unself-conscious practices result in part from the modernist impulse to view artists as disconnected from society at large. Special institutions are required to house what they produce, institutions into which uninitiated outsiders are admitted as an act of benevolence. Not surprisingly, these attitudes fail to question the power imbalances between art institutions and the communities they presume to serve. They assume that schoolchildren or homeless psychotics can appreciate, understand, and benefit from exposure to an audience of educated art consumers. An art exhibition is often deemed an emancipatory exercise in its own right, even if the newly created community "artists" have no cultural knowledge of such social rituals.

Who's Getting What?

Anthropologist Renato Rosaldo has detailed the ways outsiders can be blind to their own biases in assuming that a group has the same values, desires, and needs as it does.[6] These assumptions forge gaps between what the cultural worker theorizes will happen in the encounter and what occurs in practice. In part this is because of the largely unexamined way that artists view their own activity. The split was most pronounced at Capp Street, where the demands of the institution as a site of avant-garde display became the driving element in the artists' efforts to "help" the young people. The project originated from a funding proposal to Capp Street from the loosely knit AWOL collective (Artist and Writers Out Loud), a group that had formed originally to protest the Persian Gulf War. Although as an artists' collective AWOL had never conducted a education project, it was able to enlist the support of Jack Alter, an art teacher at San Francisco's McAteer High School—the city's magnet school for the arts. Working on a regular basis for half a school year, the primarily white AWOL group conducted the "Utopia in the Teen Age" project with Alter's predominantly nonwhite students. The themes to be addressed were "Who am I?" (what has been my social reality) and "Who will I become?" (what is my utopian/dystopian vision of the world). In weekly sessions students collected magazine images, food wrappers, play money, shoe boxes, and other materials from consumer culture, which they then collaged, wrote about, or designated as props for the exhibition. Implicit in the AWOL approach was a focus on the disempowered position of their young collaborators, as was clear in a statement the group distributed at the exhibition:

> Teenagers know what stereotypes of adolescence are recognized: gang member, star athlete, teen-mother, drug dealer, nerd, cheerleader, head-banger, skin-head, hippie, rapper, the apathetic, etc. They also know the most about the various attempts adults make to enlist their allegiance. Join the military, buy this hair care product over that one, ally your self with one fast food restaurant over another, vote for a particular candidate, etc.[7]

Hence, from the beginning the students were situated in an oppositional role, superficially similar, but actually significantly different from that of avant-garde artists. The difference between the two, of course, is that the artists chose their social location; students had it imposed upon them. The effect of this exercise in student voice, exacerbated by the race and class differences between the artists and students, was to "enlist the allegiance" of the students as producers of raw material for the exhibition.

The students' work was arranged in an elaborate installation designed by AWOL. As explained in an AWOL letter to parents, "While the artists have developed a framework and presentation system, the work of the students will be central to the exhibition." This seemingly simple division of labor further demarcated the conflicting agendas of the project: the students would work in school producing authentic artifacts of their lives; the artists would gather up these artifacts and suitably represent them to a gallery audience. The question this arrangement leaves begging in the final analysis is, Who got what? AWOL received a monetary grant from Capp Street Project to conduct its project; Jack Alter got some classroom help from AWOL; Capp Street Project got an installation it could bill as an experimental project; and the students got an art class not too unlike the one they would have gotten anyway.

The most informative component of "Teenage Utopia" was the public discussion held at the gallery to assess the project. Invited participants included AWOL members, McAteer faculty, and a range of arts educational personnel from the Bay Area, as well as the general public. Perhaps not so surprisingly, the meeting revealed that many of students had been reluctant to visit the gallery in which their work was being shown. As explained by AWOL members, the young people didn't understand the idea of an artist's space and felt uncomfortable entering one. The meeting also brought out many of the AWOL group's own misgivings about imbalances of the project as it evolved. As is frequently the case with such endeavors, the AWOL group repeatedly characterized the time spent at the school as an educational experience *for the artists*.

All of this points to the unfortunate tendency of many artists to assume they can make short-term forays into new social contexts without making long-term commitments to understanding or working in those contexts. Although laudable as a critique of art-world institutions, this attitude means that artists may not be skillful or sensitive to their new constituencies. As Victor Burgin pointed out in his essay "The End of Art History,"

> Quite simply, there is no "outside" to institutions in contemporary society; they fit together like the pieces of a jigsaw puzzle—to leave one institutional site is simply to enter another, which will have its own specific conditions and determinations. The artist who works for a trade union as an "artist" has . . . simply exchanged the problematic of one institution for that of another; in so doing he or she risks abandoning a struggle to which they could bring some experience or expertise, for one to which they are novices. Moreover, more fundamentally, they remain firmly inside the dominant discourses. The major weakness of the "art outside the institution" position is the completely empiricist and untheorized concept of "institution" with which it operates.[8]

Underexposure?

The issue of "who gets what" was much more directly addressed by Southern Exposure's "Boulevard of Dreams" project, in which a group of thirteen and fourteen year olds received an hourly wage paid by the city of

San Francisco's Conservation Corps. The predominantly African American and Latino group of teens came to Southern Exposure each afternoon after doing more conventional Conservation Corps work (picking up trash, painting park equipment, removing graffiti) in the morning. At the gallery they met with project organizer Kevin Radley, who helped them produce snapshot albums, life-sized silhouettes, customized name plates, videotapes, and maps of their neighborhoods. As with the other projects discussed in this essay, the emphasis in "Boulevard of Dreams" was on the notion of self through a process of "coming to voice." Motivating this was the belief that people's sense of worth is diminished when they are silenced by such factors as economic disadvantage or racial prejudice. Bell hooks, among others, has discussed the remarkable power of the process of coming to voice in helping people to "become subjects rather than objects" of representation—to become authors of their life stories and masters of their own fates.[9]

These notions of voice tend to be romanticized by artists, who often have an overriding faith in the value of "expression" as an emancipatory gesture in its own right. This is one reason why artists become so concerned about any limits on what they say or produce. Regrettably, there is a problem with this misty-eyed privileging of personal perspective as automatically sacred and true. As Lawrence Grossberg has suggested, the "politics of any social position is not guaranteed in advance."[10] This essentialization of knowledge based on racial, sexual, or economic identity generally produces two detrimental effects. First, it silences and invalidates external perspectives by refusing the applicability of partial or mediated experience. This can cause a failure of communication, as well as the type of moral solipsism characteristic of a single viewpoint. Second, the privileging of one form of identity tends to discount others. Therefore, a focus on race can easily elide any consideration of gender, sexual orientation, or class—and as a consequence overlook the imbricated character of these issues. While affording a form of provisional (perhaps strategic) closure, such an emphasis can produce a distorted view of the ways ideologies and oppressions operate.

In the case of "Boulevard of Dreams," this unexamined attachment to voice was evidenced in a further difficulty, evidenced in one of the project's centerpiece installations. In "Just Do It," a wall approximately twenty-five feet wide and twelve feet high was hung with dozens of broken plastic handguns, which the teenage participants had wrapped with ribbons, flowers, and pieces of colored fabric. Interspersed among the mutilated guns the students had painted such phrases as "Say No To Drugs," "Stop Racism," "This World Needs Peace," and "No More Crime." Here again, young people had been brought into a gallery and encouraged by an artist (who provided the plastic guns) to dramatize "their" concerns—in this case, street violence.

Aside from the somewhat troubling implication that these young people of color would automatically have some expertise or knowledge about this topic, the piece itself—the paucity of insight it offered—was troubling. I think this was due to the inevitable superficiality of moving a group of teens through a sequence of eight art projects in a matter of four weeks. Here again, the imperatives of creating a display overshadowed the possibility of prolonged exploration of the topic at hand, an exploration that might have resulted in responses more complex than slogans and stereotypes. Instead, the young people seem to have simply reproduced their own lack of understanding of the problem.

I raise this issue as a means of getting at my last question, which concerns the long-term implications of projects like "Teenage Utopia" and "Boulevard of Dreams." Because they are often structured around short-term exhibition schedules or fund-raising plans, such projects rarely can develop the pedagogical potential or substantive empowerment to which they aspire. As a result, their young participants often leave the project more confused about the experience than when they began.

This is often the direct consequence of arts projects that originate outside the communities they serve. Simply put, such efforts have no organic connections to the lives of those they involve. This is yet another way that the specter of the vanguard haunts the community art enterprise. As suggested earlier by Burgin, within this logic the true change agent is seen as a detached social actor who disrupts by entering from the outside. It is the vanguardist's very distance from social reality that permits a radical vision and original perspective. The contradictory implications of this should be self-evident in light of the above discussion.

This is not to suggest that projects like those reviewed here shouldn't be undertaken because of the "impossibility of knowing" a community different from one's own. Such pessimism is all too debilitating at a time when marginalized communities are for the first time finding articulation in "mainstream" contexts. The implication that teachers or artists should be silent in the face of difference is just as limiting as the suggestion that such relationships are unproblematic. Clearly one means of improving community arts education projects lies in the examination of the often unexplored power dynamics among various social actors. With this should go some collaboration in the planning of such efforts, rather than their unidirectional imposition by external agents. These are issues that teachers have been discussing for some time but that the art world has not so carefully examined. If these hybrid projects are to have a value for both the arts and education communities, then surely some benefit would result from an increased exchange over the premises, methods, and ultimate purposes of such work. Journals such as this one are a place to begin this work.

Notes

1. David Rieff, "Multiculturalism's Silent Partner," *Harper's Magazine* 287, no. 1717 (August 1993), 64.

2. American Association of Museums, *Museums: Their New Audiences* (Washington, DC: AAM, 1972), 12.

3. In a round of grants awarded to visual artists organizations at the time of these exhibitions, San Francisco Bay Area organizations received fourteen grants compared with twenty-two in New York City. See "1993 VAO Grants," *Afterimage* 21, no. 2 (September 1993), 3, 22.

4. "Boulevard of Dreams," Southern Exposure Gallery, San Francisco, CA, August 17–28, 1993; "Utopia in the Teen Age," Capp Street Project, San Francisco, CA, May 14–June 26, 1993; "The Voice of Citizenry: Artists and Communities in Collaboration," San Francisco Art Institute, Walter/McBean Gallery, San Francisco, CA, August 26–September 25, 1993.

5. Susan Hiller, "Editor's Note," in *The Myth of Primitivism: Perspectives on Art*, ed. Susan Hiller (New York and London: Routledge, 1991), 1.

6. Renato Rosaldo, *Culture and Truth: Remaking Social Analysis* (Boston: Beacon, 1989).

7. AWOL artists' statement distributed at the Capp Street Project exhibition, 1993.

8. Victor Burgin, *The End of Art Theory: Criticism and Postmodernity* (Atlantic Highlands, NJ: Humanities Press, 1986), 190.

9. bell hooks, *talking back: thinking feminist, thinking black* (Boston: South End, 1989), 18.

10. Lawrence Grossberg, *We Gotta Get Out of This Place* (New York: Routledge, 1993).

17

Punk Pedagogy, or Performing Contradiction

The Risks and Rewards of (Anti-)Transference

Robert Miklitsch

Every performance, however apocalyptic, offered palpable evidence that things could change, indeed were changing: that performance itself was a possibility no authentic punk should discount.

—Dick Hebdige, *Subculture* (1979)

The proof of emancipatory theory lies in the performance.

—Terry Eagleton, *Ideology* (1991)

In this essay I return to some issues I addressed in an earlier essay on the "politics of teaching" where I argued, among other things, that teachers can and must assume an explicit political position on *certain* topics.[1] More recently, in a paper on the Graff/Searle debate waged in *The New York Review of Books*, "*Sturm und Searle*: Intervention, Transformation, Democratization," I argued, *contra* Searle, that if "we" are intervening, whether implicitly or explicitly, in the academy, a number of difficult questions remain, such as whether, and to what degree, one should be implicit or explicit.[2] This rhetorical problem, I noted, is an important political question as well.

I want to ask and attempt to answer a related question here: if teachers are in positions of authority that they cannot simply renounce (or else abdicate part of their pedagogical responsibility), what, exactly, should they do with this authority? More to the point, what is the role of performance and (anti-)transference in the classroom?[3] Given the institutional character of these issues, I also want to take up the problem of disciplinarity. That is to say, what does a pedagogy of confrontation and contradiction, what I call "punk pedagogy,"[4] suggest about the present and future status of English studies?

Reading in critical pedagogy as I have for a number of years, I have been struck again and again by the theoreticist cast of so much of the work.

Precisely because of this trend, my strategy in this essay will be to resist the lure of theory, or at least "pure theory," in order to articulate a more concrete, site-specific analysis. The danger of this approach, of course, is that the following descriptive analysis may not possess sufficient generality. However, if the pedagogical practice described below, sometimes blow by blow, cannot be construed as a mode or paradigm, it is not, I believe, without its illustrative force.

Now, in order to say what I want to say about this "event," I need to provide something in the way of a context. This essay is a record of a course I taught at Ohio University in the winter of 1992. The course, which was titled "Introduction to Cultural Studies," was not only the first of its kind at Ohio University to focus on cultural studies but also, more importantly, the first in the English department to focus on the mass media (TV, MTV, film, etc.). This is not, I hasten to add, to claim any particular originality for the course but merely to emphasize its institutional subtext or disciplinary conditions of possibility.

To re-mark this issue, the general institutional text of a given course or curriculum raises, in turn, the more familiar question of texts (in the narrow, restricted sense). To wit, the primary texts were Dick Hebdige's *Subculture: The Meaning of Style* (1979), John Fiske's *Television Culture* (1987), Graeme Turner's *Film as Social Practice* (1988), and E. Ann Kaplan's *Rocking Around the Clock: Music Television, Postmodernism, and Consumer Culture* (1987). I'm not sure what to say about these very different texts except that whether British, American, or Australian in address, they all derive in some significant sense from what I call historical cultural studies, which—unlike that bewilderingly diverse array of discourses that now goes under the disciplinary moniker of "cultural studies"—retains an interest, however residual, in the discourse of Marxism in general and the category of class in particular.[5]

With this schematic though, I hope, functional context in mind, I want to offer a narrative of the first three meetings of the course (which met once a week, at night). The first class was uneventful—at least as I remember it—as I did my usual, not-so-usual opening-night shtick. I told the class in no uncertain terms that a lot of the *texts* were difficult—this was, after all, a class *in* theory (hence my insistent recourse to the word "text" as opposed to "work")—and, moreover, that they might well find said *texts* recalcitrant, not to say incomprehensible. I also told them that *if* they decided to return the following week, they had in effect signed the pedagogical "contract" I was in the process of verbally laying out. (I always accent the suppositional at the first meeting of a class in order to encourage students to make an active rather than passive decision about the course.)

The second meeting of the class—during which we discussed, as scheduled, the required reading (the first two chapters of *Television Culture* and the first part of *Film as Social Practice*)—was rather more eventful than the first. In fact, I think I can safely say that a number of students were decidedly put off by the "radical" rhetoric of the texts, though no student was brave or perhaps foolish enough to say so. Two citations, from the first page of each text, should suggest what I mean. First, the Fiske: "How meanings are produced is one of the central problematics of the book, but a convenient place to start is with the simple notion that television broadcasts programs that are replete with potential meanings, and that it attempts to control and focus this meaningfulness into a more singular preferred meaning that performs the work of the dominant ideology."[6] Fiske here is advancing what is now called—after Abercrombie, Hill, and Turner—the "dominant ideology thesis," which was originally formulated by the early Marx and Engels of *The German Ideology* (1845): "The ideas of the ruling class are in every epoch the ruling ideas."[7] Though this particular passage displays Marxism in all its economistic crudeness, crudeness—as Brecht knew—has a certain force, and so the above thesis, Fiske's position aside, is not without its pedagogical use-value.

The second citation, from the Turner, addresses not so much the ideology of the electronic mass media, as in the Fiske, as the industrial preconditions of the feature film: "Film is no longer the product of a self-contained industry but one of a range of cultural commodities produced by large multinationals or conglomerates whose main interest is more likely to be electronics or petroleum than the construction of magical images for the screen."[8] The use-value of this particular argument—at least for the polemical pedagogical program that I am proposing here—is that it is almost certain to offend the sensibilities of those students for whom film is simply one in a series of corporate, leisure-service commodities available to alleviate the boredom of yet another day in affluent, late-capitalist America.[9] As Greil Marcus puts it in "The Last Sex Pistols Concert" (1989), echoing the Situationists: "In modern society leisure [has been] replaced by entertainment" (13). In other words, given the pervasive influence of mass audiovisual culture on the contemporary citizen-consumer, one might argue that the historical question of leisure ("What do I want to do today?") has now given way to another, more site- and sense-specific one: "What is there to *see* today?" (Marcus 1989, 51, italics mine).

This particular question—the question of the role of the mass media in contemporary, post-Fordist society—brings me to week three and the climactic moment of the class, which occurred in the course of a charged discussion of Susan Seidelman's *Desperately Seeking Susan* (screened the previous week).[10] And here, at the risk of defusing whatever narrative momentum I have managed to work up so far, I must pause in order to provide the *critical* context within which this discussion took place. The texts—again, in the restricted sense—were "Desperately Seeking Difference," an essay by Jackie Stacey that first appeared in *The Female Gaze* (1989), and the "applied" reading of *Desperately Seeking Susan* (1985) that constitutes the "practical" conclusion to Turner's *Film as Social Practice*.

To take the latter first, part of the interest of *Desperately Seeking Susan*, for Turner, is the way the film's "feminist stance"—"the concentration on the female protagonists and the depiction of the males as peripheral to the plot"—is undermined by the concluding "invocations of conventional romance" (170). Turner puts it this way:

> The ideological invitation into *Desperately Seeking Susan* is sent by the fact that . . . Roberta's quest is not so much for a Mr. Right as for a member of her own sex who can provide a corrective and progressive role model . . . The patterning of oppositions and linkages between Roberta and Susan . . . generates a tension that is only resolved when the two women meet . . . [However,] the film seems to deflect the expectations from this meeting by immediately taking us to a more conventional romantic union between Roberta and Dez in the projection room of the theatre. (170)

If the last, romantic sequence is, as Turner notes, "only the second in a series of points of closure to the narrative" (i.e., another romantic shot of Susan and Jim in the cinema, followed in turn by a newspaper shot of Susan and Roberta, "hands aloft in a victory gesture" [171]), this sequence nonetheless marks an ideological aporia that the film repeatedly—and, arguably, unsuccessfully—attempts to resolve.

Though Stacey does not cite Turner's reading, she radicalizes his main hypothesis—"Although [*Desperately Seeking Susan*] is not . . . a female 'buddy' movie, the relations between the woman are crucial to the film" (170)—in order to address, in the wake of Laura Mulvey's originary essay on the male gaze, " '*the* lesbian look' or '*the* lesbian spectator' in popular culture."[11] Before I continue with this reading, however, let me be perfectly clear about this look/spectator with respect to Seidelman's film (since Stacey is): if the particular pleasures that *Desperately Seeking Susan* offers "female" spectators cannot be "reduced to a masculine heterosexual equivalent" (Turner's "conventional romance"), this is not to suggest that *Desperately Seeking Susan* is a "lesbian" film nor even necessarily a "progressive" one.

Rather, as in *All About Eve* (1950), *Desperately Seeking Susan* narrates one "woman's obsession with another woman": "But instead of being punished for acting upon her desires, like Eve, Roberta . . . acts upon them . . . and eventually her initiatives are rewarded with the realization of her desires" (Stacey 1989, 125). This realization foregrounds, according to Stacey, "the relations between women on the screen, and between these representations and the woman in the audience" (122), a differential relation that, not unlike the one between Roberta and Susan, escapes or at least displaces the logic of sexual difference and the "repressive" heterosexual economy this implies. Put another way: Susan is at once the "little" mirror other of Roberta and her "big" Other—the latter with a capital O, *à la* Lacan.[12]

The critical context established, we can now return to the narrative proper. In the course of my general, preliminary lecture on *Desperately Seeking Susan*, I featured—as a provocation of sorts—Stacey's "lesbian" reading of the film. While this reading cropped up only a couple of times in the ensuing discussion, Stacey's proposition retroactively refunctioned the class's reception of the film.

In fact, individual reactions to *Desperately Seeking Susan* were so pronounced that I have tried to synopsize them here:

> It's all about Roberta coming to terms with her sexuality; no, in fact it's about Roberta trying to become a different kind of woman, sort of a feminist (though the film is also about her coming to terms with her sexuality); hey, take it easy everybody, there's no need to argue over these two readings because everyone has his or her own reading and each in its own way is "correct"; it's a movie, nothing more, nothing less; right, it's just a "movie," certainly not a "work of art," and in any event, neither it nor this discussion has anything remotely to do with the "real world."

With the last *coup de grâce*, I could barely believe my ears. Here was a course about, among other things, ideology, and I was hearing the most ideologically loaded discourse imaginable, as if the class hadn't even read the material or, more to the point, hadn't really thought about it or, even more to the point, was in a complete state of denial.

Faced with this predicament, I decided to contest each of the above positions in turn. Then, in order to counter what I took to be the most overt gesture of neutralization (i.e., everybody has his/her own reading and each in its own way is "correct"), I *re*-positioned the two students who had initiated the discussion in order to effect what I hoped would be a performative contradiction. These positions—that *Desperately Seeking Susan* was all about Roberta coming to terms with her sexuality (a reading that, announced as it authoritatively was by a male student, suggested a certain self-interest) and that the film was primarily about Roberta becoming a feminist (a reading that was espoused, albeit ambivalently, by a woman)[13]—these positions, I asserted, were in conflict and no amount of intellectual benevolence would change this "fact."

Indeed, when the two students whom I had positioned and "gendered" tried to negotiate their differences, I deliberately punctuated their "debate"—again, à la Lacan[14]—insisting that rather than come to some false, "feel-good" consensus about the film, it might in fact be more productive to leave the discussion on a note of conflict.

Later, after a lot of conscience wrestling and postclass rumination, I began the following class by explaining what I had been trying to do the previous week. I explained that I had intentionally simplified people's positions—in effect, repositioned them—in order to *re*accentuate what *I* took to be the intellectual stakes of each position and the "unsaid" of the class as a whole, its performative contradicion. At which point I went through the following propositions (which I had written on the blackboard at the beginning of the class), positions, I quickly added, that should not be reflexively attributed to individual, gendered members of the class:

- *it's just a movie, like any other movie* (so what's the problem?);
- *it's not "art," it's not even a great "movie"* (so why make such a big deal about it, except maybe in a cultural studies class?);
- *it's a text about a woman coming to terms with her (hetero-)"sexuality"* (so where's the conflict, and who said anything about ideology?);
- *it's a text about one kind of woman trying to become another kind of woman in a patriarchal society* (but it's also about a woman coming to terms with her sexuality);
- *it's a text with a pretty contradictory "message"* (so you can interpret it any way you want);
- *it's a text with a specific "hierarchy of discourses,"*[15] *i.e., more "romantic" than feminist* (and if you can't see this, you're hopelessly deluded!);
- *it's a text with a specific "hierarchy of discourses," more "romantic" than feminist* (but you can read progressively against the grain of this dominant-ideological "message").

To be frank, despite my *caveat* about not personalizing these propositional subject-positions, it was pretty clear to the class as a whole whose assigned subject-position was whose. In fact, a number of students happily assumed theirs, and one position even became a running joke over the course of the quarter. I myself assumed the penultimate, mock-dogmatic critical-ideological position: "if you can't see this [that *Desperately Seeking Susan* is more 'romantic' than feminist], you're hopelessly deluded!"

At the same time, I also observed that if the last two subject-positions, mine and Fiske's, were arguably more complex than the first, they were not necessarily more correct than some of the others (say the fourth, "feminist" one). These propositions, I stressed, were not equal; in fact, some were in direct conflict, and a number were clearly more persuasive than others. The point, I continued, was to decide which position—given the textual evidence (in both the general and restricted senses of the word "text")—was the *most* persuasive or, if each of them was problematic in some way, to come up with another, *more* persuasive proposition.

Now, for some postperformance critique. The first thing I want to say about the above "scene of instruction" is that the sort of tactics and strategies I employed are risky, pedagogically speaking, as you can lose a whole class this way, and you can lose them for good. Indeed, it's not too hard to imagine what some of my students must have been thinking that third night when I rather aggressively contested their positions: What is this, some kind of intellectual one-upmanship masquerading as demystification, pedagogical oppression in the guise of a pedagogy of the oppressed, fascism as enlightenment?

As Ronald Strickland observes in "Confrontational Pedagogy and Traditional Literary Studies" (1990), conflict in the classroom can take some very unproductive forms: for instance, "monotonous authoritarianism on the part of the teacher and a deafening silence on the part of the student."[16] The net effect of just such a pedagogical impasse is that rather than opening up the space of the classroom for "productive contestation" of extant paradigms of "canonical knowledge and pedagogic authority" (292), a pedagogy predicated on conflict—on, that is, confrontation and (anti-)transference—can seriously backfire, foreclosing real learning of any sort while simultaneously reinforcing the already substantial symbolic-institutional power of the "professor."

This said, I want to invoke the little truth of the following truism: no risk, no reward. Though it would be facile and self-congratulatory to claim that this particular cultural studies class was rewarding for both the students and me (if for no other reason than such a claim cannot be effectively falsified and would therefore remain, *stricto sensu*, a claim), I do want to contend that something happened *that* night in *that* class, something *transformative*.

Transmission pedagogy, to differentiate it from a pedagogy of transformation, aims to take the student-from point A to point B (where A and B refer to the subject-positions of the student and teacher respectively).[17] Put another way, at the end of the course, the student assumes or approximates—at least ideally—the "mastery" that distinguishes the professor's position. Now, to be perfectly frank, this pedagogical scenario is, it seems to me, an entirely imaginary affair for both teacher *and* student, since the student arguably leaves the class the same as when "he" first walked in: he may have acquired some knowledge (i.e., "information"), but it is hard to see how this acquisition is qualitatively different from any other commodity or consumer service one might purchase in the marketplace. In fact, according to the classic, "reproductive" argument about education, this is the whole point of the contemporary technocratic university: to "discipline" the professional-managerial labor force to assume, docilely, its position in those occupational slots always already assigned to them by capital.

A pedagogy of transformation, or what I am calling "punk pedagogy," has a rather different social-intellectual agenda. If critical as opposed to merely technical knowledge presupposes some recognition of conflict on the part of both teacher and student, punk pedagogy makes explicit what remains implicit in Strickland's model: the role of performance (where punk, as the epigraphs at the beginning of this paper suggest, is all about performance).[18] Accordingly, the "lesson" of punk for me is that the dialectics of scholastic production is inseparable from pedagogic performance; that it is not enough, for example, merely to recognize contradiction, that one must *perform* it in the classroom. More specifically, one must perform contradiction (as I did when I repositioned various students' readings of *Desperately Seeking Susan*) because ideological formation, as Gramsci and Althusser among others have taught us, is not simply an "intellectual" matter. In short, if ideology, like hegemony, is primarily an unconscious process, critical pedagogy must engage both affect and intellect, emotion and cognition—*if* it is to be persuasive, which is to say transformative.

If performance is integral to both pedagogy and punk, I would also be remiss if I did not observe, if only in passing, that one of the things that defines punk is its status as a subculture (hence the title of Hebdige's book). Indeed, the concept of subculture is critical to any attempt to think punk pedagogy (or, less provocatively, a pedagogy of transformation) since it foregrounds an issue that is strikingly absent from Strickland's essay: popular culture.[19] I say "strikingly" because, despite its counter-hegemonic approach to Milton, "Confrontational Pedagogy and Traditional Literary Studies" not only fails to articulate the historical conditions of possibility of a postcanonical approach to English studies (the role, say, that the re-evaluation of "mass" as well as "high" culture has played in the revision of the canon) but also effectively reproduces a restricted notion of culture as such.

Thus, imperative as it is to subject the literature course and Milton in particular to a critique that "reconstructs the ideological conditions" in which both course and author are situated, such a critique invites an equally strong counter-appropriation—one on the order of an ideological return of the repressed—if it does not *reinscribe*, forcefully and insistently, the conditional place of literature itself within the larger space of the "fine arts."[20] In other words, from this media-systematic perspective, literary studies, traditional or otherwise, is only one, albeit historically dominant and now increasingly residual, satellite in the manifold constellation of the mass media. One of the after-effects of this mediatic "red shift" is that English studies (as opposed to, say, mass communications) may well be forced to assume a less avant-garde, albeit *more* critical, cultural-political role than it has in the past. At the same time, it is also apparent that departments of literature and languages can no longer rest on their cultural-capital laurels—Literature as the undisputed sign and vehicle of *Kultur*—but must actively engage electronic and mass-popular culture in all its forms.

Last but proverbially not least, I want to argue that if part of what gives punk its transgressive edge is its emphasis on resistance, "teacherly" (anti-)transference—which "negative" performative mode is the dialectical other of student resistance—is a crucial component of any pedagogy that would programmatically attempt to stage contradiction. Again, let me be perfectly clear about this practice: (anti-)transference, as the parentheses I hope indicate, always already presupposes transference. No transference, no transformation. Put another way, antitransference without some, perhaps substantial, element of transference "proper" is not only patently undialectical but, from a practical perspective, inevitably counter-productive and as such a decidedly futile exercise in negativity. Hence my tactical recourse in my cultural studies classes to what I think of as super-popular cultural texts—to, for instance, blockbuster films such as *Total Recall* or prime-time television such as *Melrose Place*[21]—which encourage a certain uncritical reception on the part of the student (where, to invoke a conventional binarism, the emphasis is on "pleasure" rather than "meaning").

In this reception context, it's also worth noting that the popular-cultural option is especially crucial if the course in question is based, as mine tend to be, on a combination of *élite* theory and popular culture.[22] That is, if the dialectic between the theoretical and popular-cultural texts is not sufficiently taut (if, for example, the students avoid the critical implications of the theory by shifting their transference from the teacher to the popular-cultural texts), the teacher may be compelled to fashion a polemical, antitransferential position in order to counter the "regressive," ideological effects of the popular-cultural texts.[23] This is, needless to say, a tricky pedagogical task, not unlike juggling three differently weighted colored balls, but any pedagogy worth its salt will be *at least* as complex.

The most intractable obstacle to "punk pedagogy" in general and (anti-)transference in particular, though, is neither texts nor students but institutions. Bluntly, to perform contradiction one must be willing to resist, among other things, the lure of popularity. In particular, one must be willing to resist the temptation to please students simply in order to get "good" evaluations or to avoid the sort of conflicts that frequently attend the introduction of such politically sensitive topics as ideology or race, class or homosexuality. This is easier said than done, of course, since the institutional apparatuses of the university—from curricular constraints to status quo departmental politics to the laissez-faire anti-intellectualism that has been so pervasive on American campuses since the early eighties—conspire, sometimes massively, against adopting just such a manifestly unpopular position. Yet as potentially self-defeating and even professionally risky as the risk of (anti-)transference may be, in certain, by no means extraordinary, circumstances it is also, as Strickland says, the "only intellectually responsible pedagogy" (294).

By way of a conclusion, I would only add that to invoke the practice of "punk pedagogy" is by no means to propose an impossibly idealistic politics nor, for that matter, its sad seductive twin, a politics of cynicism. These politics—the politics of cynicism and idealism—are, in fact, the antipodes of a pedagogy that continually affirms (self-)critique even as it recognizes the necessity of social transformation. To recollect Hegel by way of Brecht, a little cunning is by no means a bad thing. As Magiot, the communist doctor, says to the poet *manqué* Philipot in Graham Greene's *The Comedians* (1966): "Go on living with your belief, don't die with it."[24]

Notes

1. See "The Politics of Teaching Literature: The 'Paedagogical Effect,' " *College Literature* 17, no. 2/3 (1990): 90–108; reprinted in *Margins in the Classroom: Teaching Literature*, ed. Kostas Myrsiades and Linda Myrsiades (Minneapolis: University of Minnesota Press, 1994), 102–20.

2. "*Sturm und Searle*: Intervention, Transformation, Democratization," *Mediations* 16, no. 2 (May 1992): 24–29.

3. I employ the notion of (anti-)transference here rather than, say, "negative transference" because the latter usually refers to the analysand as opposed to the analyst. In other words, (anti-)transference is an effect or function of the teacher or professorial subject-position. My use of "(anti-)" is also meant to distinguish this form of pedagogical transference from a strictly clinical one. On the phenomenon of transference in general, see the entry in Jean Laplanche and J. B. Pontalis's *Language of Psychoanalysis*, trans. Donald Nicholson-Smith (New York: Norton, 1973 [1967]), 455–62.

4. Though in the last part of this essay I develop the sense in which "punk pedagogy" borrows from punk as such, precisely because it is a "way of life" (Williams) or, for Hebdige, "subculture," it is particularly recalcitrant to definition and analysis. This said, see Hebdige's *Subculture: The Meaning of Style* (London: Routledge, 1991 [1979]), esp. 106–22. For the most recent and perhaps definitive account of punk in general and the Sex Pistols in particular, see also Jon Savage's *England's Dreaming: Anarchy, Sex Pistols, Punk Rock and Beyond*

(New York: St. Martin's, 1992). Finally, on, *inter alia*, Adorno and the Clash, see the introduction to my *From Hegel to Madonna: Toward a General Economy of "Commodity Fetishism"* (Albany: State University of New York Press, 1997).

   5. For this distinction, see my "News from Somewhere: Reading Raymond Williams' Readers," in *Cultural Materialism*, ed. Christopher Prendergast (Minneapolis: University of Minnesota Press, 1995), 71–90. For a more polemical sense, see Cary Nelson's "Always Already Cultural Studies: Two Conferences and a Manifesto," *Journal of the Midwest Modern Language Association* 24, no. 1 (Spring 1991): 24–38.

   6. John Fiske, *Television Culture* (New York: Routledge, 1987), 1. In the second chapter of *Television Culture* (which was part of the reading assignment for the second class), Fiske writes: "By radicalism I mean a critical interrogation of the dominant ideology and of the social system which it has produced and underpins" (33).

   7. For the former, see Nicholas Abercrombie, Stephen Hill, and Bryan Turner, *The Dominant Ideology Thesis* (Boston: Allen and Unwin, 1980); for the latter, see Karl Marx and Friedrich Engels, *The German Ideology*, vol. 5, trans. Clemens Dutt (New York: International, 1976), 59.

   8. Graeme Turner, *Film as Social Practice* (New York: Routledge, 1990 [1988]), 1.

   9. I should note that by "those" here I mean "some students." As a group, students—even at such a relatively ethnically homogenous place as Ohio University—are by no means monolithic (as every teacher knows). In this context, I am also echoing, somewhat pejoratively, Greil Marcus's Situationist-inspired reading of punk: "In modern society, leisure (What do I want to do today?) was replaced by entertainment (What is there to see today?)." See "The Last Sex Pistols Concert," *Lipstick Traces: A Secret History of the Twentieth Century* (Cambridge: Harvard University Press, 1989), 27–152.

   10. Synopsis: *Desperately Seeking Susan* is about an affluent but unhappy homemaker named Roberta (Roseanne Arquette) who, in a fit of marital desperation, decides to track down Susan (Madonna), whose romantic life she has read about in the "personals." Susan in turn is the not-so-obscure object of desire of her traveling musician boyfriend, Jim, as well as the villain (who is trying to retrieve a pair of rare Egyptian earrings that we see Susan stealing at the very beginning of the film). When, in the process of trailing Susan in NYC, Roberta is knocked unconscious and suffers amnesia, she is taken in by Jim's best friend, Dez (Aidan Quinn), a movie-projector operator. The remainder of the film consists of a series of role reversals, mistaken identities, and screwball misadventures as Jim desperately tries to get in touch with Susan while Roberta is desperately sought by Susan, the villain, and her increasingly bewildered husband. The film comes to its happy end when Susan saves Roberta from the villain, at which point Jim and Susan are finally reunited, and Roberta leaves her husband for Dez and, presumably, a new, liberated, and liberating life.

   For a different synopsis and reading, see Lisa Lewis, "A Madonna 'Wanna-Be' Story on Film," *Gender Politics and MTV: Voicing the Difference* (Philadelphia: Temple University Press, 1990), 185–95.

   11. Jackie Stacey, "Desperately Seeking Difference," *The Female Gaze: Women as Viewers of Popular Culture*, ed. Lorraine Gamman and Margaret Marshment (Seattle: Real Comet Press, 1989), 112–29. Reprinted in *Issues in Feminist Film Criticism*, ed. Patricia Erens (Bloomington: Indiana University Press, 1990), 365–79.

   12. I am referring here to Lacan's theory and practice of the "short session." See, for example, "The function and field of speech and language in psychoanalysis" (1953), *Écrits* (New York: Norton, 1977 [1966]), 30–113, esp. 95–100. For an excellent discussion of these *séances scandées*, see John Forrester, "Dead on Time: Lacan's Theory of Temporality," *The Seductions of Psychoanalysis* (Cambridge: Cambridge University Press, 1992 [1990]), 168–218.

13. Though both of these "gendering" gestures are clearly open to the charge of essentialism, I felt that—given the circumstances—these gestures were well worth the risk. I would only add that it is also always imperative to re-mark, explicitly, *in situ*, the strategic gist of such gestures.

14. For an absolutely minimal sense of this distinction (*autre/grand Autre*), see the "Translator's Note" to Lacan's *Écrits*, xi. For a more nuanced one, see—as Lacan himself advises—the play of these terms in the *Écrits* as a whole.

15. On "hierarchy of discourses," which Fiske borrows from Colin MacCabe's influential essay, "Realism and Cinema" (1981), Fiske writes in *Television Culture*:

> A realistic narrative will contain a range of different and often contradictory discourses, which are usually explicitly recognized as such, but these are low down in the discursive hierarchy. Taking precedence over them is an "unwritten" and therefore unrecognized discourse which tells the "truth," that is, it provides us (the reader-spectator) with a position of all-knowingness from which we can understand and evaluate the various discourses of the narrative. (25)

The "unwritten" discourse" is what MacCabe calls the "meta-discourse," the "position of spectatorial privilege from which the world makes perfect realistic sense," so-called dominant specularity. For MacCabe, see "Realism and Cinema: Notes on Brechtian Theses," in *Popular Television and Film*, ed. Tony Bennett et al. (London: Open University and British Film Institute, 1981), 216–33.

16. Ronald Strickland, "Confrontational Pedagogy and Traditional Studies," *College English* 52, no. 3 (March 1990): 292.

17. See Henry Giroux, "Popular Culture as Pedagogy of Pleasure and Meaning," *Popular Culture, Schooling, and Everyday Life*, ed. Henry Giroux et al. (South Hadley, MA: Bergin and Garvey, 1989), 13.

18. For some sense of the importance of performance for punk (and, for that matter, anti-transference—with the emphasis on "anti-"), see Penelope Spheeris's *Decline of Western Civilization* (1981), which documents the LA punk milieu in the late 1970s and features such bands as X, Fear, Black Flag, Circle Jerks, and (yes, Madonna, there is a God!) Catholic Discipline.

19. For the sake of convenience, I have elided the differences here between "sub-" and "popular culture." It is now apparent—if it wasn't before—that not only are there crucial differences between mass and popular, not to say folk, culture, but that there are also important differences between subcultures (which ostensibly "contain" an element of resistance to the dominant hegemony) and what Michael Bérubé calls "leisure activities" such as watching TV. (Which does not of course mean that TV viewing is always only a leisure activity.) On the Bérubé, see "Pop Goes the Academy: Cult Studs Fight the Power," *Voice Literary Supplement* (April 1992): 13.

20. On this mediatic logic, see Fredric Jameson, *"Video," Postmodernism, or, the Cultural Logic of Late Capitalism* (Durham, NC: Duke University Press, 1991), 67–96.

21. On *Total Recall*, see my *"Total Recall*: Production, Revolution, Simulation Alienation-Effect," *Camera Obscura* 32 (Summer 1995): 5–39; on *Melrose Place*, see my "Hegemony of X: Social and Political-Libidinal Economy in *Melrose Place*" (forthcoming).

22. On the conjunction of "high" theory and popular culture, see, for example, Slavoj Zizek's *Looking Awry: An Introduction to Jacques Lacan Through Popular Culture* (Cambridge: MIT Press, 1991).

23. Here, for the sake of argument and polemic (*contra* Fiske), I am assuming a telecinematic apparatus whose dominant-hegemonic address relatively determines the site of reception.

24. Graham Greene, *The Comedians* (New York: Penguin, 1966), 177.

Contributors

Stanley Aronowitz is a professor of Sociology and Director of the Cultural Studies Program at the Graduate Center, City University of New York. He is the editor of *Technoscience and Cyberculture* (Routledge).

Carol Becker is the Dean of Faculty and Vice President of Academic Affairs at the School of Art Institute of Chicago. Her latest book is *Zones of Contention: Essays on Art, Institutions, Gender, and Anxiety* (SUNY Press).

Deborah P. Britzman is an associate professor within the Faculty of Education at York University. Her forthcoming book is *Lost Subjects, Contested Objects: Towards a Psychoanalytic Inquiry of Learning* (SUNY Press).

Henry A. Giroux is the Waterbury Chair of Secondary Education at the Pennsylvania State University. He is the author of *Channel Surfing* (St. Martin's), *Fugitive Cultures* (Routledge), and *Pedagogy and Politics of Hope* (Westview).

David Theo Goldberg is a professor of Criminal Justice at Arizona State University in Tempe. He is the author of *Racist Culture: Philosophy and Politics of Meaning* (Blackwell), and *Racial Subjects* (Routledge).

Mike Hill is a professor of English at Marymount Manhattan College. He is the editor of *Whiteness: A Critical Reader* (New York University Press) and is completing *After Whiteness* (New York University Press).

Harvey J. Kaye is Rosenberg Professor of Social Change and Development at the University of Wisconsin-Green Bay. His most recent book is *Why Do Ruling Classes Fear History? And Other Questions* (St. Martin's).

Douglas Kellner is a professor of English at the University of Texas at Austin. He is the author of *Articulating the Global and the Local: Globalization and Cultural Studies* (Westview) and *Media Culture: Cultural Studies, Identity and Politics Between the Modern and Postmodern* (Routledge).

Cameron McCarthy is a professor of Education and Cultural Studies at the University of Illinois. He is the author of *Uses of Culture* (Routledge) and editor (with W. Crichlow) of *Race, Identity and Representation* (Routledge).

Robert Miklitsch is a professor of English at Ohio University in Athens. He has published articles in *the review of Education/Pedagogy/Cultural Studies* and other journals.

Claudia Mitchell is a professor of Education at McGill University in Montreal. She is the author (with Sandra Weber) of *That's Funny, You Don't Look Like a Teacher! Interrogating Images and Identity in Popular Culture* (Falmer).

Douglas D. Noble is the Director of Research at the Cobblestone School in Rochester, New York, and author of *The Classroom Arsenal, Military Research, Information Technology, and Public Education* (Falmer).

Jacqueline Reid-Walsh is a professor of Education at McGill University. She has published several articles in *the review of Education/Pedagogy/ Cultural Studies* and other journals.

Susan Searls is a graduate student of English at the Pennsylvania State University. She has published articles in *the review of Education/Pedagogy/ Cultural Studies* and other journals.

Sharon Todd is a postdoctoral fellow at the Ontario Institute for the Study of Education, University of Toronto. She has published articles in *the review of Education/Pedagogy/Cultural Studies* as well as other journals.

David Trend is Dean of Creative Arts, De Anza College in California. His most recent book is *Cultural Democracy: Politics Media and New Technology* (SUNY Press).

Kakie Urch is a graduate student in English at the Pennsylvania State University. She has published articles in *the review of Education/Pedagogy/ Cultural Studies* and other journals.

Jeffrey Williams is a professor of English at East Carolina University. He is the author of *Narrative, the Question of Theory, and the English Novel* (Cambridge University Press), and editor of *PC Wars: Politics and Theory, in the Academy* (Routledge).